In Search of Lost Meaning

The publisher gratefully acknowledges the generous support of the Humanities Endowment Fund of the University of California Press Foundation.

In Search of Lost Meaning

The New Eastern Europe

Adam Michnik

Edited by Irena Grudzińska Gross
Translated by Roman S. Czarny, with a Foreword by
Václav Havel and an Introduction by John Darnton

UNIVERSITY OF CALIFORNIA PRESS

Berkeley   Los Angeles   London

University of California Press, one of the most distinguished university presses in the United States, enriches lives around the world by advancing scholarship in the humanities, social sciences, and natural sciences. Its activities are supported by the UC Press Foundation and by philanthropic contributions from individuals and institutions. For more information, visit www.ucpress.edu.

University of California Press
Berkeley and Los Angeles, California

University of California Press, Ltd.
London, England

Library of Congress Cataloging-in-Publication Data

Michnik, Adam.
    [W poszukiwaniu utraconego sensu. English]
    In search of lost meaning : the new Eastern Europe / Adam Michnik ; edited by Irena Grudzinska Gross ; translated by Roman S. Czarny, with a foreword by Vaclav Havel and an introduction by John Darnton.
        p.   cm.
Includes index.
ISBN 978-0-520-26923-1 (alk. paper)
    1. Social ethics.   2. Social ethics—Poland.   3. Poland—Politics and government—1980–1989.   4. Social change—Europe, Eastern.   5. Social change—Poland.   6. Europe, Eastern—Politics and government—1945–1989.   7. Europe, Eastern—Politics and govern-ment—1989–   8. Europe, Central—Politics and government—1989–   I. Grudzinska Gross, Irena   II. Title.
    HM665.M53413 2007
    303.48'4094380904—dc22

                                                            2010040640

Manufactured in the United States of America
20   19   18   17   16   15   14   13   12   11
10   9   8   7   6   5   4   3   2   1

This book is printed on Cascades Enviro 100, a 100% post consumer waste, recycled, de-inked fiber. FSC recycled certified and processed chlorine free. It is acid free, Ecologo certified, and manufactured by BioGas energy.

CONTENTS

FOREWORD

About Michnik

This piece was originally written for Elzbieta Matynia's book
Michnik-Havel *and appears here with her permission.*

I have known the name of Adam Michnik since 1968. I remember vividly how back then, listening to the news from Radio Free Europe about the events in Poland, I heard about the crackdown at Warsaw University—and the names Jacek Kuroń and Adam Michnik. In Prague at that time, the "Prague Spring" was at its height, and I was worried that we only cared about ourselves and were not interested in what was going on in neighboring Poland. I tried a bit to raise awareness about the Polish events. I think by then it was becoming clear that to disengage from the Soviet grip and get rid of their totalitarian rule would be extremely hard to do on our own, and that something of that kind could not become a real hope until we put our efforts together and made it clear that the motto "divide and rule" would have no effect on our countries.

Later on, Adam and I became friends, and now—for years already—I have been reading his articles with great zest. Whenever I find myself unable to follow Polish affairs, I look up what Michnik is writing. In short, for me he is the intellectual conscience of the Polish nation, a conscience, however—and this is important—that does not have a gloomy face but is characterized by a capacity for impartiality, irony, and playfully witty turns of phrase.

Adam and I first got to know each other personally at those secret—and now rather historic—meetings in 1978 along the Czechoslovak-Polish border. Since that time, many dramatic events have unfolded; one day he'd go to prison, another time it would be me. But always—if I may say it this way—we were both tugging at the same end of the rope. Adam, furthermore, founded *Gazeta Wyborcza*, which is most likely the one genuinely independent media organization in post-Communist Europe. If he had done nothing else besides all of that, it would already have been a great accomplishment.

But from the standpoint of history, even more important than his roles as editor in chief or member of parliament is the fact that Michnik continues to be a most insightful and astute commentator on current affairs, an embodiment of free reflection, a man who observes politics not just from some highly placed vantage point but—so to speak—from within.

I am very happy to hear that his third book is being published by the University of California Press, as I am certain that it will help many in the West better understand what happened and what is happening now in our part of the world.

Václav Havel

EDITOR'S NOTE

The book now before you pertains to the astonishing post-cold war transformation that Eastern Europe has been undergoing for the last twenty years. That transformation is shown here from an especially illuminating vantage point. The author, Adam Michnik, is one of the best-known East European dissidents. But the 1989 revolutions did not spell the end of his political activities. He became very influential as a politician, journalist, writer, and historian. The changes in his role as well as the political changes in East Central Europe are reflected in successive books by Michnik that have been published by the University of California Press. The first one (*Letters from Prison*, 1985) was an in depth, combative analysis of what later turned out to be the last years of the Communist regime in Eastern Europe and of the Soviet Union. The second (*Letters from Freedom*, 1998) dealt with the next stage, which Michnik called "the velvet transformation," that is, the installation of the new democracies in the region. It now seems that the transformation was not very velvety after all, and the present book deals with the remarkable defeat of the elites that led the peaceful handing over of power of 1989. So while Michnik's first book was written from the point of view of an oppositionist to the Communist regime and the second from that of an implementer of the new order, the third finds him again in the opposition, this time against the groups in Polish political life that are most radically anti-Communist. The book's author is an active participant who gradually becomes more of an observer and who searches to understand what mistakes were made, what we can learn from historical and political analogies and from Poland's past and literature. It is a very personal volume, very sober, and sometimes bitter, and, as usual with Michnik, extremely intelligent and interesting. We know what 1989 tore down; we are learning here what was built in its stead.

The book has three distinct parts. The first part, Anniversaries, offers a double perspective: it invokes the main events of the anti-Soviet and anti-Communist rebellion as seen contemporaneously and compares this picture to the way the society thinks about those events today; in other words, it looks at how the politics of today changes the perception of the past. The scope of this analysis reaches beyond Poland, as Michnik discusses as well the fiftieth anniversary of the 1956 revolt in Hungary and the shift in the entire East European region away from the Left toward the New Right. The author ponders the appeal of the East European parties and groups openly proclaiming the need to break with the "velvety" nature of the transformation. The second part, The Work of Hatred, is an analysis of the new political climate that these parties and groups imposed upon the Polish social scene. It describes the rise of the conviction that Poland and Poles fell victim to exploitation by post-Communist elites, left-wing European Union bureaucrats, and immoral political and economic dealers. In the last chapter in this part, Michnik looks to the period when Poland lacked national independence in order to find the sources of the vitality of this climate of victimhood. The chapter is an original interpretation of Romantic national myths and their revival in the situation of national sovereignty. The third part, The Complex Polish-Jewish Matters, is devoted to issues of memory of Polish–Jewish relations: the debates about the 1941 massacre of the Jewish inhabitants of Jedwabne by their Polish neighbors and the continuous conflicts about the 1946 Kielce pogrom.

The book is thus a profoundly personal and often melancholy inquiry into the mechanisms of change and transformation whose final shape is still open, and still fascinating. It throws light not only on the events in question but also on the thinking of one of their most important protagonists. In fact, all of the chapters have been written "in the moment," having first appeared in *Gazeta Wyborcza*, the newspaper of which Michnik is editor in chief. It is history in the making.

Because the book is immersed in contemporary politics and recent history, Michnik gives a hearing to many voices and liberally quotes from many sources. As a historian, he invokes documents and declarations of political and religious leaders, often printed in hard to find volumes. His authors range from Józef Piłsudski, Claude Lévi-Strauss, and Hannah Arendt, to Władysław Pobóg-Malinowski, Tomáš Masaryk, and Václav Havel. Most of the purely political quotations come from newspapers, especially from *Gazeta Wyborcza, Rzeczpospolita*, and, for older quotations, from *Trybuna Ludu*. He is also steeped in literature, quoting and referring to the poetry of Shakespeare, Stanisław Barańczak, Gyula Illyés, Adam Mickiewicz, Jarosław Iwaszkiewicz, Czesław Miłosz, and others. The novels of Stendhal, Stefan Żeromski, and Wojciech Kuczok are referred to, as is the *Dictionary of the Polish Language* by S. B. Linde. And this is only a partial list. Not all of the quotations have been found by the editor, but all of the authors and titles are clearly identified. I include a partial list here.

In Chapter 5, quotations from the following texts were used: Hannah Arendt, *The Origins of Totalitarianism*, New York, 1951; Janusz Stanisław Gruchała, Tomasz G. Masaryk, Wrocław 1996; Gustav Le Bon, *The Crowd: A Study of the Popular Mind*, 1896; Claude Lévi-Strauss, *Tristes Tropiques*, Paris, 1955; Daria Nałęcz, *Sen o władzy. Inteligencja wobec niepodległości* [Dreaming about Power. Intelligentsia and Independence], Warsaw, 1994; Józef Piłsudski, *Pisma - mowy - rozkazy* [Writings, Speeches, Declarations], vols. 1–8, Warsaw, 1930–1931; Władysław Pobóg-Malinowski, *Najnowsza historia polityczna Polski* [Recent History of Poland], vols. 1–3, Warsaw 1990; Adam Pragier, *Czas przeszły dokonany* [Past Perfect], London 1966; Paweł Zaremba, *Historia dwudziestolecia 1918–1939* [History of the two decades 1918–1939], Paris, 1981; Emil Zola, "J'Accuse", *L'Aurore,* January 13, 1898; and Stefan Żeromski, *Przedwiośnie,* Warsaw, 1925.

In Chapters 6 and 7, quotations come from the following texts: John Paul II, *Pamięć i tożsamość* [Memory and Identity], Kraków 2005; Karol Wojtyła, *Poezje, dramaty, szkice* [Poetry, Plays, Essays], Kraków 2004; Adam Boniecki, *The Life of Karol Wojtyła,* Kraków 2000; Jakub Andrzejewski (Andrzej Paczkowski), biographies of Czesław Miłosz, Juliusz Mieroszewski, Sergiusz Piasecki, Antoni Słonimski, Krytyka, 13/14, Warsaw 1983; Jerzy Giedroyc - Juliusz Mieroszewski, *Listy 1949– 1956* [Letters],Warsaw 1999; Michał Głowiński, *Mowa w stanie oblężenia* [Speech under Siege], Warsaw, 1996; Czesław Miłosz, *Przygody młodego umysłu* [Adventures of a Young Mind], ed. A. Stawiarska, Kraków 2003; Cyprian Norwid, *Pisma wszystkie* [Collected Works], Warsaw, 1968; Joanna Pyszny, *Boje na łamach* [Fights on Newspaper Pages], Wrocław 2002; Peter Raina (ed.), *Kościół w PRL: Kościół katolicki a państwo w świetle dokumentów 1945–1989* [Church in People's Poland. Catholic Church and the State in Documents 1945–1989], Poznan, 1994; and Marek Skwarnicki, *Mój Miłosz* [My Miłosz], Kraków 2004.

Quotations in Chapter 9 come from the following sources: A deposition of Jechiel Alpert, Halama, August 4, 1967, edited by Ida Fink, manuscript; Ryszard Gryz, "Attitude of the Catholic Church in the Case of the Pogrom of Jews in Kielce" in Nasza Przeszłość, *Studia z dziejów Kościoła i kultury katolickiej w Polsce* [Our Past: Studies in the History of the Church and Catholic Culture in Poland], Kraków, vol. 93, 2000; John Micgiel, "Kościół katolicki i pogrom kielecki" [Catholic Church and Kielce Pogrom], in *Niepodległość* [Independence], New York, vol. 25, 1992; Ronald Modras, *The Catholic Church and Antisemtism, Poland 1933– 1939*, London, 1994; *Bożena Szaynok: Pogrom Żydów kieleckich 4 lipca 1946* [The Pogrom of Kielce Jews], Intr. Krystyna Kersten, Warsaw, 1992; and Rev. Jan Związek, "Biskup Teodor Kubina" [Bishop Teodor Kubina] in *Wiadomości Diecezjalne Archidiecezji Katowickiej* [News from the Katowice Church District], 2001.

The author of the book and its editor would like to thank Stanley Holwitz for his exceptional, long-standing editorial leadership, John Darnton for his introduction, Roman Czarny for the translation, and Jolanta Benal for her exemplary editing of the text of the book. Information about events and people mentioned in the chapters may be found in the Glossary.

Irena Grudzińska Gross
Princeton, May 2010

INTRODUCTION

Michnik

"Twenty-five years ago, in August 1980, Poland changed the face of the world," Adam Michnik writes in his chapter "In Search of Lost Meaning": "I close my eyes and see it—it was a beautiful time with beautiful people. I was thirty-four years old and convinced that my generation was writing an important chapter in history."

Now I close my eyes and see the Michnik of those days. He has curly brown hair, a rumpled look, a bit of stubble that suggests he's been up all night, the pallor of someone who's spent a lot of time behind bars. His eyes dart around, half nervous, half mischievous. His words pour out quickly, trying to keep up with his thoughts. He has a rat-a-tat stutter that, paradoxically, lends his words more urgency and more power. His cigarette ash falls over his brown jacket, which was once perhaps fashionable, and a cloud of smoke encircles his head. He exudes energy and a sense that anything is possible.

Our first, hurried meeting takes place on a street corner in 1979. We talk in French about the dissidents in Prague and the Czech movement Charter 77. He looks at me, suspiciously, I think. I'm a Western correspondent *based* in Poland. Who ever heard of such a thing? How could I be here without being compromised? I ask: Could the movement spread to Poland? He shrugs and grins for the first time. Anything's possible.

September 1, 1980. The Gdańsk accord establishing Solidarity has just been signed, and as part of the agreement political dissidents are released. It's drizzling and the blue-and-white gates of Rakowiecka prison open to release them in twos and threes. Suddenly, there he is! A huge smile across his broad face. Hugs and shouts. Prisoners only minutes before, they are pinching themselves. Later, Solidarity T-shirts are passed around.

Three months afterward, workers have gone on strike at the giant Ursus tractor factory outside of Warsaw. It's a complicated dispute pitting Solidarity against the core power of the Communist Party—the prosecutor's office and the secret police—and tempers run high. Thousands of workers crowd a meeting hall. Everyone wants to speak. It's decided each person will be allotted two minutes. Michnik bounds up. "I n-n-n-need four m-m-minutes!" he shouts. Everyone laughs.

Later he takes the floor. The workers' speeches have been spiraling to ever-larger demands. One worker has just said that if the Russians don't like the way things are going, that's too bad. Maybe the Russian troops should be tossed out of the country. Michnik explains the facts of life. "We don't live on the moon," he says. Slowly, bit by bit, with doses of history, appeals to common sense and the authority of "a known anti-socialist element," he calms down the crowd. Eventually the crisis is resolved.

June 1993, in the newly independent, democratic Poland. Michnik is running *Gazeta Wyborcza*, the most important paper in the country. He writes editorials, attends conferences, and travels east and west meeting political leaders, activists, and philosophers. He's older, a bit heavier. In his office, he uncorks a bottle of cognac, pours out two glasses, puts his feet up on his messy desk, and looks like a man who never doubted he'd end up on top but who is still somewhat amazed that it's all happened so fast. "When I was growing up," he says, "I learned that we were surrounded by three countries—the German Democratic Republic, Czechoslovakia, and the Soviet Union. Now look, they've all disappeared!"

Adam Michnik is one of a number of people—along with Václav Havel in Czechoslovakia and Janos Kiš in Hungary—who changed the ideological map of Europe. They brought democracy to what used to be called the Eastern Bloc. But the case could be argued that Michnik and a dozen or so of his compatriots, including Lech Wałęsa, stand alone, because Poland was the most audacious. It was the first country to pull the brick out of the monolithic wall of Communism.

Solidarity did not spring up by itself. It grew from the theoretical framework that they laid down—most notably an alliance between workers and intellectuals. Under the careful guidance of a "self-limiting revolution," it turned from a free trade union into a mass movement for liberalization that offended, but managed to fend off, the Soviet Union. It survived for sixteen months before being repressed by martial law in December 1981, and then it continued through a process of continual dialogue between the people and "the power," moving from underground to aboveground and eventually taking over the government.

Michnik was involved in every step of that delicate dismantling and reconstruction. He helped plant the seed of freedom with his ideas, he helped nurture it with his protests, and then, once successful, he helped harvest it—by serving in the parliament in a democratic Poland and using the forum of the newspaper to argue for morality and dignity and against mindless, self-defeating vengeance and retaliation. Amazingly, but characteristically, he established a working relationship with General Wojciech Jaruzelski, the dictator who imposed martial law.

Michnik, born in 1946, seemed to turn into the enfant terrible of Poland through a combination of background and temperament. He is Jewish—his grandparents on his father's side were killed by the Nazis—and, with a father who was politically active and a half brother who was a military judge during the postwar Stalinist period, he had a Communist legacy. As a child, he was active in the "red" scouts, a Communist youth group, and he took the slogans of justice and truth literally; these experiences and habits of mind served to deepen his disillusionment when he began to encounter contradictions and learn the true history of Poland's past and her relationship to the Soviet Union, taught in the streets and homes, as opposed to the official history taught in schools.

At age fifteen, he founded a discussion club called "Seekers of Contradiction" to bat around big ideas such as humanism, but it was branded subversive and was disbanded. At age eighteen, he was arrested for the first time, serving two months in detention, for disseminating a document, "An Open Letter to the Party," critical of the authorities. Two older men, Jacek Kuroń and Karol Modzelewski—who would also later play a role in founding Solidarity—were sentenced to prison in the same episode. As for many people, 1968 was a pivotal year. It brought both the Warsaw Pact invasion that snuffed out the Prague Spring, thereby showing the iron fist of international Communism, and a homegrown protest that led to Michnik's expulsion from Warsaw University in the midst of an ugly, officially sponsored, anti-Semitic campaign.

This was the beginning of his life as an open dissident. As he told Michael Kaufman, a *New York Times* reporter, years later: "This is the point where I said to myself, 'Halt, stop. I do not want to have anything to do with the system. I am no longer the heretic. I cut my umbilical cord to communism. What they are for, I am against.'" It was also, not coincidentally, the start of a long-running cat-and-mouse game with the rulers. For two years Michnik was given menial work as a welder in the Rosa Luxemburg lightbulb factory, a job that gave him experience and confidence in dealing with workers. Altogether he would end up spending more than six years in prison. But he profited handsomely from the time, using the quiet of detention to compose his political works. For the authorities, it was a losing proposition either way—outside of jail, he was a tireless agitator; inside, he was a dangerous political theorist. Meanwhile, he continued his studies. In 1975 he earned an MA in history as an extension student at Poznań University.

In 1976, together with Mr. Kuroń and a handful of others, Michnik founded the most important dissident organization in the Eastern Bloc. It was called the Workers' Defense Committee (KOR) and it was intended to provide food and help for the families of the workers who had been brutally suppressed during protests. In reality, it was something much more important—it was the beginning of a bridge between intellectuals and workers, who would eventually join forces to bring the regime to its knees.

This notion of inclusiveness, the idea of seeking out common ground and forging alliances, is central to Michnik's political thought. It was sounded eloquently in one of his most important books, *The Church, the Left, and Dialogue,* which was smuggled to Paris for publication in 1977. In a nutshell, he perceived the Catholic Church to be a protector of Polish sovereignty and a fount of dignity and so proposed that political activists, who were largely atheistic workers for human rights, join forces with it to confront the regime. These ideas laid the groundwork for the spirit of Solidarity three years later.

Michnik's writings, including those penned in prison, are noteworthy for their clear thinking, their passion, their thoughtful resort to historical analogies, and their pragmatism. He is not one to see the world in unyielding blacks and whites, villains and heroes, bad people and good people. It is in the way he detects all the shades in between—and yet still holds fast to the eternals of truth and justice—that his humanism comes through. Perhaps more than anything, his philosophy of achieving "normality"—his belief that one can be free if one simply acts free—was the guiding spirit of Solidarity. The workers who went on strike in the Gdańsk shipyard in the summer of 1980 were able to take on the armed power of the state because they all did it together and because they were soon supported by factory workers and miners throughout the country. They became free men and women by following the simple, yet exceedingly brave, injunction to act like free men and women.

No person embodies this principle—that one can become what one wants to be by being it, and that one can become free by being free—more than Adam Michnik. It was indeed a beautiful time and he, in the full bloom of his youthful optimism, like all of the other Poles who made it happen, was indeed a beautiful person.

John Darnton

PART I

Anniversaries

CHAPTER ONE

Poland at the Turning Point

Fifteen Years of Transformation, Fifteen Years
of Gazeta Wyborcza

We are the witnesses of a miracle. Let us consider what the Polish prayer sounded like twenty years ago.

> Dear Lord, make Poland have freedom instead of dictatorship; dear Lord, make Poland have a democratically elected parliament; make television and radio, the press and publishing houses free of censorship; open our borders and give us a free market economy; dear Lord, make Poland stop being a satellite country, make the Soviet army leave Poland, and allow Poles to become members of NATO and the European Union by their own choice.

We, however, when we were penniless and starting to publish *Gazeta Wyborcza,* could only pray that our attempt did not end in complete humiliation. And that our paper—the first daily published by the people of the democratic opposition and by those who traced their roots to the Solidarity underground, who had come back from banishment or simply from prison—would win the struggle for readers' hearts and manage to survive at least those most difficult years of transformation.

And the good Lord granted us those unrealistic wishes. He gave Poles what they dreamed of.

Then why, after fifteen years of freedom, are we Poles so furious? And why are we, the staff of *Gazeta Wyborcza,* who registered such an unbelievable success, we, the beneficiaries of the Polish transformation, the darlings of fortune, also so furious?

This will be a personal account, as I feel partially responsible for the fury of my compatriots as well as that of my friends from *Gazeta*.

I

As early as 1980, at the time of the first Solidarity, when Providence seemed to start smoothing out Poland's rocky destiny, we were asking ourselves, following the lead of the poet Juliusz Słowacki: "Poland, but what sort of Poland?" And we answered, full of uncertainty: a self-governing Poland, a multicolored one, grounded in Christian tradition, socially just; a Poland friendly to her neighbors; a Poland able to accept compromise and moderation, realism and loyal partnership, but un-willing to accept slavery or to be spiritually tamed; a Poland with the conflicts that are normal in a modern society but permeated with the spirit of solidarity; a Poland where intellectuals defend persecuted workers, and workers' strikes demand cultural freedom; a Poland that treats herself with pathos and irony, so often attacked, but never subju-gated, so many times crushed but never defeated; a Poland that has now regained her identity, her language, and her face.

Today we ask ourselves the very same question: What is left of that dream of Poland? We are still asking, and that is why we are so furious.

II

We believed in the myth of the emancipation of labor, and we be-lieved that those who worked in the big factories would take them over. That dream proved to be an illusion. The logic of emancipation was simply replaced with the hard laws of the free market. The strikers who brought us freedom—the workers in the mines and the steel industry and in the shipyards and the refineries—were the first victims. It was not their fault, but they have paid the biggest price. Their work was as good as before, but still they faced the specter of unemployment. We had no idea how to reconcile the pursuit of real economy with care for the people who, through no fault of their own, fell victim to that market.

It is not a situation specific to Poland, but nowhere was the opposition so deeply rooted in big factories as in Solidarity. Those people have every right to feel they were betrayed, even though the major "shock therapy" economic reform under Leszek Balcerowicz was the only way to break the cursed chain of backwardness.

III

We believed in Solidarity. It was the only instrument able to force the Communist authorities to negotiate Poland's way out of dictatorship. But Solidarity, this wonderful federation of people united in opposition to the Communist regime, was not able to come into its own in the new reality. What was worse, it vacillated between replicating the behaviors learned in the years of dictatorship and taking the place of the former leading power. Strikes and demonstrations clashed with the demands to take over the workplace. At one time it was the Polish United Workers' Party (PZPR) that decided who would enter the power structure. Then Solidarity wished to do exactly that. It wanted to decide who was going to be the governor, the director, the head of the post office or registry, the president of a university, or the administrator of a hospital. At the same time, Solidarity did not have a clue about how to be a trade union in a country that had just undergone such a great democratic transformation. These sorts of difficulties are understandable—such a transformation had no precedent whatsoever.

In free Poland, Solidarity was gradually more and more marginalized, and many Solidarity supporters felt cheated.

IV

Solidarity had a wonderful asset: Lech Wałęsa, who personified the dreams of millions about freedom, justice, and solidarity. This electrician with the Virgin Mary lapel pin was able to fascinate great crowds and make them enthusiastic about him, but the very same Wałęsa destroyed his own heroic and grand image by his ruthless and relentless pursuit of the presidency, in which he destroyed the government of Tadeusz Mazowiecki and publicly offended Jerzy Turowicz. It was Wałęsa, the national hero of our history, who first employed the rhetoric of boorishness that found so many followers later on.

Wałęsa was an unpredictable and incompetent president, although we will always remember that he consistently stood for the free market economy and for a Polish orientation to the West. And nothing will ever erase the fact that Wałęsa changed the history of Poland from worse to better.

V

For many years we believed in the Catholic Church as a great protector of freedom. We shall never forget the wise heroism of the primate Stefan Cardinal Wyszyński, who was able to combine Christian witness with the sense of the common good. In those years, to us, *Tygodnik Powszechny*, edited by Jerzy Turowicz, the monthly *Znak*, edited by Hanna Malewska, and the monthly *Więź*, edited by Tadeusz Mazowiecki, were the faces of the Church. The elevation of Karol Wojtyła to the papal throne solidified our conviction that the Catholic Church, which always has been a symbol of protest, would never become a symbol of compulsion. The martyrdom of the priest Jerzy Popiełuszko solidified our feelings that the Church represented everything that was best in Polish spirituality.

And that was a mistake. After 1989, it became apparent that the Catholic Church represents both what is best and what is worst in Poland.

The ghosts of triumphalism, intolerance, and xenophobia once again raised their ugly heads. A substantial part of the Church chose to use the language of contempt and hatred toward dissenting thinkers. From the pulpits came calls to vote for the extremist parties that advocated destruction. True, this period lasted only a short time, but it was long enough to plant the seed of fear of what the clergy is capable of.

Today, thank God, the Church speaks in a different voice. Today, the Church talks about pluralism, dialogue, and tolerance. It declares openly that the European Union (EU) is not a disaster for Poland but a great opportunity. And that is very good. But do not be surprised that we still remember that the Polish bishops once took a different tone.

VI

Solidarity was formed in August 1980, when a great wave of strikes ended in an agreement. The idea of a compromise and the idea of a "common Poland" became a fundamental component of the Solidarity ethos. We said at that time that this conflict would not produce winners or losers; that August, we claimed that Poland was the winner. And in spite of what followed—martial law, the tragedy at the Wujek mine, and the casualties of Lubin—this ethos of a Poland constituted by a grand historic compromise was retained as we entered the new epoch in 1989. Our banners bore statements of honesty, courage, and work for Poland rather than for entrenched interests. We believed we would build a magnificent, just Poland.

Soon enough, a different language surfaced among us. There came a time of demands for reckoning, although there was more talk about settling accounts, more fear of settling accounts, than there was any real reckoning.

Questions about historical justice are always sensible. Those victimized and degraded by dictatorship have a right to be angry, especially when people who were part of the overthrown dictatorship splendidly arranged their lives in the new reality. Such is the natural law of every revolution. And it applies both to the people of the democratic opposition and to Solidarity, as well as to the people of the Catholic Church. The former had a moral right to declare after years of oppression "It's our fucking turn now!" while the latter could declare "Until now it was the Communists, set in place by Moscow, who ruled; now Catholic Poland will be ruled by Catholics." I understood and shared that emotion, and I was also among those who believed that the former dictators should be punished while the victimized and degraded should somehow be rewarded, and that the latter deserved to feel that justice had been done and their virtue rewarded. If I took a stand against lustration and decommunization, I did it in spite of my own feelings and sentiments. I was fully convinced that a revolution that seeks historical justice consistently and wishes to execute it properly nevertheless ends up with the execution of a monarch, as in Britain; with the guillotine, as under the Jacobins; or with simple terror, as under the Bolsheviks. In a nutshell, begotten of freedom, it ends in dictatorship.

I can understand the psychological need for revenge on the participants in the former regime. However, I am not capable of understanding the politicians who exploited that need and started a cold civil war that only resulted in pathetic accusations against two former presidents as well as against others who served Poland well and now stood accused of having been agents of secret police.

I have opposed these ideas many times, often going far overboard. I regret the overkill of some of my gestures and statements. Many of my friends hold it against me. Many others never understood it, and many simply condemn it. I will try to explain now, because I feel guilty.

Let us take the example of General Czesław Kiszczak, who was chief of the security apparatus at the time of martial law and is humanly and morally responsible for the excesses wrought by the functionaries of his department. And we know that they did terrible things: they shot workers, fomented plots, broke people's characters (and forced them to violate their principles), and trod on their consciences. I tried to include all of that in the open letter I wrote to General Kiszczak from Warsaw prison in December 1983. But this is not the end of General Kiszczak's biography. Later on, he became one of the architects of the Round Table agreements and was loyal to the Polish democracy as minister of internal affairs in the government of Tadeusz Mazowiecki. Since he was the head of the security apparatus, he could have caused the Round Table talks to devolve into a fiasco by ordering any provocation by his agents at any given time. But he did not, and he saved the compromise struck at the Round Table. I think we should not forget that. That is exactly why, when asked by two excellent journalists during an interview with General Kiszczak and me if he was a man of honor, I said yes.

That answer was nonsense. It is not up to me to judge who is and who is not a man of honor. I should have said: "General Kiszczak played a negative role at the time of martial law, but his role at the time of the Round Table negotiations was very positive." After all, it must be easier to be the head of a repressive agency in a Communist country than to transcend the horizon of one's own biography and cooperate at the disassembly of a dictatorship.

I also should have added that the people who ruled Poland in 1981 (and who introduced martial law) had a right to make their own decisions based on the fear of Soviet intervention. They were even obligated to remember the burning of Budapest in 1956, the occupation of Prague of 1968, and, finally, Afghanistan.

Had I said that, perhaps I could have avoided much criticism, for which my friends and colleagues from *Gazeta Wyborcza* paid dearly. Today I am saying I am sorry.

VII

Many of my friends reproach me for my overly kindhearted attitude toward post-Communists, that is, to the Social Democracy of the Republic of Poland (SdRP), led by Aleksander Kwaśniewski, and the Democratic Left Alliance (SLD), led by Leszek Miller. I would like to explain my point of view.

Alexis de Tocqueville wrote about the France of a hundred and fifty years ago that both conservatives and their opponents have a predilection for public office because they desire to live off taxes, and that this hidden illness undermines all governments. I maintained that if the philosophy of opportunity for everyone were the principle governing a free Poland, then that opportunity should also be available to post-Communists. After all, ordinary opportunists were members of the Communist Party, but the party also had members who wanted to change things for the better. I did not think the proper attitude toward people who wanted to participate in and build a democratic Poland should be a total boycott and ostracism. On the contrary, I perceived many SLD politicians as sometimes inconsistent allies of the process of modernization. I thought that the post-Communist formation should be treated just like all the others, and that we should remember what divides us but also seek that which unites us.

Where the SLD had once been invested in a reasonable post-Communism that aimed toward Western social democracy, it finally became just another party in power, distributing privileges and benefits. Today, the SLD leaves the public sphere in a welter of infamy, corruption scandals, and ineffective unnecessary reforms (and the lack of necessary ones). Leszek Miller himself admitted that he dismissed Ewa Milewicz's warning that the SLD was "the party with less leeway." The SLD was a party of people who thought they were allowed to do anything, and it was a party open to "capable people; regrettably, capable of anything."

The SLD revived the Polish People's Republic's greed and its custom of contempt for the law, as well as its corrupt cronyism. Established in the climate of the PZPR's defeat and uniting many valuable people from the previous regime, the SLD was taken over by the immortal Comrade Weasel, who is cowardly toward the powerful and arrogant toward the weak and who is merciless and cynical.

Many people today criticize me for liking President Aleksander Kwaśniewski. And I want to say to them, I do not regret my gestures;

I have no doubt that he was a very good president. Kwaśniewski kept Poland on the road to the North Atlantic Treaty Organization (NATO) and the EU; he consistently protected the principles of parliamentary democracy and, simultaneously, tried to stitch together post-Communist Poland with post-Solidarity Poland.

Many people hold it against me that I publicly declared my liking of Leszek Miller and my conviction of his honesty. Miller himself defined our relations as "close familiarity." He spoke the truth; such was the case. I have never lobbied on his behalf at *Gazeta Wyborcza* or with Agora (the publisher of *Gazeta Wyborcza*), and he never pressed me to gain media support for his government. I have never tried to "go easy" on Miller, although I have often been accused of it, even at editorial meetings. I treated him just as I did other prime ministers—with respect but also with criticism. We at *Gazeta Wyborcza* criticized harshly anything he did that we saw as a mistake. We criticized the dismal reform of the national health care system; we criticized the senseless conflict with the National Bank of Poland and the Monetary Policy Council; we criticized his government's incomprehensible personnel decisions, and, finally, we criticized the draft of the bill on mass media. In the end, we supported every single government whenever it was doing something good for the Polish state.

I have always maintained, with certainty, that Leszek Miller had nothing to do with the corrupt offer made by Lew Rywin (see the Rywin entry in the Glossary); I reiterate that, in my opinion, Miller is an honest politician. It is also my opinion that he applies in daily life the legal principle of presumption of innocence, which would be an asset for every man, or for a lawyer, but is disastrous for a prime minister. Miller defends his political friends with die-hard loyalty, on the ground that they are innocent until found guilty in a court of law. And that is his mistake. A politician is guilty as soon as he becomes involved in an ethically ambiguous situation. Therefore, his defense of both Aleksandra Jakubowska and Mariusz Łapiński, his political friends who were involved in the case, was inherently wrong.

I confess I have trouble evaluating Leszek Miller. I admire him because he grew up poor and worked his way to the top. And I also remember his stand on Kosovo. When the majority of the SLD party opposed the intervention there, Miller, with utter determination, forced a resolution supporting it. I also remember the matter of Jedwabne. Apart from the members of the Freedom Union, Miller was the only party leader who actually came to Jedwabne to acknowledge the truth. His principled attitude toward anti-Semitism must not be forgotten.

Heads of state leave in a variety of ways. Leszek Miller left as a head of state who tolerated scandalous corruption. But it must be emphasized that, owing to his determination, the post-Communist electorate voted for Poland's entry into the EU. Under his rule, Poland returned to economic growth, and he had the courage to subject the flat tax to public debate. We should not forget all of that.

VIII

I am fully aware that *Gazeta Wyborcza* paid a higher price for its publication in the case of the Rywin scandal than it ever had before. The whole matter came as a complete surprise to us. We had never expected to be approached with a corrupt proposal; we had never expected that anyone would suspect us of being able to solve our (as well as others') problems through a bribe. Apparently Lew Rywin and his principals were not the only ones who assumed that we were capable of unprincipled behavior, as that opinion was shared by a substantial portion of the public in our country.

I neither envisioned it for myself or for any one of us. For that lack of imagination, for that cocky certainty that the *Gazeta* had a positive image, I have paid a high price, and so has the *Gazeta*. We had our hides whipped. I regret the mistakes made, which might have misled a large portion of the public, but I do not regret the principal decision—we documented the attempt to buy us, and, by publishing the whole truth, we subjected it to open judgment. Yes, the corruption had to be documented and exposed. Yes, it had to be fought, and fight it we did. The work of an investigative commission, brought into being because of our articles, allowed for the identification of the "power yielding group" behind the corruption offer. The investigation succeeded mainly due to a few members of the commission and particularly as a result of the courage and extraordinary honesty of one of the members of the commission, Tomasz Nałęcz, to whom I bow my head in admiration today.

Initially we did not connect the demand for a bribe with the conflict surrounding the proposed media bill (which would ban Agora from buying certain media outlets); we just did not understand the nature of the "power yielding group." The "power yielding group," after all, was not synonymous with the SLD, although it is true that without the acquiescence of SLD leaders in the corrupt actions of their colleagues, the "power yielding group" would never have had the nerve to send Rywin to convey their scandalous, foolish proposal. Through the publicly broadcast sessions of the parliamentary commission, everyone who wanted to could see how cynical they were, how dangerous for Polish democracy.

IX

Polish democracy found itself facing a great opportunity but also a great danger. The opportunity is, obviously, provided by the EU. The spectacular growth in enthusiasm for populist parties is the danger. Populism feeds on fear. This fear is born of unemployment and the fear of unemployment; populism preys on frustration and disillusionment. Democracy is perceived as senseless chatter in the parliament. The market is associated with exorbitant profits made by some and the poverty of others, as well as with corruption or acquiescence in corruption. The conviction that everything is ruled by thieves is a dangerous one, but nothing justifies that view more effectively than tolerance of corruption.

Populism feeds on the dream of security, while democracy and the market economy offer freedom and responsibility for one's own life.

X

Stefan Niesiołowski, a politician of the Polish Right, known for his sharp tongue, wrote not long ago: "Various suspect types, former Moczar followers, communist collaborators, people who at the time of the People's Republic were quiet as a mouse, people of whom nobody knew where they were and what they were doing, today speak like heroes of the struggle for independence, like great patriots, and announce that they are the only true Poles, true Catholics and steadfast anti-communists. They brutally and mercilessly attack all those who for various reasons do not share their views. They reveal their opponents' shady histories and unclear (that is, Muscovite) origins." Therefore, we are angered to see the ethos of a democratic and honest Poland going to pieces.

It is difficult not to note the overall disappearance of belief in honesty and disinterestedness in public life, difficult not to notice the general view that everything is just a dirty game of self-interest and a Gombrowicz-like war of masks. One of the leaders of the Civic Platform Party (PO) asked at the hearings regarding the Rywin scandal: "Why are we talking about democratic values and not about the Agora business?" I replied that I believed in democratic values but that I had only limited knowledge of the Agora business. My interrogator just smiled knowingly. I realized then that, to him, base or material motives could be the only possible explanation for anybody's behavior.

Nobody believes in anybody or anything anymore. We observe the dramatic fall of all moral authority, a fall to which the politicians of all stripes have worked together to harmoniously contribute. It is impossible today to speak about a political opponent with respect; it is impossible to seek a compromise that would lead to the common good; it is even impossible to converse without an internal conviction that our adversary is but a cynical cheat.

I watch it with despair. There is an increasing lack of clarity and more and more obliteration of the border between truth and lies. The effort of trying to understand the adversary is sometimes replaced with the effort of trying to destroy the adversary. The Round Table, the instrument of disassembling dictatorship by way of negotiations, is called treason; fifteen years of transformation, which in spite of many mistakes and failures ultimately brought great success to a free and democratic Poland, are presented as a series of national disasters after the pastoral of Soviet domination and Communist dictatorship. So what should the average person, fearing the specter of unemployment and the actions of local power brokers, believe in?

Stendhal's character, Lucien Leuwen, a banker by profession and an MP by chance, has just brought about the fall of a government that he earlier helped form. In a conversation with his wife, he deliberates over the situation, analyzing his own options and the chances of making his son a prefect. The banker's wife asks innocently: "Wouldn't it be beautiful to do much good and not take anything in exchange?" "No one is going to believe that," replies the banker. "Monsieur de Lafayette played that role for forty years and he was always just a step shy of the ridiculous. Our society is too morally putrefied to appreciate such things. Three fourths of Paris would have loved Monsieur de Lafayette, had he stolen some four million" (Stendhal, *Lucien Leuwen*, 1834).

Sometimes I cannot help thinking that Stendhal's picture of the French restoration describes our Polish reality to a tee. And that picture explains so well why we are furious.

XI

However, we are not furious alone. All of the post-Communist countries are going through similar disillusionments and frustrations—the whole democratic world keeps talking about an institutional crisis, democratic deficits, and the growing dangers.

Twelve years ago I attended an international conference in Kyoto. Alexander Yakovlev, one of the godfathers of perestroika, also was a participant. One day, having observed closely our Japanese hosts, I said to Yakovlev: "Look, they have democracy but they are so disciplined that they don't have any freedom. In our countries, it is just the opposite." I gave Russia as an example. And yet I happen to be a true anti-Soviet Russophile. I do like Russians and I am at ease in their company. I love Russian literature, which often in life has served as a source of strength and hope for me.

Today, I am afraid of Russia. I am afraid of a Russia that leans dangerously toward autocracy. Obviously I do not share the opinion of many of my Russian friends, that Putin is as autocratic as Brezhnev was. In my opinion, that is absurd, like saying that Chirac is as bad as Pétain. Still, it is with apprehension that I observe how the Putin administration, under the lofty banner of fighting corruption, destroys oligarch after oligarch, simultaneously eliminating pluralism in the media and wrecking the institutions of civic society. It is with anxiety that I watch the Russian parliament become merely ornamental and political parties turn into pure fiction.

Obviously the process of stabilizing the country after the shock of the collapse of the Soviet Empire must be complex and full of traps. Nobody has ever learned how to swim without actually entering the water, but it is nevertheless disquieting when the pro-Western language of official Russian discourse hides an autocratic and imperialist message.

I wish Russia to follow a pro-Western path, because the institutions and customs of a democratic state wait at the end of that road. However, like nearly every Pole, I fear the return of the imperialist way of thinking in Russia. Therefore, I have always maintained that Polish membership in NATO and the EU should be an overriding priority.

We at *Gazeta Wyborcza* supported a pro-Western orientation in Polish foreign policy, but we also took great care to ensure that Poland's eastern border did not become another iron curtain. Therefore, we were open to the changes happening in Russia, Ukraine, Byelorussia, and Lithuania.

XII

Today few people are enthusiastic about the condition of democracy in the Euro-Atlantic world. We constantly hear that American democracy is endangered by the peculiar Judeo-Christian fundamentalism of the Bush administration, and we keep hearing about the danger posed to European democracy by the spirit of Berlusconi.

The epoch of globalization brings with it the crisis of the welfare state, the spectacle of politics transformed into a media beauty contest, and the specter of structural unemployment and corruption. The rise of populist rhetoric has been observed. In the opinion of Edward Luttwak, no party in the West, whatever its political program, can face the challenge of turbocapitalism. The people of those countries are unwilling to pay taxes to support those who do not work, and to feed the crowds of bureaucrats who serve as intermediaries in this assistance. Daniel Bell notes a resurgence of new populist parties in Europe; when traditional institutions and democratic procedures fail, irrationalism grows. And Zbigniew Brzezinski maintains that today the greatest danger to stability is posed by the conflict between the insolubility of social problems and the cult of material affluence and consumption, a conflict heightened by the main providers of mass culture and by the promulgation of self-indulgence as our chief ideal. As we can see, nobody in the world has found a cure for today's crisis of democracy.

The observer from Central Europe seeks a prescription in his own experience. In the face of the growing totalitarian danger of the 1930s, Karel Čapek noted that in facing the contemporary world, the intelligentsia had three options: shared guilt, cowardice, or martyrdom. As a possible fourth way he added not to betray one's own spiritual discipline even in the most trying circumstances. Could we help the world in any way?—he asked. He believed there was still a chance to win or lose.

Perhaps that is the best recipe for the imperfect world in which we must live. A world of imperfect democracy is still much better than a world of imperfect dictatorship. A dictatorship, regardless of what it might call itself and what ideas it might claim, is no answer to a threat. The liquidation of democratic institutions and customs cannot make it possible to prevail over the terrorist, fundamentalist Islam that has declared war on the values of our world. A tenacious defense of pluralism and tolerance is the only way.

XIII

Freedom brought us the necessity of settling our historical accounts. Therefore, we at *Gazeta Wyborcza* wrote about the difficult Polish–Lithuanian, Polish–Ukrainian, Polish–German, and Polish–Jewish conflicts. We were often accused of slandering Polish history. We have never accepted that. We have always been of the opinion that through sorting out our history, Poland, one of the few nations of our region, has passed on the test of our democracy's maturity.

When we ponder the condition of our democracy today, it is good to reflect on Polish vicissitudes in the twentieth century. Such reflection is a cause for both pride and bitterness. Let us be reminded of the euphoria after Poland regained its independence in 1918; of the unity we mustered in the 1920 war with the Bolsheviks; of the magnificent resistance of the Armia Krajowa (AK), or Home Army, and the underground state during the Nazi occupation; of the magnificent resistance of Stefan Cardinal Wyszyński and the Church to Communist oppression; of the great success of October 1956, when Poland managed to throw off its Stalinist shackles but, owing to wise, self-imposed restraint, avoided the fate of the Hungarian Revolution; of August 1980 and our collective revolt in the name of freedom and self-determination; and of the Round Table. We can be proud of all of these.

But there have also been quite a few dark chapters in our history: factiousness and depravity; the assassination of President Gabriel Narutowicz and Piłsudski's May Coup of 1926; the Brest trial and the Kartuz–Bereza detention camps; the "bench ghetto" for Jews at universities and the "pacification" of Ukrainian villages; the corruption and egotism of a substantial part of the political class—these vices found expression even at times of grave danger.

Years ago, Professor Stanisław Pigoń, the eminent scholar and great patriot, recalled in the book of his reminiscences a certain incident typical of this dismal tradition: the tradition of arrogance and impudence of the rulers. He described a summer 1939 visit by a group of Jagiellonian University professors with President Ignacy Mościcki. At that time, "The danger of a German invasion loomed distinctly on the horizon. Among others, Professors Bujak, Lasocki, Glaser, Pigoń, and Stanisław Estreicher were in the group....Bujak and Lasocki talked about the unsettling situation in the countryside. Farmers...did not trust the government led by the prime minister, whose hands were stained with the blood of strikers.... Witos, so necessary for the country at the moment, was not allowed to return....Glaser interjected a similar point regarding Korfanty....Estreicher made things absolutely clear... we can be saved only through uniting the whole nation and thereby exerting maximum resistance...the regime should be changed immediately in order to prepare for an all-out effort under the leadership of a national defense government. "The president," continued Pigoń, "sat there looking glum and angry....He complained of how badly he was mistreated in Poland as a president. He was bound by the Constitution to be responsible to God and history. And he felt responsible only to his own conscience." He dismissed our objections brusquely. Witos could return if he wanted to but nobody was going to change the system of law just for him. There was a court verdict against him and if he returned, he would have to report to the prosecutor to serve his sentence.... The president was particularly passionate about Korfanty. He held quite a grudge against him: Korfanty was a trickster, an adventurer whose own interests were his only guide....He rejected Estreicher's reasoning totally. All of that was nonsense. Polish politics, both external and internal, were in perfect condition.... The defensive capability of Poland had been placed in utterly reliable hands: if any aggression came, we would fight it and win. As for bitterness and internal disturbance—it was a misunderstanding. There was no such thing, and the nation was united behind the government."

Pigoń continued: "We listened to him, downcast; no one tried to stop that flood of cynical euphoria.... Finally, completely resigned, we stood up ready to leave. The short-tempered Estreicher alone could not bear it and said in a raised voice: 'Mr. President! Allow me to point out to you that your eyes see badly and your ears hear badly.'"

Later on, Pigoń said of President Mościcki: "History made a giant leap forward. Our eminent leader was forced to take to the Zaleszczyki road [that is, escape into exile] in a magnificent limousine. He was in a hurry but had judiciously managed to find in a drawer an old document certifying his Swiss citizenship. In the secluded land of Tell he was able to peacefully confront the highest tribunal of his own conscience. He cannot have been too worried about the verdict" (Stanisław Pigoń, *Fragments of Memory*, 1968).

I dedicate this story, told by a Polish scholar about the Polish president of prewar Poland, to all Polish politicians.

XIV ·

We at *Gazeta Wyborcza* have written about all of these things over the last fifteen years, the lifetime of our existence. We are as old as Polish democracy. We have tried to cocreate it, to support it, protect it, and accompany it from a critical distance. We have checked up on Polish democracy. It must be admitted, however, that with our criticism went a peculiar self-imposed restraint. We have been of the opinion that Poland faces a historic opportunity in joining NATO and the EU, and for the sake of that opportunity we were more cautious in our statements regarding prime ministers Jerzy Buzek and Leszek Miller and the president Aleksander Kwaśniewski than normal journalistic practice would require. Often we whispered, alluded to, and understated what should have been shouted out loud. We thought that matters divide into important, most important, and—finally—fundamental. In the name of the fundamental we were more cautious when writing about the important and most important. Thus the moment Poland joined the EU was also a key one for us, as we no longer had to restrict ourselves.

Today, I can clearly state that the fundamental goals of my political formation and my generation have been accomplished. We have a free Poland, well anchored in international democratic structures. Now the main task should be to address the primary matter: saving Poland from the rule of a coalition composed of populists, post-Communists, and post-nationalist pseudo Catholics. The specter of a coalition between the Self-Defense Party and the League of Polish Families Party, which under the banner of Catholicism—and contrary to the frank opinion of John Paul II and the episcopate—rejects the EU, may be disturbing but cannot be paralyzing.

We shall do whatever is necessary to block the boorishness and demagogy that may end in dictatorship and plain stupidity. However, we fully realize that Poland is not an exception here; these phenomena are common to all of European democracy.

We shall wrestle with them, just as other countries do.

And, for the time being, we are still furious.

CHAPTER TWO

In Search of Lost Meaning

The Twenty-Fifth Anniversary of
the Solidarity Movement

Twenty-five years ago, in August 1980, Poland changed the face of the world. I close my eyes and see it—it was a beautiful time with beautiful people. I was thirty-four years old and convinced that my generation was writing an important chapter in history. When recalling those days, I reach for my notes, as I do not trust my memory any longer. Too much bitterness and sadness have accumulated in my memory in these last few years; so I am not quite sure I am doing the right thing in writing up bitter remarks that do not quite match the atmosphere of that special anniversary.

Władysław Frasyniuk, my friend, the head of the workers' protest in Wrocław in August 1980, and later a legendary leader of the underground Solidarity movement, imprisoned during the period of martial law, recently appealed for the celebrations to be conducted in amity, with "all grudges set aside" and "no talk of traitors." I would like to write that way but I am unable to. I do not believe in the unity of that time and I do not want to—nor can I—celebrate with those who draw their knowledge of the democratic opposition and Solidarity from the archives of the Security Service, who treated police denunciations as if they were gospel truth. I feel soiled by them.

The experience of that time, historical and personal, cannot be spoken of in the language of police denunciations. Therefore, we ourselves must attempt to comprehend what we managed to accomplish. We must regain the sense of our own biographies.

I

Last year, the Nike Prize, Poland's most important literary award, went to Wojciech Kuczok for his novel *Muck*. The thirty-some-year-old writer told "a story of family hell," that is, the history of a Polish family, just an average provincial one. However, in this novel, superficially educational and moral, one can detect, just as in the cases of Balzac or Flaubert, a picture of a country of which the protagonists speak and think reluctantly, when they do so at all.

In the Poland of Kuczok's novel, there are no great ideas; there is no class struggle or bright future. There is no God, honor, or Motherland either. This Poland is a sad country of sad and uninteresting people. To quote the author, people are "hollow: they have their roots and their branches but they are hollow inside; they shut themselves off in that hollowness" and lock themselves away from the world. This world is ruled by a whip with which a father beats his son for educational purposes; the whip brings "excruciating pain." It is the whip with which the Old Man deals blows to the Young, and the strong beat reason into the weak. And the Young, beaten and weak, can only master a cry: "Dad, stop beating me!"

The Young, having been beaten with the whip, was then subjected to a lecture about how he is of the generation "spoiled by history" because, unlike the Old Man, he did not live through the war. In place of the experience of war, the Young was given the lesson of spittle. As early as his school days, spitting was customary; "spittle was the most effective teacher." One could expect to be spat on "from all sides, straight into the face, when an opponent ran out of words." Spitters were ubiquitous:

"I felt their breath on my back"; "They kept spitting while I crossed the street"; "They would mark me."

A whip at home and spittle away. This period lasted for a long time—such was the Polish home.

And then that home grew old. It grew old in an ugly way, much uglier than the way people age. "Homes grow old in a sneaky way; senescence hatches in them bit by bit, and then annexes whole territories. Home senescence gets out of control; it stops being visible to the householders, while arriving guests can sense it in the mustiness on the very threshold or in the corridor."

It was with that same mustiness that the home of Communist Poland, the Polish People's Republic, was dying out. The People's Republic was a country whose international politics, army, and police were subordinated to decisions made in the Soviet Union. It was a country ruled by the Communist *nomenklatura*, by police surveillance, imposed ideology, fear, and hypocrisy. People were beaten up and spat on by this system. With the help of some alcohol, one mustered the courage to express one's hatred of everything and everybody. The Communist system nurtured this covert hatred and skillfully preyed on what is evil and weak in a person. Timid pettiness, opportunism, apathy, and cynicism were common. On a daily basis, the instinctive reflex of repugnance toward the all-encompassing moral quagmire slowly disappeared. Yes, it stank of mustiness then.

II

In August 1980, Poland breathed in fresh, clean air—with both lungs. A mighty wave of strikes flooded the whole country. The strike at Gdańsk Shipyard, inspired by the democratic opposition and supported by intellectuals and the Catholic Church, led to the famous Gdańsk Accords and the establishment of trade unions independent of the Communist regime. This was not a superficial concession, such as had been displayed in the past, but a complete delegalization of the system of Communist dictatorship. The system, having claimed to be a dictatorship of the proletariat, was morally disqualified by a mass protest movement of the workers. If the label "revolution" properly applies to a great change preceded by mass social protests and real paralysis of the regime's apparatus, then we can speak of the "August Solidarity revolution." But above all, August 1980 was a celebration of Polish democracy as it restored meaning to the sense of human freedom, dignity, and truth.

I spent the period of the August strikes in prison, incarcerated, along with many other members of the democratic opposition, by the Security Service. "They" still believed—as all dictatorships do—that police can actually control history. On August 31, the Accords were signed that effectively ended the strike. On September 1, we were freed and found ourselves in a completely different country. Instead of mustiness, we smelled the wonderful aroma of freedom. My notes then, made in the thick of events, mention "the calm determination of the strikers, the spontaneous discipline, and the maturity of the workers' demands." I noted that the strikers demanded "a substantial change in the system of exercising power but stopped just before the limits marked by the Soviet military presence." I noted: "The workers fought for the rights and interests of the whole society, for social rights and improvements in the standard of living, for citizens' rights and freedom of speech, for the right of self-determination and independent trade unions, for moral rights and the release of political prisoners."

I pondered "with appreciation the fact that the authorities chose the road of negotiation instead of a power struggle." In addition, in the thick of events, I noted the Polish double bind. "The latest events," I wrote, "have proved that Polish society could not continue in a condition of progressing hypocrisy, enslavement, and pauperization—nor did it want to go on in that state. It is a justifiable reason for national pride that we have been able to restore our rights in the most reasonable of possible ways." Still, how Poles lived depended not only on their aspirations but also on Soviet domination, which was accepted by the West. Hence the assumption that "the non-negotiable aspirations of

Poles to freedom and self-determination must be realized in such a way that military intervention would hurt the Soviets more than refraining would." In a nutshell, I believed in some form of broad autonomy and democratic liberties existing within the Brezhnev doctrine. And I think that was the horizon of the whole Solidarity movement then.

Those were the days, and those were the words.... The cheering crowds, hungry for truth, appearing at meetings in factory and university halls—it was like the most beautiful of dreams come true. For us, the people of the democratic opposition, who lived through the student protests, the anti-intellectual and anti-Semitic witch hunts, the police repression of March 1968, the massacre of workers on the coast in December 1970, their repression during June 1976, and finally the harassment of those who worked in the Workers' Defense Committee (KOR) and other social initiatives, it was a long-awaited moment of satisfaction and vindication. After years of the whip and the spittle, of vileness, of desolation and cynicism, our actions found their existential and historical meaning—without the KOR and the democratic opposition, there would have been no magnificent, bloodless, and victorious August 1980. It was mostly the people of the KOR who led the Gdańsk strike.

And it was by no means easy for us—the security apparatus poisoned our lives with arrests and beatings, by banning us from working in our professions, by blackmailing us, and by using smear tactics. They tried to dig up whatever dirt on us they could find; they fabricated compromising material, slung mud at us, set us against each other, and harassed us with provocations. Many were not able to withstand the pressure; they would withdraw from activism, fall apart, or leave Poland for good. The bravest of us were continually dragged through the mud— the materials fabricated to discredit Jacek Kuroń or Jan Józef Lipski would probably suffice to wallpaper the whole Palace of Culture. Not a single one of us imagined then that many years afterward, when there was no Security Service, People's Republic of Poland, or Soviet Union, that those Secret Police archives would take on a life of their own, and that the beautiful time of beautiful people would turn into the muck of Secret Service denunciations.

But Poland's bloodless Solidarity revolution was truly beautiful—it was a carnival of freedom, patriotism, and truth. That movement managed to reveal what was most valuable in people—their tolerance, nobility, and kindness toward others. That movement built and did not destroy; it returned dignity to people and did not prey on the urge toward retaliation. Never before and never again was Poland to be such a nice country, its people so free, equal, and congenial.

III

It was the time of three Polish miracles: the election of Pope John Paul II and his visit to Poland in June 1979, Lech Wałęsa and Solidarity, and, finally, the Nobel Prize for Czesław Miłosz. For years we had been repeating that it was not enough to wait for a miracle—one has to work for it. And in 1980 Poles saw the results of that work.

At the end of the pope's visit in June 1979, I noted: "Something strange happened. The very same people who were frustrated and aggressive while waiting on line to do their daily grocery shopping were transformed into a cheerful and jubilant community, and became citizens full of dignity. They rediscovered this dignity within themselves and together with it their sense of personhood, self-determination, and power. The police disappeared from the streets and an exemplary order prevailed. Society, incapacitated for so many years, regained the joy of self-determination." John Paul II said "Have no fear!" and people stopped fearing.

June 1979 was a harbinger of August 1980, therefore, the workers' revolution carried crucifixes and portraits of Pope John Paul II. "Thus history," said Leszek Kołakowski ironically, "mercilessly mocked theory."

The Polish pope and then the Polish shipyard worker took the first bricks out of the Berlin Wall, together with the Polish writer who was honored with the Nobel Prize. Czesław Miłosz, the poet and exile, incisively exposed the workings of the "captive mind," told the world about his home ground, enslaved Europe, and spoke up loudly in defense of the Baltic nations subjugated by the Soviet Union. For thirty years his books circulated in illicit copies and underground or émigré editions— Miłosz was an icon of the democratic opposition.

John Paul II became a symbol of the best aspect of the Polish Catholic Church. The Gdańsk strikes and Lech Wałęsa became a culmination and a symbol of the rebellion of the Polish workers. Czesław Miłosz became a symbol of Poland's dissenting intelligentsia.

These were the three hallmarks of three tendencies within Solidarity: that which accentuated the national and Catholic character of the movement; that which personified the workers' movement and their demands; and, finally, that which emphasized democratic and humanistic values. These were neither contrary nor conflicting—we perceived them as complementary. But even then they bore the germ of future divisions.

All of that has changed the image of Poland in the world. Poland, perceived usually as a country of reckless cavalrymen charging tanks and as a country of drunks and reactionaries and anti-Semites and prigs, became an important, attentively observed, respected place. It was not only our courage that was admired but also our prudence; not only the patriotism and honor of Poles but also their moderation and sense of realism.

The self-limiting Polish revolution did not try to assume power in the state. Solidarity proposed a self-governing model of the Polish Republic—from enterprises to townships, and from townships to the institutions of the central state. There was quite a bit of realism in it—an impetus to act incrementally and to avoid open confrontation— but there was also quite a lot of delusion, for such a model of democracy functioned nowhere in the world. What is important, however, is that Solidarity remained open to seeking nonconfrontational solutions. Simultaneously, the Communist authorities—admittedly, under constant and brutal pressure from Moscow—were unable to offer any sensible model of coexistence. The regime grew weaker day by day. In order to save itself, and perhaps to save the whole country from a Soviet intervention, it reached for the ultimate countermeasure. On the night of December 13, 1981, martial law was introduced. The leaders of the labor union were imprisoned and Solidarity outlawed.

IV

Pushed underground, Solidarity endured seven long years. It survived repressions; some of its activists capitulated dramatically, while many went abroad. It owed its survival to the attitude of its leaders, especially Lech Wałęsa; to the behavior of its underground leaders, mainly Zbigniew Bujak; to the staunch refusal by those interned—Jacek Kuroń, Karol Modzelewski, Bronisław Geremek, and Tadeusz Mazowiecki—to capitulate; to the stance of Pope John Paul II and of brave priests; to the support of international public opinion; and to the hundreds of thousands of people who did not want to renounce the dream of a free Poland.

It survived also thanks to reason—Solidarity engaged in the struggle while rejecting violence, and it never stopped declaring its willingness to compromise. It never allowed itself to be broken or pushed into the extremism of a fanatical sect that feeds on the sense of injustice and the drive for revenge. It was absolutely consistent with its own values— from the beginning, in August 1980, it declared that it wanted to create, not to destroy.

Those were seven years filled with underground work and repressions, everyday risk and helplessness. We used to repeat a joke, probably borrowed from our Czech friends in Prague: What needs to happen for the Soviet troops to leave Poland? There are two possibilities: the rational one and the miraculous one. The rational one is that St. George who killed the dragon will come to the River Vistula and chase away the Soviet army. And the miracle?

They leave on their own.

Gorbachev's perestroika, from our perspective, was a true miracle. Initially it aroused suspicion—we had no reason to trust declarations made by the Soviet leader. But eventually hope arrived. The unrest in Russia created new prospects for change in Poland and other countries.

The connection between perestroika and Solidarity was obvious to me, although, I suppose, it was not that obvious to Mikhail Gorbachev. The Solidarity revolution was for the Soviet system the same thing the Reformation was for the Catholic Church—a challenge to all the dogmas of the institution that yet did not challenge the dogma of the faith itself. The Soviet system responded with its own counterreformation—a reply that assimilated all the critical trends of the reformation in order to save the institution itself. The Soviet debates featured themes well known from August 1980 and later months—demands for the truth about the Stalinist past and the economic situation, demands for freedom of speech and pluralism, and demands for reforms and the rule of law.

Leaders of the Polish United Workers' Party (PZPR) diligently studied the Soviet newspapers. They must have found the new language intriguing and disturbing. At the same time, they understood how much more maneuvering room they had. Two waves of strikes in 1988 were the last warning signs. Then the Polish authorities proposed the Round Table talks. As a result, Solidarity was legalized and free, though elections held in June 1989 were not truly democratic. Solidarity triumphed in those elections, the Communists surrendered power, and it all happened without a single barricade, without a single shot fired, without a single casualty. The spirit of August '80 triumphed—the dream to gain independence without violence or fanatical hatred.

The Solidarity revolution ended and the period of transformation began.

The historian and essayist Jerzy Jedlicki wrote a few years later that it was a historical artistry of the Polish anticommunist opposition of the 1970s and '80s to limit the immediate goals of civil struggle in its consecutive stages and to skillfully strike tactical compromises. He believed that due respect was owed also to the other side, because a truly ruthless authority would not have acceded to such methods. That agreement, he said, was a masterpiece of political ethics and its example might very well have spared Eastern Europe torrents of heroically shed blood.

I share Jedlicki's opinion. However, mudslingers are legion today. Foreigners often ask why. Indeed, it is hard to fathom.

V

Let's see: on August 1944, the Warsaw Uprising started; after sixty-three days of heroic fighting, it ended with a capitulation and a complete catastrophe. The flower of Polish youth perished, thousands of civilians were killed, the capital of Poland was completely ruined, and the political benefits equaled zero. Yet today we publicly worship, honor, and build monuments to that act of Polish patriotism, politically fruitless though paid for with so much blood. At the same time, the success of the Round Table, which paved a peaceful road to freedom for Poles—and not only for Poles—is sometimes treated as a malicious conspiracy and high treason.

Foreigners frequently ask why Poles are unable to take pride in what was magnificent and brave, wise and rational, and accomplished before the eyes of the entire world. Can Poles only worship the defeated, the fallen, and the murdered?

Alexis de Tocqueville observed once that although we may be used to the changeability of the human character, we may still be surprised at great changes in the moral disposition of a given nation, when egoism replaces sacrifice and indifference replaces passion. I often pondered the words of the great Frenchman while following the vagaries of Polish history over the past fifteen years, when the fight for freedom ended and the time of divisions and power struggles began. It was a period of demagogic promises and base accusations of treason, a time of corruption scandals and the rat race, of intrigues and vested interests, of contempt for the law and of mudslinging at those who rendered the greatest services.

At the same time, it was the best fifteen-year stretch in the last three centuries of Polish history. So, on balance, what is the outcome of the Polish transformation?

The workers who demanded civil rights in August 1980 have all those rights today, although their lives are often dramatically difficult and the conduct of owners of private enterprises occasionally recalls the unfettered capitalism. Nevertheless, workers have a right to unions independent of the apparatus of power. Another story is whether the unions are able to use those rights skillfully, whether they can renounce nostalgia for their former might and stop repeating the forms of protest they used when fighting dictatorship. In those years, each strike, street demonstration, and blockade was a means of weakening and undermining the Communist regime. Now one needs to find different ways of securing rights in a democratic country. Are trade unions today able to reject the temptation of populist rhetoric, to cease making demands that are impossible to fulfill, and to stop entering into alliances with xenophobic parties and enemies of the European Union (EU)? Can they formulate a program of employee benefits within the reality of a private economy, high unemployment, and progressing globalization? Let us leave these questions open. Obviously this is not an exclusively Polish problem. The whole European trade union movement is somewhat at a loss in searching for a new way to function in a united Europe.

Farmers enjoy all of the rights they once sought as well, but they are afflicted by the fear of foreign competition and of the inevitable changes in the structure of the Polish countryside. Intellectuals and artists also won full rights—they are no longer choked by ideological bans or censorship; they write what they wish and they publish what they want. But they fume at the diminishing government expenditure on science and culture. Their voice, so important and distinct during the dictatorship, today disappears in the cacophony of the words and sounds of mass culture.

The Catholic Church was granted all of the rights it demanded during the dictatorship, and certain privileges as well. However, the shepherds today lament that their flock does not obey the Church's imperatives. And within the sphere of politics, the voice of the Church has ceased to be decisive—the faithful do not respond to the pre-election appeals of the bishops and parish priests but, rather, vote in accordance with their own interests and liking.

So although all gained the rights for which the people of August '80 fought, no one is pleased with free Poland. In Wojciech Kuczok's novel there is a monologue by the old K.: "What terrible thieving times these are; they cheat a man in broad daylight.... Oh, if I were in charge, I would root out this plague, wipe it out completely."

VI

The waves of discontent are illustrated by the results of consecutive parliamentary elections. This proves, after all, that the system is functioning properly—society won the right to peaceful transfers of power, and it uses this very right. The problem is, however, that a miracle is expected with every change, although the time of miracles is long gone. Initially the miracle was to be the overthrow of the Tadeusz Mazowiecki government and the election of Lech Wałęsa as president. Then the return of post-Communists to power would fulfill people's nostalgia for the full employment and social security of the epoch of the People's Republic.

The frustration caused by unemployment and the loss of social security is accompanied by frustration of another type: justice has not been done. Many former activists of the democratic opposition and Solidarity, often highly distinguished activists, feel anger when they watch the brilliant financial careers of the people of the former regime. They see the growth of organized crime, spreading corruption, and the cynicism of the servants of the former regime, and they start looking for guilty parties. Often they say that the Solidarity revolution was betrayed or unfinished; their solution is to hunt down the agents of the old Secret Services and to search for them in police archives. Over and over they repeat that wrongs have not been righted and justice has not been done. And they are not mistaken—the damage has not been repaired; the crime has not been punished, nor has the virtue been rewarded properly.

Even worse, the fundamental idea of the Solidarity revolution—the design of a self-governing republic, from the individual enterprise through districts and towns all the way to the central state institutions—has been replaced with a system of parliamentary democracy and a market economy based on private property. The time of selfless heroism is gone—the ethos of solidarity has been driven out by the spirit of entrepreneurship and competition. The nobility of community workers and their daring and chivalry have not only become rare commodities but are little valued on the Polish market. Slyness and brutality, as well as ruthlessness and impudence, have become much more effective in these new times. Intrigue skillfully poses as nobility, and fanaticism dresses up as a defense of principle. No wonder that the people who gave their best years to the fight for a free Poland feel so much frustration.

However, the point is that every major revolutionary change raises hopes and expectations that cannot be fulfilled. In this sense, every revolution is unfinished or betrayed, and none brings about the punishment of sinners and the gratification of the virtuous. And may the good Lord save us from revolutions that truly balance vice and virtue and become completed. The completion signifies a guillotine or a firing squad. The compensation for suffered harm invariably brings new harm, often more cruel than what came before. It would be enough to examine the vicissitudes of the revolutions of the past two centuries. Whoever wants ultimate justice should remember that only executions are ultimate.

VII

At the beginning of 2005, Poland was shocked by the publication of a long list of Secret Service functionaries, agents, and people whom the

Secret Service had wished to recruit or failed to recruit. The names were listed at random, and it was impossible to discover how they had been categorized. Thousands of people felt slandered, and this was only the beginning of the show. Since then, the press and television have unceasingly disclosed more and more names of alleged agents drawn from the police archives.

The shocked Władysław Frasyniuk, an indisputable hero of the Solidarity revolution, wrote: "I cannot have remained silent when Lech Wałęsa found himself pilloried when accused of cooperation with the secret police when the out-of-control lustration of several politicians, including the current president, began, as well as that of the current and former prime ministers, who had previously been vetted and cleared; when they said that Zbigniew Bujak had been a 'gateway for secret service in the underground.'"

Wojciech Kuczok concluded his novel *Muck* with a telling appeal: "May the fucking lightning strike and burn it all forever!"

"But on that day," continues Kuczok, "instead of lightning they encountered muck: they suddenly sensed an awful stench all over the house, all the way to the attic; they sensed it unexpectedly and got worried and started calling out and asking what stank so badly, as if suddenly alarmed that perhaps their consciousnesses started rotting away.... They came down and opened the door a bit, and the shit-laden water flowed over to the neighbor, who stood on lower ground; the stench struck them with doubled force. The women whimpered weakly: Jesus! The septic tank must have run over."

Defiling the Solidarity revolution and its protagonists through the Secret Service archives is for some a heroic deed and for others a grenade thrown into a septic tank: some will get killed, some will be hurt, but surely everyone will stink like hell. So, here we are, injured, frustrated, and smeared, to celebrate the twenty-fifth anniversary of the August Solidarity revolution.

One can only hope that the Polish organism will reject the poison of falsified history and of a despicable axiology of the public life. One can only hope that in the aftermath of this cascade, some way of retrieving the lost *sense* will be found, and that we will be able again to talk rationally about what we once found the courage to do. After all, the bloodless disassembly of the Communist dictatorship, the regaining of sovereignty, the building of a parliamentary democracy and market economy, economic growth, the joining of NATO and the EU, stable borders, and good relations with our neighbors and ethnic minorities—that is not so little, is it?

Therefore, twenty-five years after August '80, I repeat to myself what the inimitable Antoni Słonimski taught me: Poland is a country of miraculous and unexpected events; in the Polish pot, both the devil and the angel are cooking.

Anything is possible in Poland—even changes for the better.

CHAPTER THREE

Rage and Shame, Sadness and Pride

The Twenty-Fourth Anniversary of the Imposition of Martial Law

For many years I feel rage on December 13—Solidarity, proved helpless, could be knocked out by a military coup. I feel shame because we didn't manage to prevent that dark scenario, because on a weekend night I let the authorities arrest me in front of my house when I should have had the foresight to hide. And I feel sadness, because Poland lost her great historical chance to sway history. But these feelings are coupled with pride because we managed to survive. Today, however, I feel regret that this anniversary is no longer an occasion for reflection and reverie on the convoluted paths of Polish history but instead gives rise to displays of reprisal and resentment.

This year we also celebrate the fortieth anniversary of a memorable proclamation by Poland's bishops, who twenty years after World War II extended their hands toward their German counterparts in a gesture of forgiveness and reconciliation. Are we then able, a quarter of a century after the introduction of martial law, to extend a gesture of forgiveness and reconciliation to our fellow Poles?

I

I've often wondered what martial law grew to symbolize. It was undoubtedly a symbol of the Communist state's victorious suppression of the mass movement Solidarity—a movement for democracy, citizens' rights, human rights, and a society's self-determination. It was a symbol of the defeat of the philosophy of dialogue and compromise born out of the August 1980 agreements. Finally, it was clear and most probably final proof of the ideological and moral illegitimacy of the Communists in power as geopolitics and unchecked military and police brutality became the only means of their survival. Martial law was a disaster for the Communist system. But at the same time, it became a disaster for the democratic movement which, despite its own rhetoric of omnipotence, was unable to defend itself effectively against the sudden and surprising blow. The imposition of martial law laid bare the false hopes of Solidarity's leadership, and its (and our) illusory sense of might. That defeat produced humiliation and helpless rage—frustration, resentment, and despair. Some were pushed into radical talk full of empty clichés. Others, devoid of hope, were pushed into private life, sometimes into capitulation and even emigration. It is important, however, that Solidarity was not broken; the leadership of its underground structures managed to survive the waves of oppression and the destructive power of despair and did not allow itself to be pushed toward extremism but, rather, consistently rejected violence. It managed to lead the supporters of Polish democracy to better times.

Is that really so obvious? To me it is. But I do realize that I am not an objective narrator relating the events of the time. I was a witness and participant, and nobody is a reliable witness in one's own case.

II

Several different accounts exist of the reasons for martial law and its historical context. Let us start with two classical ones.

On December 13, 1981, General Jaruzelski proclaimed: "Our Motherland is on the edge of a precipice. The cradle of many generations, the Polish home, reborn from the ashes, is being ruined. State structures have ceased to function. The struggling economy is subjected to new blows every single day.... Any prolongation of this state of affairs will inevitably lead to catastrophe and complete chaos, to poverty and hunger.... In the face of such a situation, to do nothing would be a crime against the Nation. We need to say: Enough! We must say it today, when we know the date is approaching of mass political demonstrations, including demonstrations in the heart of Warsaw, called to mark the 'December events' [workers were killed by government forces in December 1970]. That past tragedy must not be repeated. We must not allow—we have no right to allow—the announced demonstrations to become a spark from which the whole country may catch fire.... May this tormented country, which has experienced so many disasters and endured so much suffering, see not so much as one drop of Polish blood spilled."[1]

Twenty-four years later, after quoting the proclamation, General Jaruzelski added: "I read these words with an aching heart, because blood was spilled. Perhaps it was not a 'river of blood,' which was a real danger at the time; but nine miners from the Wujek mine died. It is a human tragedy and I bow my head in sorrow over it." In his proclamation of martial law, Jaruzelski also announced that "there would be workers' 'Solidarity.'" Those words remained but an empty promise.

Stanisław Barańczak, the eminent poet of my generation, reacted to the introduction of martial law with the poem "Restoring Order" (Stanisław Barańczak, *Restoring Order*, 1982):

> According to unverified
> reports. Which need to be treated
> with caution. According to
> unverified reports,
> which came in

1. Martial Law Declaration, *Trybuna Ludu*, December 14, 1981.

late due to
adverse snows and barricades.
According to
unverified reports,
they have gone too far
in the rapacious snatching of
breath into their lungs, they have lost
the sense of reality in refusing to
accept the boot,
the dialogue between brass knuckles and jaw
has been violated,
and the latter must be blamed.
According to unverified
reports, one should not wonder.
One should not wonder, really,
at the decisive reaction.
The reaction prompted
by the will to restore order,
so everybody knows
their place.

Thus, with irony and sarcasm, the poem commented on the war proclaimed by our nation's own generals against us, the citizens, the Solidarity
movement, Polish civil society, and the Polish will to be free.

Others commented on martial law in a different way. Caspar Wein-
berger (secretary of defense in the Reagan administration) called Jaruzelski a Soviet officer in a Polish uniform. This sharp rhetoric was supported by the conviction that Moscow played a crucial role the decision
to declare martial law. In 1984 Alexander Haig (then former U.S. secretary of state) expressed the opinion that dominion over Poland was for
Moscow a *casus belli*. "Poles themselves," he wrote, "cannot become masters of their own fate as long as the Soviet Union opposes it while enjoying overpowering force.... There has never been any doubt that the
popular movement in Poland will be crushed by the Soviet Union. The
only question was when and by what measure of brutality." François

Mitterrand, the president of France, who saw no possibility of squaring the Polish circle, reasoned along similar lines: "I always saw only two and not three options: Either the Polish government would restore order in the country, or the Soviet Union would. The hypothesis that Solidarity might win was purely fictional. Had that victory actually happened, the movement would have been wiped out by the Soviet army."

Meanwhile, in the streets of Warsaw, they were saying this about martial law: "A band of gangsters attacked the madhouse."

III

If proverbs and sayings are indeed the wisdom of a nation, then it is worth considering that statement about "gangsters" and a "madhouse." On the one hand, we have the authorities, who have gone from a philosophy of dialogue and consensus to the decision to attack their partners of yesterday like gangsters and brigands. On the other hand, there is the Solidarity camp, powered by a wave of revolutionary attitudes and behaviors, which evolved, contrary to their initial intentions, from the logic of self-restraint and compromise to an unbounded radicalism with no sense of reality or responsible good judgment.

In a communiqué dated November 26, 1981, the Polish Conference of Bishops warned: "Our country is facing great danger. Dark clouds loom over it and threaten civil war." The caution in these words is clearly directed not only toward the Jaruzelski regime. On December 7, the primate of Poland, Cardinal Glemp, told high-ranking representatives of Solidarity: "1. Gentlemen, such politics exceeds the mandate given to you by the workers. If you wish to engage in pure politics, establish an executive committee of Solidarity and do not drag the whole labor union into the game. 2. You are not taking the psychology of the nation into account. 3. You have not considered the international and economic situation." Undoubtedly this concern over the possibility of internal confrontation and a Soviet intervention dominated the bishops' attitudes.

Within the ranks of Solidarity, attitudes were much more diverse. Although at first the prevailing view was that peaceful coexistence must be established between the labor union structures and the authorities, it soon appeared that the latter backed down only when strikes were threatened and meanwhile did everything and anything possible to divide, antagonize, and weaken Solidarity. These ends were served by media smear campaigns and the provocations arranged by the Secret Service apparatus, hence the increasingly common conviction that the authorities always acted in bad faith, and that since it was not possible to discuss reforms honestly, reform could be achieved only through pressure.

All of the aforementioned were accompanied by the travails typical of any young revolutionary movement that was just beginning to institutionalize. Solidarity activist Bogdan Borusewicz analyzed this situation right after the introduction of martial law and was blunt and outspoken. "The movement was overgrown," he said in October 1983, "with all the negative features of the system: intolerance of dissent, suppression of criticism, and a primitive variety of chauvinism.... A cult of the leader flourished: in first place was the top dog, Wałęsa, who was immune to criticism; behind him came the leaders in every province and in nearly every single factory. Within Solidarity there appeared a wing that could only be compared with [the extremist organization] Grunwald or [the extremist publication] *Rzeczywistość*. The 'true Poles' of Solidarity also promulgated totalitarian ideology, though it was not colored red.... At a certain moment, the democratically elected activists of the union lost touch with reality."

Of the many self-critical analyses that emerged from the Solidarity camp, for example, the great "Critique of the Solidarity Mentality," by Sergiusz Kowalski, it is Borusewicz's tersely expressed insight that seems most accurate. Today, regrettably, a different treatment of historical accounts seems to dominate. Instead of reflection on the mechanisms of Solidarity's conflicts, we find accusations of spying for the authorities which, we are told, are the key to understanding Solidarity's history. In that fascination with the reports and denunciations to the Communist Secret Service, I find a strange national nihilism of sorts and a peculiar contempt for the heroes of Polish history and Polish national tradition. Why should the alleged evidence of the Secret Service have more weight than the accounts given by the heroes of the Solidarity movement? Why are the documents of Communist investigators and agents cited continually and persistently rather than the testimony of Lech Wałęsa, Zbigniew Bujak, Bogdan Borusewicz, Władysław Frasyniuk, Bogdan Lis, Tadeusz Mazowiecki, Bronisław Geremek, Stefan Jurczak, Jerzy Buzek, and Jacek Kuroń—to mention only a few names? After all, Solidarity was the European continent's largest mass freedom movement of the twentieth century. It was a movement of millions for emancipation and civil rights, the movement of a grand return of Poland to the main currents of history for the sake of rebuilding national identity and human dignity. That movement has shaken the world, and the movement's leaders and activists deserve gratitude and praise, not dirt dug out of the archives of Communist agents.

Today, when I read or listen to the ugly accusations that Lech Wałęsa, with whom I have often been at odds politically, cooperated with the Communist Secret Police, a fear grows within me. It is the fear that, before our very eyes, Polish baseness is being revived, so well described by (the writer) Melchior Wańkowicz. The best of our people have been attacked by it, starting with Thaddeus Kościuszko, through Józef Piłsudski, and all the way to Czesław Miłosz. This very baseness gradually invaded large parts of Solidarity in the fall of 1981, when the movement began to resemble a "madhouse."

IV

And what about the "band of gangsters"? In May 1981, Wacław Piątkowski, the head of the International Department of the Central Committee of the Polish United Workers' Party (PZPR), gave the following assessment of the situation to the envoy of Erich Honecker, the first secretary of the Communist Party of the German Democratic Republic (GDR): "Poles are in such a state emotionally that they not only betray their own interests and country but also present the gravest difficulties to the commonwealth of socialist countries, and endanger world peace. The degeneration of the Party is much advanced." What was happening was "a betrayal of the Party and of Poland. [First Secretary Stanisław] Kania is incompetent. He is just a passive tool...devoid of political principles. Jaruzelski is a hollowed-out puppet, taking pride in the fact that he is the prime minister. Nothing good should be expected of him." In the early summer of 1981, Michał Atłas, the head of the administrative department of the Central Committee of the PZPR, said in a conversation with a different envoy of Honecker: "Wojciech Jaruzelski plays an extremely negative role today. The anti-Soviet generals are his closest collaborators. We must prepare to face the fact that the decisive positions in the Party leadership will be taken by anti-Soviet factions. Poland is not a credible partner in the Warsaw Pact.... If the countries of the socialist fraternity do not begin to help in some way, I see no chance for socialism in Poland." The sense of both statements is clear: help from the comrades was needed, not only against Solidarity but also against the Jaruzelski regime.

Any attempt to interpret the aforementioned statements brings us to two fundamental questions: What was the PZPR? How was it perceived by the people of that time? Those years must not be extracted "from the whole history of the civilized world and looked at as a backwater locality, a maudlin, sadness-inspiring spectacle.... Every historian must enter that epoch in order to become familiar with the people who created it and who were actors in history. It is imperative to connect with the people whose work is to be assessed, with the people who are to be described, and with the people who are to be criticized."

These words come from an eminent man who not only described history but also created it—Józef Piłsudski. Accepting his point of view, one needs to ask if the People's Republic of Poland was then a backwater torn out of world history? Was it a sovereign country whose citizens decided their fates? Was it at least a sovereign dictatorship, like Franco's Spain or the Greece of the "black colonels"?

The answer is a resounding no. The Poland of 1980–1981 was ruled by the logic of Yalta, modernized by the Brezhnev doctrine of "limited sovereignty." The People's Republic was a country whose first government after World War II was installed by the Red Army. It was a nonsovereign nation, ruled like a dictatorship, whose leaders were condemned to fundamental obedience of Big Brother in Moscow and had little room to maneuver. So what was the moral and civic condition of a Pole in such a country? After the Yalta Conference, that Pole had no hope of being the householder of his or her own country. In keeping with the decision made by the world powers, the real householder would be Josef Stalin, and Communist puppets were to rule Poland by his authority. The hope of sovereignty was taken away from the Poles many times: when the Communists falsified the results of the referendum in 1946 and the parliamentary elections in 1947; when the pitiful remnants of political and cultural pluralism were liquidated and Stanisław Mikołajczyk had to flee to England to save his life; when the heroes of the Home Army and the Polish Socialist Party were condemned in Stalinist show trials; and when the primate of Poland, Stefan Cardinal Wyszyński, was imprisoned and the Soviet marshal, Konstanty Rokossowski, was made commander in chief of the Polish army. When all of this was happening, the democratic countries of the West did nothing to assist Poland, having forgotten that it was among the Allies from the first day of the war until the very last.

In 1956, the year Khrushchev spoke at the Twentieth Congress of the Communist Party of the Soviet Union, a smidgen of that hope was revived in the Pole. But the Soviet tanks in Budapest and the carnage of the Hungarian Revolution precisely defined the limits of that hope: it was possible to live but only within a zone adumbrated by the dictatorship of the Communist Party, controlled by Moscow. The Pole was reminded once more how strict was that control—in August 1968, when Soviet tanks, with the help of the Polish army as well, choked the Prague Spring in Czechoslovakia.

V

The lessons of limited sovereignty and the dictatorship of the Communist Party were well learned by the Poles—especially by those who created that authority and supported it, who came to terms with it and thought it would last forever. But what were those Poles like in 1980 and 1981? They were no longer idealists and ideologues who believed in the bright future of Communism, in Communism the liberator of humanity through world revolution. Apart from actual Soviet agents and people who saw in Soviet protection their only chance of furthering their careers, they were usually pragmatists, whose aims were measured by their strength and who saw Poland's future and her real *raison d'état* in harmonious coexistence with the Soviet Union. This was the lens through which they evaluated every action of the democratic opposition and of Solidarity. They were prepared only to make superficial concessions, including the admittance of some ranking Solidarity activists to the world of authority as the price of eliminating the "anti-Communist extremist" wing, a group to which I was privileged to belong. This pragmatism was accompanied by conservatism—the authorities wanted the kind of reform that would keep everything the same. They had no plan whatsoever for real democratization in which there would be a place for independent and self-governing trade unions and unfettered public opinion.

Those in power were not all of one mind. The faction led by Stanisław Kania and Wojciech Jaruzelski believed for a long time that the Solidarity movement and the wave of demands for democracy Solidarity could simply be waited out. Later they believed that the movement could be co-opted, corrupted, divided, and fractured from within. The regime had no plans for a "historic compromise" with Solidarity; it was probably neither willing nor able to strike such a compromise. But it was ready to grant all sorts of substantial privileges to the Catholic Church, which in the context of the time was considered a sign of flexibility.

Besides the faction centered around General Jaruzelski, there was also a strong and popular movement among party apparatchiks for radical action resembling the Czechoslovak "normalization" after 1968. These party members advocated strong-arm tactics and wanted to use the police and military to fight Solidarity. They opposed compromise and any concessions, and they provoked and kindled conflict after conflict, starting with opposing the registrations of Solidarity bylaws, through the arguments about the Independent Student Associations and Solidarity of farmers, the imprisonment of leaders of the Confederation for an Independent Poland (KPN), an investigation against the members of KOR, and the Bydgoszcz provocation of March 1981. The proponents of force repeatedly asserted the need to combat the counterrevolution, and they secretly tried to convince the envoys of Brezhnev, Honecker, and Husak not to stop exerting pressure on Poland. Those people were ruled by fear of the waves of political demands coming from Solidarity, day after day. Michał Atłas, as mentioned earlier, the head of the administrative department of the Central Committee, was undoubtedly an exponent of this policy. Its mouthpiece was the weekly *Rzeczywistość*, and Moscow was its true sponsor.

On October 21, 1981, a functionary of the Central Committee of the Soviet Communist Party, Konstantin Rusakov, said to Honecker: "The [Committee...] has regularly and in a timely fashion supported the positive forces within the Polish United Workers' Party. We visited half the provinces, provided the weekly *Rzeczywistość* with paper, and tried to move things along in Poland." Many years later, General Jaruzelski commented that that activity might have become, "in a given situation, a germ for some sort of coup d'état."

VI

Consequently, General Wojciech Jaruzelski, with admirable courage, assumed personal responsibility for the introduction and application of martial law. He has presented his reasons many times, recently in the book titled *Pod prąd* [Against the Current]. The book synthesizes the general's reasoning and at the same time serves as documentation, or perhaps as his argument in his own defense before the Tribunal of History. Such documentation, by nature subjective and one-sided, nevertheless contains much information and interpretation worthy of reflection or polemic.

Regrettably, Jaruzelski's arguments met not with sensitive polemics but with an announcement by a prosecutor from the Institute of National Remembrance (IPN) that there would be an investigation of crimes committed in the administration of martial law, crimes to which statutes of limitation would not apply. That particular prosecutor's charge I consider a dark chapter of Polish public life. When an IPN prosecutor can make the decisions about the complex and tragic weave of Polish history, I perceive a return, both moral and mental, to the epoch when [Communist] prosecutors decided what was or was not "the crime of fascist tendencies in pre–World War II Poland." Those were sad times marked by ignominious deeds. Having said that, I will engage in polemics with the general.

The general reasoned that a key role was played by two developments: Solidarity's actual rejection of the proposal of the Military Council of National Salvation of November 4, 1981, offered at the meeting between Jaruzelski, Wałęsa, and Primate Józef Glemp, and the big political demonstration planned for December 17 in the heart of Warsaw. These two events allegedly prompted the decision to impose martial law.

I find it difficult to agree unequivocally with this assessment. The proposal by the Military Council, unaccompanied by any plan of reform, must have been read by Solidarity as a mere gesture to manipulate public opinion—a façade engineered to mislead the movement, to foment internal conflicts, and to disarm and paralyze it. As for the demonstration planned for December 17, it would not have been the first angry one that year, and none of the previous ones had led to open war with Solidarity. I do not imply that the general consciously deviated from the truth. Just the opposite: I am convinced that he truly believed what he wrote. But the real reasons, in my opinion, were different, and I find them in the general's book, though disguised and mentioned only in passing.

I think that the true motivation for the December 13 decision was the Jaruzelski regime's fear of losing control over the apparatus of power. That fear was evoked, admittedly, by the specter of social unrest; more importantly, though, it was correlated with the growing pressure from Moscow, laced with blackmail and threat and with the potential to provoke an intraparty coup. Moscow exerted pressure both openly and covertly.

On September 17, 1981, on the occasion of the forty-second anniversary of the Soviet invasion of Poland after the Molotov-Ribbentrop Pact, a joint communiqué of the Central Committee of the Soviet Communist Party and the Soviet government stated that the two bodies

must draw the attention of the Central Committee of the Polish United Workers' Party and the government of the People's Republic of Poland to the growing anti-Soviet attitude in Poland and its intensification, which has reached a dangerous level.... The Solidarity convention was a forum for spreading libel and defamatory statements about our country. Anti-socialist forces are striving to produce an atmosphere of extreme nationalism in Poland, giving it a decidedly anti-Soviet character. We must examine why the official authorities in Poland have not so far undertaken appropriate and decisive measures to terminate the hostile campaign against the Soviet Union, with which the People's Republic of Poland is connected by friendly relations and treaty obligations. The Central Committee of the Soviet Communist Party and the Soviet government are of the opinion that continued tolerance of any manifestation of anti-Soviet attitudes will cause tremendous damage to Polish–Soviet relations, and contravening Poland's treaty obligations and undermining the vital interests of the Polish nation. We expect the leadership of the Central Committee of the Polish United Workers' Party and the government of Poland to take decisive and radical steps to put a stop to malicious and anti-Soviet propaganda as well as to any actions directed against the Soviet Union.[2]

2. *Trybuna Ludu*, September 18, 1981.

Everyone and anyone who remembered the Soviet declarations of 1968 directed at and addressed to the leadership of the Czechoslovak Communist Party and the leaders of the Prague Spring knew only too well what such language meant. General Jaruzelski probably knew it best.

Let us go back to the previously cited Michał Atłas. At the beginning of December 1981, he made the following comment about Jaruzelski and his people to Honecker's envoy: "If the leadership procrastinates any longer, it means they want the defeat of socialism. Then it would be necessary to call the Seventh Plenary Assembly of the Party to change the leadership." Mirosław Milewski, the secretary of the Central Committee and a member of the Politburo, according to Jaruzelski "a man who enjoyed a particular insight and trust of the allies," said at the December 1 Politburo meeting, "We have observed developments in our country that to a great degree resemble the scenario of the Hungarian and Czech events. May it not be too late to act."

This comparison was simply a reminder for Jaruzelski of the trial and execution of Imre Nagy, the Hungarian leader of the rebellious Communists in 1956, and of the kidnapping of the handcuffed Alexander Dubček from Czechoslovakia to Moscow in August 1968. These were not pleasant reminiscences.

VII

My strongest objections to Jaruzelski's book are related to what he says of the state's practices under martial law. Since this is a topic worthy of its own chapter, I will limit myself to a few obvious and abbreviated remarks. It is not only a few dozen victims that we bow our heads to. The enumeration and assessment of the mistakes, nonsense, and plain baseness certainly deserve something more than generalization and euphemism. After all, it is not true that martial law paved the way for a historic compromise and for the Round Table discussions. Martial law included a strategic plan of Kádárization—the Hungarian model of breaking the resistance of independent society, after which the country would take the road from the Communism of tanks and executions to the Communism of goulash and universal conformity. So it was intended to liquidate nearly all independent institutions—I say "nearly" because the independence of the Catholic Church was respected—and to use them to create new façades.

And these plans were put into practice: the Polish Writers' Association, the Polish Journalists' Association, and even the Association of Polish Artists and Designers were abolished and replaced with pro-regime mouthpieces. All of this was accompanied with provocations by the Secret Police, lies and smears, illegal wiretaps, blackmail, and other violations of human dignity and character; show trials prostituted the Polish rule of law. With us, the members of Solidarity, the authorities wanted to discuss only one subject: the capitulation that was to destroy our reputations. True, the regime was not bloodthirsty. But is that enough of a compliment for the people who ruled Poland unrivaled for those few years?

VIII

At the conclusion of his book, Jaruzelski says: "Given the reality of that time, and particularly in view of international conditions, we had reached the limit. Solidarity had come to the end of its road of far-reaching aspirations, demands, and unstoppable, unchecked revolt. The authorities could retreat no further from the principles of the existing system— which they had already modified to some extent—or from the need for internal security. The language could not be created for an authentic political dialogue. The level of mutual aversion, if not outright hatred, was growing and finally reached a peak....Martial law might have not been introduced had the world and Europe, and Poland's near neighbors in particular, been different at the time." So says General Jaruzelski. One could say that for his regime the introduction of martial law was the only way to avoid being destroyed by the vehemence of the Solidarity revolution, through an intraparty coup, or by Soviet intervention.

Avoiding that particular intervention certainly was in Poland's interest, and in Solidarity's, although the generals surely did not introduce martial law in order to earn our gratitude. It does not change the fact, however, that owing to the Solidarity revolution the Communist system registered the biggest defeat in its history. In introducing martial law, the Communists admitted the defeat of that ideology as they had to resort to violent means—their own or the Soviet brand. What is more, Solidarity, subjected to repression, pushed underground, its members forced to emigrate, did not capitulate to the violence but survived, preserving for better times the Polish desire for freedom, and it rejected violence and kept the spirit of compromise intact. Meanwhile, Poland managed to avoid a Soviet intervention that might have resulted in thousands of casualties.

Such are the facts. One can judge them in a variety of ways. But the fundamental question still needs to be posed: What price would Poland have paid had General Jaruzelski chosen to play the hero, following the example of the Communist Hungarian prime minister Imre Nagy? Most probably, he would have ended hanging from the gallows as his Hungarian counterpart had; perhaps today he would be praised as a hero; maybe he would have had a few statues erected in his memory. But Poland would have paid a tremendous price for that heroic gesture— it would have lost not the few dozen tragic victims of martial law but probably a few dozen thousands, and a consequent "lost generation" of young Poles. In a clash with Soviet military power, Poland had no chance whatsoever, and nobody in the West would have risked a military conflict with the Kremlin. Can politicians afford to sentence their own country to such a hopeless war, expose it to such a risk, to the outcome of that proverbial game of Russian roulette, played out on a national scale? The wisdom of the underground leaders of the Solidarity was that they chose a means of resistance that enabled the avoidance of bloodshed and still managed to preserve the ability to create and institutionalize an underground civic society.

IX

That fight lasted many long years. Solidarity stubbornly refused to capitulate and repeatedly expressed a readiness to sit at a negotiating table.
In the meantime, the regime's radical notions of healing the Polish economy ended in a fiasco, and the international horizon shifted dramatically.
In the Soviet Union, the regime of Mikhail Gorbachev implemented the
policies of perestroika and glasnost. After two waves of strikes in 1988,
organized by Solidarity, General Jaruzelski and the leadership of the
PZPR, freed from the specter of Soviet intervention, decided to negotiate with the opposition. Such was the genesis of the Round Table.

At this juncture, let us disregard the motives of the respective leaders of the Communist Party and Solidarity. Let us assume outright that
their motives were ignoble—one side wanted to best the other. Let us
assume that the Communists simply wanted to preserve their authority
by co-opting a part of the Solidarity elite. And let us assume that the
leaders of Solidarity wanted to improve the situation of the opposition
weakened by the years of repressions and hopelessness, as well as by the
apathy of a portion of the society.

Nevertheless, the results of the Round Table were a resounding success, the kind that made the world spin. The compromise allowed, through
semi-democratic elections, the transfer of power and the peaceful dismantling of the dictatorship. This monumental event, which nobody
had believed possible, came into being as a result of the discussions.
Poland was the first member of the Soviet Bloc to establish a non-
Communist government and to pave the way for the "Fall of Nations"
in 1989 nearly all over Europe. It was here in Poland that the first bits of
the Berlin Wall were taken apart, and the pedigree of the famous Velvet Revolution can be traced back to here as well.

The Round Table was the most important and successful Polish political accomplishment in the twentieth century, and it was achieved
without shedding blood. It was jointly achieved by the wing of the

Communist Party that wanted to save the system by reforming it, and by the people of Solidarity who wanted to abolish that very system. Both sides sat at the Round Table to strike a grand historic compromise between the Poles themselves. And that compromise signaled the true end of martial law. At the same time it marked the beginning of the end for the Communist system in Poland and Central Europe.

Every compromise is full of difficulty and has many opponents. The more unexpected, surprising, and revolutionary it is, the more criticism it may draw. Critics among the authorities were simply not able to accept the fact that after forty-five years the Communist Party had relinquished its hold on power. Władysław Gomułka's declaration that "power once gained shall never be relinquished" proved to be rubbish. The critics on the Solidarity side grieved that instead of a spectacular storming and seizure of the Communist Bastille there followed only peaceful elections and a quiet handover of power. The latter never accepted the fact of compromise with their former adversaries—they expected restitution and justice for years of degradation and abasement, and they sought revenge, not reconciliation.

That grieving is the source of all the talk of alleged conspiracy and betrayal during the Round Table, talk that persists to this very day. This chapter is no place to refute such mad reasoning—which, after all, is not the first madness of its sort in Polish history. In 1920, at the time of the Polish–Bolshevik war, Józef Piłsudski was accused of maintaining a secret telephone line to the Kremlin through which he could engage in some nefarious plot. One should not allow hearsay and madness to govern policy. Let us say just the following: What "nefarious plot" paved the way for Polish democracy and sovereignty, for a free market economy and open borders, and for membership in the North Atlantic Treaty Organization (NATO) and in the European Union (EU)?

Let us repeat emphatically: there was no plot. The deliberations of the Round Table effectively ended Polish–Polish hostilities. And that compromise, its effectiveness and durability, Poland owes to the ability of the elites of that time to think in terms of the common good. At the most trying and crucial moment, the Polish elites passed the test of patriotism and responsibility.

This was made possible by two leaders: Lech Wałęsa and Wojciech Jaruzelski. Their biographies, although so different, call for the pen of a first-rate chronicler; they illustrate the paradox, the drama, and the idiosyncrasies of Poland's vicissitudes. Both had to struggle against the stereotypes inherent in their own biographies and their own formations, both managed to carry out the true compromise, and both deserve the gratitude of the Polish people.

The situation might have taken quite a different turn. It could have been like Beijing on June 4, 1989, when the tanks choked the mass movement for Chinese freedom in the ill-fated Tiananmen Square. Or it could have been like Romania, which witnessed a bloody massacre. Or like Algeria and Burma, where, after the powers that lost in a first round of elections martial law was introduced and the winning opposition was sent straight to prison. In Poland things took a different turn. Poland, who for two centuries had been surprising Europe with her heroic and uncompromising fight for freedom, now surprised the world with her ability to reach a compromise that brought unprecedented results.

X

I do not wish to dodge the question of the moral significance of what happened on December 13, 1981. I grew up in the generation and the ideological formation that never acceded to the logic of dictatorship and that opposed that dictatorship, believing that rebellion against enslavement is morally justified, intellectually sensible, and potentially politically effective. Hence I can honestly repeat today, although I try to refrain from the rhetoric of the old veteran, that I am proud to have been among those, initially few in number, brave enough to challenge the system of lies and oppression. It does not necessarily follow, however, that we should abandon a critical attitude and a historian's perspective with respect to that time. Nor do I forfeit the obligation to honor the intrinsic dignity of our opponents, which all human beings deserve. In a lecture delivered in 1924, Józef Piłsudski said the following on the era of the Polish Insurrection of 1863:

> When I ponder the history of 1863, I always feel that it invariably tries some in the court of public opinion in order to extol the merit of others. One cannot hold it against Zygmunt Padlewski that he was unaware that just a few years later a new epoch would arrive in Europe and that Prussia's overwhelming might would bring it a hegemony of arms and would make technical innovation a monopoly of the powerful. To judge Padlewski would be as ridiculous and preposterous as to judge Wielopolski and his followers for their inability to foresee that in the years 1904 and 1905 Japan would defeat the mighty Russians, or that in the year 1925 somebody named Piłsudski would discuss him and Zygmunt Padlewski in the hall of the Vilna Theater.... He would talk about one and the other with equal ease, uniting them in a commonwealth of Poles, into the same style of that generation, into a union of people who believe that Poland as a country with established borders is a living thing, and not only living but able to create real things.

So said Piłsudski.

Let me repeat: "uniting them in a commonwealth of Poles"— Zygmunt Padlewski, the heroic leader of the insurrection against Russia, and Aleksander Wielopolski, the conspiracy's deadly enemy, who established conscription in order to make the uprising impossible. These words of Piłsudski provided me with crucial inspiration when I formed my opinions of Lech Wałęsa and General Wojciech Jaruzelski.

XI

Exactly for that reason, I read strident calls for revenge with displeasure, particularly when General Jaruzelski is the object of the attacks. What is so characteristic is that among those calling for retaliation are few authentic heroes of the democratic opposition. Rather, most of these people are better known for their circumspection at the time of martial law, a state that demands special compensation now, when courage seems to be much less expensive.

The well-known German psychotherapist, Bert Hellinger, pondering the phenomenon of revenge, said this:

> All those who think of themselves as better are suspect to me. Let us exam-
> ine the attempts at reconciliation with the past in East Germany....I have
> noticed that it is almost a rule that real victims are not enraged like those
> who had never been victims and now are claiming their mantle. They
> think it is a point of honor to express their fury at the oppressors, though
> they themselves never suffered but rather chose to hide in the crowd at no
> real risk to themselves. Hence, a very peculiar sort of arrangement exists
> here between the enraged and the evildoers, and the former feel much
> better than the latter. It used to be that the latter felt better as they were
> powerful enough to attack others and destroy them.

The opinions of the German psychologist are worthy of consideration,
at least by those who want to break the unending chain of harm, revenge, and resentment, and especially by those who wish to break with,
as John Paul II put it, "the lethal logic of retaliation."

The guilt of the former authorities is obvious to me—it has been
often declared and will be brought up again many times. But today we
are witnessing a consistent chain of guilt on the other side, the side of
the enraged accusers and avengers. Obviously their guilt is of a different kind, reflecting different times. But the disdain for the human dignity of an opponent, the disregard for material truth, and the replace-
ment of sensitive debate with prosecutorial investigation—all of that
leads us to suppose that the gene of Bolshevist villainy, the gene of
Homo sovieticus, is deeply rooted in Polish public life. After the calamity
of Communism with an inhuman face, we detect the features of anti-
Communism with a Bolshevist mentality.

This does not bode well. We are about to enter the twenty-fifth year
since the declaration of martial law. Soon it will be seventeen years since
the inauguration of the Round Table talks. Is anybody with any sense
able to imagine that a prosecutor in a free Poland would have started an
investigation of the perpetrators of the 1926 coup twenty-five years after
the fact? What sheer idiocy and clear absurdity!

Polish historical quarrels will remain alive for quite some time. To this day we debate the meaning of the national uprisings of the nineteenth century, and we assess the value of the 1926 coup, the Brest trials, and the 1944 Warsaw Uprising. We shall continue quarreling about martial law. But it is high time we stopped hunting for criminal responsibility. Let us allow prosecutors to pursue corruption, larceny, organized crime, and serious robberies but not political opponents from half a century ago. May the identifying mark of Polish democracy become not the spirit of retaliation but that of mercy. William Shakespeare put this emblematic passage into the mouth of a character in *The Merchant of Venice*:

> The quality of mercy is not strain'd,
> It droppeth as the gentle rain from heaven
> Upon the place beneath: it is twice blest;
> It blesseth him that gives and him that takes:
> 'Tis mightiest in the mightiest: it becomes
> The thronèd monarch better than his crown;
> His sceptre shows the force of temporal power,
> The attribute to awe and majesty,
> Wherein doth sit the dread and fear of kings;
> But mercy is above this sceptred sway;
> It is enthroned in the hearts of kings,
> It is an attribute to God himself;
> And earthly power doth then show likest God's
> When mercy seasons justice.[3]

I should like to dedicate the aforementioned passage to the new president of the Republic of Poland, Lech Kaczyński. And I should like to say to him: Mr. President, please terminate this sad spectacle of investigations and revenge trials. Please draw up an act abolishing them, which would make Poland worthy of her great tradition—a state without witch hunts, without political trials, a country of tolerance and compromise. Please make that the identifying sign of your presidency. Let us give ourselves a chance to become better.

3. Shakespeare, *The Merchant of Venice,* Act 4, Scene 1.

CHAPTER FOUR

The Bitter Memory of Budapest

The Fiftieth Anniversary of the Budapest Uprising

On November 1, 1956, a few minutes before 8 p.m., Prime Minister Imre Nagy spoke on the radio to make a memorable appeal to the Hungarian nation:

> The Hungarian national government, imbued with profound responsibility toward the Hungarian people and history, and giving expression to the undivided will of the Hungarian millions, declares the neutrality of the Hungarian People's Republic. The Hungarian people, on the basis of equality and in accordance with the spirit of the UN Charter, wish to live in true friendship with their neighbors, the Soviet Union, and all peoples of the world.... The century-old dream of the Hungarian people is thus fulfilled.... We appeal to our neighbors, countries near and far, to respect the unalterable decision of our people. It is true indeed that today our people are as united in this decision as perhaps never before in their history.[1]

These words, declaring Hungary's withdrawal from the Warsaw Pact, settled the matter of Soviet–Hungarian confrontation. In that

---

1. C. Gati, *Failed Illusions: Moscow, Washington, Budapest, and the 1956 Hungarian Revolt* (Washington, DC: Woodrow Wilson Center Press; Stanford, CA: Stanford University Press, 2006), p. 10, footnote 102. Subsequent page numbers given in this chapter are from this text.

confrontation, Hungary had no chance at all. By demanding national and human rights, Imre Nagy challenged the Soviet superpower.

On October 23, a demonstration several thousand strong was held at the monument of Józef Bem, a Polish general who immigrated to Hungary after the defeat of the Polish November insurrection of 1830 and became a hero of the Hungarian Spring of Nations. In the name of freedom, Hungarians demonstrated their solidarity with Poland and the Polish October, read patriotic poems, and remembered Polish–Hungarian friendship.

On November 4, Soviet troops entered Budapest to drown the revolution in blood. The drama of the Hungarian nation extended over those few days.

Was the defeat of the Hungarian Revolution inevitable? What did that revolution mean for Poland? Who, in reality, was Imre Nagy, the symbol of that revolution for many years?

I

Charles Gati, who emigrated from Hungary in 1956 and later taught at an American university, searches for answers to those questions in his book *Failed Illusions.* He goes back to the events of half a century ago in order to recall "the damned problems," to evaluate the mistakes and lost chances of all the participants in those events: the American administration, the Soviet authorities, the Hungarian government of reform Communists, and the insurgents themselves.

His brilliant analysis of American policy has a devastating conclusion: Washington had no coherent policy at the time. There existed only official declarations full of empty promises, the belligerent and demagogic rhetoric of Radio Free Europe (RFE), and the games accompanying the election campaign in the United States.

Richard Nixon, then vice president of the United States, said at a top-secret National Security Council meeting in July 1956 that "it wouldn't be an unmixed evil, from the point of view of U.S. interest, if the Soviet Union's iron fist were to come down again on the Soviet bloc, though on balance it would be more desirable, of course, if the present liberalizing trend in relations between the Soviet Union and its satellites continued" (p. 69). The strategic horizon of American policy at the time was such: things would be better if they were better; but should they get worse, that would be acceptable as well. Hungarians could not count on any real assistance. They could count only on themselves. Meanwhile, Hungarians treated the commentaries of RFE as the voice of Washington, D.C. They gladly listened to the attacks on Imre Nagy who, according to RFE commentators, was guilty of "treason" and "bore the mark of Cain on his forehead." At the revolution's decisive moments, when the fate of a potential compromise with Moscow was at stake, they also listened to the declaration of "Away with the Russians!"

Gati is of the opinion that such voices contributed to the confusion among insurgents; they made it difficult to reach an agreement with the Nagy government, and they sharply narrowed the government's room to maneuver. Was that inevitable? The dynamics of a revolutionary process usually preclude compromise. However, as Gati points out, Poland did not experience a Soviet intervention. Poles were in equal measure rioting in the streets, yet they, the Catholic Church, and the émigré community (including RFE) gave ear to the appeals for restraint and truly supported Władysław Gomułka. In the face of that situation, Khrushchev chose a compromise.

On October 30, 1956, he also elected to strike a compromise with the Nagy government. Gati wrote:

> What changed Khrushchev's mind was *that Hungary was not going to be another Poland.* Hungary did not want to be on a longer leash; it wanted to be on no leash at all. In Poland—because of signs of realism and the coincidence of cooperation among the Communist Gomułka, the Catholic Stefan Cardinal Wyszyński, and Radio Free Europe's calm Jan Nowak—the people, despite their strong idealistic tradition, accepted the half-measures that were being offered to them. In Hungary, Nagy was no Gomułka, Mindszenty [the Hungarian primate, who was imprisoned at the time of Stalin's rule] was no Wyszyński, and RFE's Hungarian Desk was not led by Nowak.

On October 30, Hungarian Communists were not in charge of their country; worse yet, they no longer tried to be in charge. Two critical events of the day in Budapest—the lynching of secret police officers in Republic Square in the morning and announcing the return to the multiparty system after lunch—appear to have convinced Khrushchev that Nagy and other Communists were too weak to maintain order." (pp. 188–89)

On October 31, a decision was made to intervene. The following day, Soviet troops crossed the Hungarian border.

II

At the outset of the Hungarian Revolution, I was a ten-year-old child. I recall the sadness in my home and remember the conversation in which my mother convinced me to give all my savings to aid Hungarian children. I organized a collection at my school, and that was the first political act of my life.

I have indelible memories of the long lines of people in the streets waiting to donate blood for the Hungarians. I pored over the Polish papers in the last months of 1956 and the shocking reports by Wiktor Woroszylski, Hanka Adamiecka, Krzysztof Wolicki, and Marian Bielicki. I read essays and analyses by Hungarian writers, many of whom later became my friends. In time I met the outstanding leaders of the Hungarian democratic opposition: Geörgy Konrád and János Kiś. I devoured Hungarian literature and was fascinated by Hungarian films. I found bits and pieces of the tragedy of 1956 everywhere. I shall never forget the wonderful essay by Kiś on the Kádár normalization. In the 1970s, we had started cooperating with the Hungarian opposition and issued their writings in samizdat. Over and over, year after year, I said to myself: "A Pole and a Hungarian are like two brothers."

And finally there came June 1989, the day of the ceremonial rehabilitation of Imre Nagy.

Charles Gati, who was present in Budapest on that very day, writes: "The mood at the square was surely encouraging, even inspiring. The people, having taken pride in living in what was widely called the 'best barrack in the Communist camp' and enjoying the meager freedoms granted to them by Kádár's semiauthoritarian regime, suddenly appear to have recovered the long-suppressed memories of real freedom in 1956. Did they finally stand tall, or did it only seem that way? More than a single drop rolled down my face. For the second time in my life, I experienced history in the making" (p. 226).

I also stood on the Square of the Heroes in Budapest that day. I was deeply moved by that demonstration honoring the murdered heroes of the Hungarian Revolution. That day brought the fulfillment of my dream of thirty-three years ago—that justice be served. Such dreams hardly ever come true.

III

The Hungarian Revolution, like every revolution, had two different faces: a joyful face and a dark face. The joyful face was the triumph, however short-lived, of freedom and truth. The dark face was the exploding hatred that turned into cruelty. October 30 in Budapest marked events as tragic as they were revolting. It all happened on Republic Square, right in front of the municipal headquarters of the Communist Party.

Gati writes:

Rumors had spread that morning throughout Budapest that there were secret catacombs under the pavement in front of the [police] building. Soon enough a huge crowd gathered, and some people claimed to hear the cry of prisoners calling for help. Armed rebels tried to enter the building to find the secret corridor to the underground jails, but they were arrested. In the ensuing battle, members of the secret police guards sent there to protect the building opened fire on the crowd in the square. Army tanks arrived; the shooting escalated; secret policemen were dragged out of the building and lynched; and Imre Mező, head of the Budapest party committee and a Nagy supporter, was also killed. There were no catacombs, and no political prisoners were found in the vicinity. (p. 177, n. 62)

That lynching served for years as an argument to discredit the Hungarian Revolution. But it is worth remembering: a revolution against oppression should not only evoke joy and hope—it should also evoke fear of revenge and hatred.

IV

Imre Nagy became a symbol and an icon of the Hungarian Revolution. János Kádár, who under Soviet auspices became dictator of Hungary, for years remained its villain. Both were Communists, but Nagy experienced some rather unpleasant history while living in Moscow. Both were victims of the politics of Matyas Rákosi, Stalin's governor in Budapest. Nagy lost his high-ranking positions, while Kádár was imprisoned. The latter was freed on Nagy's orders in 1954, during Nagy's brief tenure as prime minister. In the fall of 1956, the revolution raised both men to the very top of the power structure. On November 1, Nagy publicly declared Hungarian independence, having agreed on this step with Kádár. Later, they dramatically and forever parted ways. Nagy was interned in Romania (having been taken there from the Embassy of Yugoslavia, where he sought asylum). In 1958, he and his comrades were tried at a Stalin-like tribunal and sentenced to death. The sentence was carried out.

Gati wrote:

> Nagy, who was uncertain of himself during the revolution, became—on the road to the gallows in 1957–58—decisive, resolute, strong-willed, and unyielding. As he bravely confronted his interrogators and the so-called judges of the Hungarian kangaroo courts, he showed himself to be a genuine hero and a patriot who stood up for his beliefs. This is all the more remarkable not only because of his Muscovite past but also because if, after the Soviet intervention, Nagy had formally resigned and accepted Kádár's Moscow-installed government, he would have been allowed to live; he might have even played a role in Hungarian political or academic life. In-

stead, he did not cooperate with his jailors; he did not confess his political sins. On several occasions, he stubbornly refused to sign the minutes of his testimony and went on [a] hunger strike when his tough interrogator did not allow him to relate his side of the story. (p. 224)

At the trial, he never broke down. "As if he had expected the record of the trial to become public one day," Gati wrote, "he fought for his legacy. He declined to ask for clemency. In his last memorable words, he appealed to 'the international working-class movement' to clear his name. He died a genuine martyr and the only good Bolshevik the world has ever known. Thus the simple truth about Nagy is that he was a Communist true believer who became a loyal Hungarian. The more complex truth is that he was a Communist who became a patriot while remaining a Communist" (pp. 224–25).

This biography is worth comparing with János Kádár's. Kádár disappeared from Budapest on November 1. Until then, he had supported Nagy; he supported reinstatement of a multiparty system and voted for the declaration of independence. In a radio speech recorded before his disappearance, he proclaimed "the glory of our wonderful revolution." Soon afterward, he received word that the Kremlin had decided to suppress the revolution.

Gati wrote:

Kádár and [Ferenc] Müennich were being offered [by Moscow] the two top jobs. They knew that leading members of the Old Guard—notably Rákosi, [Ernoe] Gerő, and [Andras] Hegedüs—were in the Kremlin eager to return and take over the country's leadership. Their choice, therefore, was either to become traitors or to effectively hand over Hungary to the Stalinist diehards.... Kádár left Budapest without telling his wife where he was going. Professional politicians and detached analysts might call it a sensible choice under incredibly difficult circumstances, adding, perhaps, that this was what a politician who was a patriot had to do. In the real world, where decency and integrity also mattered, Kádár revealed himself to be a man with a bottomless capacity for expedient rationalization—and a man without a moral compass. (p. 193)

If we add to these remarks that Kádár was responsible for the slaying of Nagy and other leaders of the revolution, then it is difficult to question the author's assessment.

V

Charles Gati's fascinating book starts with an epigraph well worth quoting: "You must not deprive a people of their illusions" (p. 1). These words were spoken by Prince Kunó Klebelsberg, the Hungarian minister of culture during the 1920s, in a conversation with a historian. The prince was explaining why he had refused to allow new documents to be published that implicated the widely admired hero of a national insurrection in 1848 against Austria as in reality being an Austrian agent. Gati thinks that in the name of truth, people should be deprived of illusions. But he approaches the matter as a historian and not as an inquisitor who wishes to finish off his hated adversaries.

He writes:

> Consider the answers to these questions. Was Nagy at one point a Stalinist true believer and a Soviet secret police informer? Yes. Was he a popular—if also a Communist—prime minister between 1953 and 1955? Yes. Were many of his supporters disillusioned Communists who had once loyally served Stalinist causes? Yes. Did they prepare the ground for an anti-Soviet revolution? Yes. Was Nagy both a patriot and a Communist during the revolt and in captivity afterward? Yes. Did he and his associates lead that revolution ineffectively, even incompetently—but to the best of their ability? Yes. As for the United States, did Soviet aggressive behavior after World War II call for vigorous U.S. countermeasures? Yes. Did the U.S. government hope to liberate the Soviet satellites in Central and Eastern Europe? Yes. Did Washington prepare for the moment when some sort of diplomatic or economic, let alone military, assistance would be requested? No. Did key officials in the White House and elsewhere believe the slogans they uttered, or were they hypocrites? A few were true believers, most hypocrites. Did U.S. propaganda mislead the Hungarians? Yes. Did the United States let them down? Yes. (p. 20)

An evaluation of Russia's conduct must be similarly complex—Khrushchev de-Stalinized Russia as much as he wanted to, but Hungarians, unlike Poles, crossed the threshold of de-Stalinization acceptable to the Kremlin.

Returning to Polish matters, Gati quotes the well-known American analyst Walter Lippmann, who wrote in July 1956 that "it is not in our interest that the movement in Eastern Europe should go so far that no accommodation with Russia is possible.... In the interest of peace and freedom—freedom from both despotism and from anarchy—we must hope that for a time, not forever but for a time, the uprising in the satellite orbit will be stabilized at Titoism" (p. 164). The Polish émigré leaders Jerzy Giedroyć, Juliusz Mieroszewski, and Jan Nowak-Jeziorański expressed similar views, though with a focus on Polish interests. In this context, the evaluation of Władysław Gomułka must be unambiguously positive.

The problem, however, is very complex. Gomułka's stance indeed saved Poland from a Soviet intervention, and for that he deserves commendation. Yet the very same attitude led the way to "creeping despotism" and the curbing of civic, political, religious, cultural, and scientific freedoms. The progressive elimination of reform politicians, the intensified censorship, the elimination of academic freedom, the rows with the Catholic Church, the conflicts with the intelligentsia, the disgraceful anti-intellectual and anti-Semitic campaign of 1968, and the bloody massacre of the shipyard workers in December 1970—such was the dreary balance of the fourteen years during which Gomułka held power.

Is it not a sad paradox that in 1968 Kádár's Hungary was a much more liberal country than Poland? "Goulash Communism," the offspring of the lost Hungarian Revolution, unexpectedly proved to be much more humane than the Gomułka regime, the brainchild of the Polish October.

I do not claim that the bloody Soviet intervention served Hungarians better than the bloodless evolution of Poland from the liberation in October of '56 to the bloody December of '70. But I do claim, and it is an important conclusion drawn from those events, that no success is given to a nation once and for all, and no defeat is final. It may happen that defeat becomes the mother of reason, and that success breeds mental laziness and conformism. The memory of the bloody Hungarian Revolution pushed the rulers and the ruled to be moderate. Moderation in turn may lead to reasonable courage and unreasonable cowardice. In Poland and in Hungary, we witnessed both.

VI

The great Hungarian poet Gyula Illyés wrote in his famous poem "A Sentence about Tyranny" (in translation by George Szirtes):

> in tyranny's domain
> you are a link in the chain,
> you stink of it through and through,
> the tyranny IS you.

The Communist system was tyranny. In my circle, we realized that early on, although perhaps we didn't see it clearly enough at first. Until March 1968, we believed it was possible to reconstruct and reinstate the ideas of the Polish October. But long before that, we desired not to be "a link in the chain"—we chose opposition. The memory of the Hungarian Revolution, as well as of the Prague Spring of 1968, supplied us with a twofold lesson. First, resistance is possible—after all, it actually happened. We claimed that a system that defended itself with falsehood and oppression had to be attacked with the weapon of truth and not with violence. Second, change was possible but would be limited as long as the Soviet Empire existed. Therefore, the forms of opposition proposed and the changes made should be such that people could feel freer and the specter of Soviet intervention avoided.

Gati wrote:

> That is not to say that if only three of the four major players in the Hungarian drama—the revolutionaries, the Hungarian government, and the

United States—had proceeded more creatively or more cautiously, Moscow would have allowed the revolt to achieve its objectives. If those three key players had acted more prudently—seeking to gain a few yards instead of risking all for a touchdown—the Kremlin might not even have allowed a semi-free and semi-independent Hungary to emerge. We will never know. What we know is that in 1956 illusions and pent-up frustrations guided all four participants' actions. Cool heads did not prevail in Budapest, in Washington, or of course in Moscow. Emotions reigned, and wisdom was in short supply. In the end, instead of winning a bit of elbow room, as happened in Poland, the Hungarians ended up with little or nothing to show for their extraordinary bravery. (p. 209)

That particular passage from Gati's work was very dear to me. The Hungarian Revolution was for the people of my generation a call to nonconformism and courage, while the memory of it was an appeal for moderation and calculation.

VII

The dispute about the heritage of the Hungarian Revolution is one about political legitimacy. Regrettably, it is not unlike a dispute between hypocrites.

"Today's ex-Communist socialists," writes Gati, "identify with Nagy and claim to be his heirs and of 1956 too—as if their predecessors had nothing to do with suppressing the revolt, supporting the Soviet intervention, and, in 1958, organizing the juridical murder of Nagy and hundreds of revolutionaries. By contrast, today's anticommunists—some of them political impostors and turncoats who before 1989 cooperated with the Communist regime—do not know what to make of Nagy's Communist past, disparage his associates, and passionately deny the revolution's socialist goals" (p. 20).

Gati quotes with approval the words of Viktor Orbán that were spoken at the Square of Heroes in June 1989: "'We cannot understand that those who were eager to slander the Revolution and its prime minister have suddenly changed into great supporters of Imre Nagy. Nor can we understand that the party leaders, who made us study from books which falsified the Revolution, now rush to touch the coffins as if they were charms of good luck'. Paradoxically," comments Gati, "Orbán, then a fiery anticommunist and deeply pro-Western liberal, changed his spots and became a fiery anticommunist nationalist in a few years" (p. 226, n. 2).

A nationalist must face a difficult choice. In the name of defending the myth of a national revolution, he may glorify Nagy, thus making him a patriot without sin, or, in the name of defending the myth of the Hungarian people, always without sin, he may remove Nagy from the pantheon of national heroes, subjecting him to the ritual of posthumous lustration and decommunization because, as a Communist, by definition Nagy cannot be a hero of Hungarian history. Any which way, a nationalist will pick a myth instead of truth.

But this is not the only trouble he will encounter. Hungarians, just like us Poles, worship their defeats and their hero martyrs. They glorify them instead of cool-headed statesmen who seek compromise. Imre Nagy was a representative of exactly this ethos. "He was more impressed," writes Gati, "by the likes of Sándor Petőfi (the radical poet and hero of the 1848–49 revolution against Hungary's foreign oppressors, for whom the only choice was between slavery and freedom) than he was by the likes of Ferenc Deák of the 1867 compromise with Austria, whose opportunism did not yield Hungary full independence yet sparked not only an economic boom but also an extraordinary architectural renaissance in Budapest that is visible to this day" (p. 217). Today, when reverence is expressed for the Hungarian Revolution, which ended in utter defeat, we often hear of a "moral victory." With all due respect, may fate spare the Hungarians, as well as us Poles, any more of those "moral victories."

VIII

"Bravery without wisdom amounted to childish romanticism," writes Gati, "and what was needed was both courage to shake off the Communist oppressors and shrewdness to make them give up their positions without a fight" (p. 217). In 1989, we mustered enough courage and smarts, both Hungarians and Poles. But can we enjoy that bloodless victory? Or, perhaps, do we still prefer our "moral victories"—the Warsaw Uprising and the Hungarian Revolution? This is the question that makes the history of the Hungarian Revolution pertinent today. Richard von Weizsacker, the president of the German Federal Republic, said that to remember means to think about the past so intensely and truthfully that it becomes a part of oneself. This is a great challenge to our love of truth.

So what, then, is the truth of our times? Actually there are quite a few truths, so let us examine them. Charles Gati, an exile for whom the Hungarian Revolution always remained a thorn in his heart, desperately tries to tell the true story rather than a falsified or mythologized one. Contrary to the quoted opinion of Count Klebelsberg, he thinks that "responsible scholarship *should* try to deprive people—Hungarians, Americans, or Russians—of their historic illusions" (p. 21). However, since historical illusions are much more durable than thoroughly documented historical truths, I do not predict any immediate success for Gati. But I must congratulate him on his courage and persistence.

Another truth is the conviction—always relevant—that one can accomplish more in public life when "valor goes hand in hand with reason and prudence," and also when one promises people what is real, and not what is unreal though highly desired. That is the condition of an "idealist devoid of illusions," according to Gati. In the Polish tradition it was called "sober enthusiasm."

I got lucky—I lived in a circle of "sober enthusiasts" or "idealists devoid of illusions." Today I am afraid there remain a much smaller number of such people, as if the spiritual climate has changed. Persistent seekers of truth have been replaced with professional mudslingers. An idealist devoid of illusions will be driven out by a scoundrel without scruples. Is there still a place in public life for an idealist who cares to do something for the common good?

The idealist devoid of illusions has always followed one rule: do not succumb to despair. After my Hungarian friend János Kiś, I shall therefore repeat: democracy is not only about free elections, though democracy is impossible without them. Democracy is also about a permanent dialogue that is a dispute between values and the methods by which they are realized. It is also a debate about the past, historical truth, and the valuing of the freedom to search for that truth. Only thus do we pay true homage to those who fought for that truth and died for it.

PART II

The Work of Hatred

CHAPTER FIVE

The Sadness of the Gutter

Claude Lévi-Strauss wrote in his *Tristes tropiques,* also translated as *A World on the Wane,* that soon after Columbus's discoveries, the Spanish colonizers established a commission to ascertain whether the natives were people or animals. They asked: Are the Indians capable of independent living, just like the Castilian peasants? The answer was in the negative, and the conclusions of the report were obvious: It was better for the Indians to become slaves than to live like free animals. At the same time, Lévi-Strauss stated, the Indians occupied themselves with catching white people and drowning them, then guarding the drowned bodies for weeks to see whether their corpses were subject to decay.

I

In comparing the practices of the two sides, Lévi-Strauss observed that the white people were led by knowledge of the social sciences, while the Indians had recourse to the natural sciences. White people decided that Indians were animals, while the Indians suspected that white people might be gods. And Lévi-Strauss concluded that, considering their equal ignorance, the conduct of the Indians was certainly more worthy of human beings.

Lévi-Strauss described a conflict between civilizations—people do not understand each other, they are not able to talk to each other, and therefore they are not capable of any compromise. They understand only the language of war. This state of affairs has its consequences—we speak to an adversary, but we fight with an enemy. An adversary can be persuaded and a compromise can be struck with him; an enemy has to be annihilated, trampled, and drowned in the gutter. That is why in a world of war the language of the gutter dominates and the customs of the gutter rule.

II

"Gutters full of stinking mud," "a foul-smelling gutter"—these are phrases cited by Samuel Bogumił Linde, the author of the *Dictionary of the Polish Language*, phrases that date to the early days of Polish writing. The language of the gutter is the language of impurity, just as it was in the bygone past. Later on it became the language of abuse and cruelty. It is a language that has always soiled, denigrated, and dehumanized; sometimes it has even killed.

III

In December 1922, the Polish Diet (the lower house of the nation's parliament) elected a president of Poland. After 123 years of slavery during the partitions, after the bloody Great War, and after the victory over the Bolsheviks, a sovereign parliament of the Polish Republic elected a head of state. This moment crowned the process of rebuilding an independent Poland. The parliamentary clubs had nominated their candidates. Finally, after a few rounds of voting, Gabriel Narutowicz won. The candidate of the Center-Left Peasant Party-Liberation (PSL "Wyzwolenie"), supported later by the Polish Socialist Party and the Polish People's Party "Piast," Narutowicz defeated Maurycy Zamoyski, the candidate of the National Democratic Party. Narutowicz also won the backing of the Bloc of National Minorities.

This choice of president did not meet with universal approval. On the contrary, it triggered an ugly wave of hatred; the Polish gutter questioned the decision made by the Polish parliament. One day after the election the press published a declaration by the leaders of the National Democratic Party saying that Narutowicz had been imposed on the presidency by the "votes of foreign nationalities," votes that the Polish nation must perceive as a "violation" and a "grave insult." The National Democratic press argued that Narutowicz was not connected with Poland: "he could not even speak Polish properly." Rather, he was "a protégé of Jewish financial circles." The Reverend Kazimierz Lutosławski asked rhetorically, "How dare the Jews impose their president on Poland?" Stanisław Stroński claimed indignantly that Narutowicz "puts himself forth as a representative of the Polish state thanks to the Jewish–German–Ukrainian vote," and that the choice "is amazingly thoughtless, defiant and inflammatory." Other publications accused Narutowicz of being a Mason and a heathen.

One's blood runs cold when reading these texts. No wonder, then, that we recall them rarely and reluctantly. It is because something extraordinary happened. To be blunt, the politicians of the rightist National Democracy ended up in the gutter. They declared the parliamentary choice invalid and argued that because Narutowicz had been elected by the "Jewish vote" he should not accept the office or take the presidential oath. What this really meant was that a certain category of the population of a multiethnic state was to be refused the right to participate in the parliamentary election of a president.

Narutowicz was a man of great talents and abilities. At one time a pro-independence conspirator, he was later a professor at the technical university in Zurich, in the department of hydro-engineering. He was a true European, well acquainted with the reality and philosophy of Western Europe, and with the example of Switzerland's good school of democracy. There, writes the émigré historian Paweł Zaremba, he learned to speak "with everybody about everything, on the condition of sticking to a defined topic. He was unique in the world of Polish politics, in that respect and also because he did not treat ideological differences as an insurmountable obstacle to achieving an agreed-upon and concrete goal. He believed in the power of persuasion."

This was the man described as being imposed on the presidency by Jews, Germans, and Ukrainians. "The nation," wrote Stroński, "in whose veins blood flows, not liquid manure, must be appalled when it is shown arrogantly and with sarcasm that the most important and dearest institutions of its newly recovered state are decided by the hostile foreign nationalities." Along with articles in the press came a torrent of telegrams to Narutowicz demanding his resignation. Dozens of anonymous letters showered him with abuse and warned him of a "miserable death." At mass demonstrations, people shouted in the streets: "Down with Narutowicz!" and "Shame on him!" At rallies, National Democratic Party leaders repeated over and over that "Poland has been violated."

Historian Władysław Pobóg-Malinowski writes:

On Monday, December 11, long before the swearing-in ceremony scheduled for noon, a crowd, a few thousand strong, composed mostly of youngsters led astray, started gathering in the vicinity of the parliament building. Some made barricades out of street benches and school desks to block the president's route to the National Assembly; others blocked MPs and senators on the way to the Diet; those who belonged to the parties supporting the president-elect were showered with abuse, sneers, pokes in the ribs, and shouts that the Assembly would not convene because there would be no quorum. The socialist MP Piotrowski was severely beaten. MP Kowalski, a Jew, fought his way into the Diet, blood oozing from a head wound.... In light of all this," continues Pobóg-Malinowski, "those around the president decided to ask him to play it safe and go to the Diet not by way of Aleje Ujazdowskie but rather along Myśliwiecka and Górna streets, where there was no crowd. The president categorically declined.... The procession set out with only a slight delay. The police sat on their hands; an advance unit of light cavalrymen removed the barricades. The crowd blocked the president's route and greeted him with hostile shouts, whistles, and curses; soon clumps of mud and icy snow began to fly; some actually hit the president. A few bold youths jumped onto the steps of Narutowicz's carriage and were thrown off immediately by the chief of protocol, S. Przeździecki, who was accompanying the president. Once the carriage made it past the opened-up barricade, the screaming mob ran after it brandishing sticks, and from the rear and sides the crowd kept throwing clumps of mud and snow....In the Diet many benches were empty as the Right...refused to participate in the session of the Assembly and sent only one representative who managed to hurl a few words of abuse at the president-elect....Pale and deep in shock, he...swore [the oath of office] on the ebony crucifix in a strong, steady voice.

It is awful to read all that after so many years. But it was only a prelude to the real drama. Right after the swearing in, the camp of "true Poles" demanded that the president step down. Stroński, in an article entitled "The Obstruction," wrote that it was Józef Piłsudski who came up with Narutowicz to block the reforms in the country. Other National Democratic papers published articles in the same vein. Soon afterward, during a visit to the Zachęta National Gallery of Art, President Narutowicz was shot to death by Eligiusz Niewiadomski, a painter and critic, loosely connected with the National Democrats. The killer explained in court that although the real target was Piłsudski, "Narutowicz's assassination was a step in the fight for Polishness and for the nation. He died by my hand as a victim of the machination whose arena was the Diet—the Left did not want an independent man to become president. They wanted a man who would keep the country in anarchy, and by voting as a bloc with Jewry they have managed to get one." Accounts of the trial cited Niewiadomski's "heroic stand" and "sacred convictions" and spoke of the "tragedy of a man who loved Poland above all." Once the sentence of death was carried out, many people requested masses for the soul of the assassin, "the victim of patriotic duty." Władysław Konopczyński, an eminent historian who came out of the National Democratic movement, added a few years later: "The dignified conduct of the offender won him the admiration of many passionate hearts, although everyone admitted that he had harmed the nation, and the National Camp in particular." The historian failed to mention whether the "passionate hearts" also lamented the fact that only a substitute was killed and not the real target: Józef Piłsudski.

IV

Piłsudski, a legendary man, the chief of the state, had read and heard so many foul lies about himself that he decided enough was enough. Soon after Stanisław Wojciechowski was elected as the new president, Piłsudski decided to remove himself from the political scene. He was shocked by the villainy pervading the world of Polish politics. When saying good-bye to his associates in the Bristol Hotel in Warsaw in July 1923, he pronounced these memorable words:

> There was this shadow, running around me—it would sometimes overtake me and at times stay behind. There are many such shadows; the shadows have always surrounded me. Those shadows, inseparable from me, have walked with me step for step, stalking me and mocking me. Whether on a battlefield, in my peaceful work at the Belvedere, the presidential palace, or in the caress of a child—the shadow inseparable from me pursued me and persecuted me. It is a wretched, ghastly midget on bandy little legs, spitting out his dirty soul, slandering me from far and near, sparing nothing that should be spared—my family, my human relations, my nearest and dearest—dogging my every step, aping me and making faces, turning my every thought upside down; this ghastly midget has crawled after me like a fiend not to be parted from me, bearing flags of all types and colors, sometimes foreign and sometimes of our own country, shouting out platitudes, twisting up his ghastly mug and inventing unbelievable stories; this midget has been inseparable from me, a companion who has stuck by me through thick and thin, in ups and downs, in victories and defeats.... This gang, this crowd picking at my honor, sought blood. Our president was murdered after street brawls, which diminish the value of work in representation, by the very same people who earlier had displayed such filthiness and so much hideous, vulgar hatred when dealing with the first representative, elected through a free process. Now they have committed murder.

It is not difficult to feel Józef Piłsudski's fury and pain, fury and pain born out of moral shock. However, it is difficult to avoid the impression that Piłsudski's reply to the National Democratic witch hunt employs language far removed from the language of democratic debate. From then on, he invariably perceived his political adversaries as "scumbags, scoundrels, and thieves." Pobóg-Malinowski wrote years later that 1922 was a turning point for Piłsudski. "The Right's murder of Narutowicz and the complete impunity of the chief instigators led the Marshal to the conviction that nothing can be achieved in Poland through kindness and persuasion, that force and extortion are the only way and that one has to be tough and ruthless."

Before Gabriel Narutowicz was murdered with a bullet, he had been murdered with words. Along with him, the spirit of democratic debate was murdered too. "No Polish king has ever stood on a scaffold," wrote the poet Cyprian Kamil Norwid. Such was the message of Polish historical tradition. The assassination of Narutowicz implied a break with the unwritten imperative of the Polish national community. Until then, only treason, understood as purposeful activity for the benefit of a foreign invader, was punishable with moral infamy and ostracism, while death was a punishment reserved for those who committed high treason, and not for people whose goals diverged from the status quo. The assassination of a president meant that the value of an independent and democratic state as a common enterprise had been challenged, while individual interest had beaten the collective interest. And that was a new quality.

V

Several months later, the writer Stefan Żeromski was being murdered with words. That happened toward the end of 1924, after the publication of *Przedwiośnie* [The Early Spring], a bold, wise, and bitter novel. The book, in the opinion of Tomasz Nocznicki, a cofounder of the peasant movement, was written "in dismay that this free and independent Poland has so many jackals, hyenas, predators and executioners, and regrettably so few human beings."

The right wing immediately reacted to the book. A National Democratic columnist, referring to the participation of the main character, Cezary Baryka, in the demonstration at the Belvedere, asked: "If that's early spring, what comes with the real spring?" And, naturally, he provided an answer:

> Obviously, in the spring, Poland should bloom with the crimson flower of the Soviet state security services, in the dungeons of which the comrades, very nice woman doctors, will poke out the eyes of young Polish officers while the perfumed men of the Cheka will start manufacturing white gloves made of skin peeled off the hands of our generals. The encroaching conquerors of the world will bayonet and eviscerate those hideous Polish hags who once had the nerve to turn them down, while they, urged on by fashionable Jewesses, will wipe out many a group of Polish prisoners. And comrade Lulek will take up residence in the Wawel as the Polish Lenin.

Żeromski explained to no avail: "This is to state clearly that I have never been a proponent of revolution, in other words of murdering people for the benefit of something, property or money. In all my writings, and in *The Early Spring* in particular, I have condemned the Bolshevik massacres and torture. I have never called on anyone to take the road of communism; rather, in my literary work I have tried, as much as possible, to prevent the spread of communism and to warn, horrify, and deter." An idle argument: the Polish gutter did not listen to arguments. It stuck to its guns and knew better, as usual. "What's said in the book through the mouth of a communist about Polish prisons may easily, when translated into a foreign language, become an accusation against Poland, for the author has never disowned that accusation." The gutter honestly believed that the duty of a writer was to defend a penal system that tortured Communist prisoners.

But Żeromski was not only accused of propagating bolshevism, he was also accused of pornography: "Let Mr. Stefan Żeromski, since he cannot liberate himself from the influence of either pagan or bolshevist culture, remain faithful to his religion of sensual debauchery, but he really should not propagate corruption among his brother Poles." A member of a religious order, writing under the pseudonym Sodalis Marianus, proclaimed *The Early Spring* "one of the most harmful books in our literature." And, he added, "the most zealous Bolshevik could not have written a book advocating communist revolution as cunningly as this." Furthermore, "sensuality here borders on lasciviousness and cynicism."

Fortunately, not all of Poland was flooded by the gutter. On May 3, 1925, Stefan Żeromski was awarded the Grand Cross of Poland Restored (*Polonia Restituta*). The gutter immediately voiced its indignation. The writer, argued the gutter, had received the Grand Cross "for the communist tendencies of his latest book" and "for glorifying moral and physical debauchery." But "in the Polish heart there was no place for Bolshevist sympathies," because "a Pole ideologically submerged in this quagmire stops being Polish" and "becomes a kind of Soviet larva preying on the Polish land and spreading its poisonous breath." Żeromski was admonished to "get rid of the excessive humanism that remains deep inside you: it blurs the horizon for you, confusing your judgment and your views of the good of the Polish nation. You may remain a socialist or even a communist, but you must completely reject Jewish elements and all Jewish ideology. You may even become the devil incarnate, but be our own native devil and not the one ... with *payot* sidelocks. So, sir, reject all sympathies for half-Poles and sever any relations with them." Stefan Żeromski as a writer of the Jews and half-Poles? How peculiar.

The witch hunt went like clockwork. "In Poland," wrote Ksawery Pruszyński twenty years later, "it is not the wars that are well-organized but the witch hunts." The gutter sucks all in like quicksand, often even fine people. Earlier I quoted the words of Stroński and Konopczyński. And Karol Hubert Rostworowski, a writer of a high order, asked viciously: "What is the world going to get out of *The Early Spring?*" Rostworowski forgot to add that the world would learn a lot about the nature of the Polish gutter from the debate surrounding *The Early Spring.*

VI

At the threshold of Polish modernity we find magnificent symbols: the self-organization of society, the victory over the Bolsheviks, the reunion of the organic state that had been divided during the partitions, and the most democratic constitution in Europe at that time. We rightly take pride in all that. However, within the same period, we also find scandal, the gutter, and murder, and such symbols should always make us think.

The gutter is not a specifically Polish phenomenon; it is universal. It is advisable to learn from the lessons of others, for example, from France, the country of Pascal, Montesquieu, Napoleon, Chateaubriand, the country that produced the Declaration of the Rights of Man. In that very country, toward the end of the nineteenth century, Alfred Dreyfus, an officer of the general staff and a French Jew, was falsely accused of spying for Germany and was sentenced to life in prison.

The fight to clear Dreyfus and shame those who falsely accused him deeply divided French public opinion. Emile Zola's addresses won particular renown, starting with his famous "J'accuse!" Zola considered the verdict against Dreyfus a disgrace to France. In his defense of the condemned, he was led by the patriotic and honorable motives natural to a French writer who stands for the most precious values of his homeland. He observed with anxiety how the gutter flooded his democratic country. With disgust he noted the surging anti-Semitism that "desecrates our epoch."

As for the behavior of the gutter, Zola put it bluntly: "What a mad combination of obsession and stupidity, what a whirl of crazy ideas and corrupt police work!" He said it straight:

> It is a crime to seek support in the despicable press and to turn to the defense of the rabble of Paris. It is a crime to accuse of wreaking havoc those who want the pure France to lead the march of free and just nations. It is a crime to confuse the public opinion and use it in despicable work, making it delirious. It is a crime to trickle poison into the minds of the lowly and the meek; it is a crime to kindle the passions of reaction and intolerance, while sheltering behind the odious anti-Semitism, of which the great and liberal France, the country of the right of man, will die if not cured. It is a crime to use patriotism for the work of hatred.

Zola was dragged through the mud—the French gutter was highly dependable. He was accused of being a foreign agent; it was claimed that he was not ethnically French, that he slandered the state, the Church, and the army, that he was a libertine and a Mason, and that he worked for an international Jewish conspiracy aimed at the destruction of France. He was put on trial, and crowds of "real Frenchmen" gathered before the court, sparing no abuse or threat. The ferocious witch hunt and the climate of moral terror forced him to leave France. He was stripped of his Legion of Honor. But he was not silenced. In "Open Letter to the Senate" he wrote that in the France of his day nobody had the courage to see "the matter in accordance with the laws of justice and for the good of France. No one has this kind of courage; everyone trembles at the thought that they might incur a torrent of abuse from anti-Semites and nationalists." Zola died before the case was fully resolved with Dreyfus's exoneration. Nevertheless, he became a symbol of democratic, tolerant, and honest France.

Hannah Arendt reminded us years later that some people have been able to resist monarchs and have refused to make gestures of submission to dictators, but only a precious few have been able to resist the crowd and stand alone against the masses, daring to say no. Zola was such a man. All of France should tip their hats to the ashes of the writer.

VII

Tomáš Garrigue Masaryk, the first president of Czechoslovakia, was also such a man. Prior to becoming president, he learned the taste and the smell of the Czech gutter.

First came the matter of the so-called Hanka manuscripts, considered the most important Czech literary relic, dating to the thirteenth century. They were discovered at the beginning of the nineteenth century by Václav Hanka, an eminent scholar of medieval Bohemian history. The manuscripts played a highly important role in forming the Czech national consciousness in the nineteenth century. Regrettably, Hanka had forged them. A group of Czech scholars, including Masaryk, publicly questioned the authenticity of the manuscripts (also known as

"Královédvorský Rukopis," or "The Love Song of King Václav"). They started a storm in the gutter. The "true Czechs" decided that to call the manuscripts a forgery was synonymous with the thesis that "those who awakened the modern identity of Czechs were fools and swindlers," and that the matter of national rebirth was a "fraud and great stupidity."

Masaryk was accused of acting on behalf of Germany. There were even charges that he was not an ethnic Czech, that he did not understand the Czech soul, that he advocated "nihilism," and so he should be removed from the university where he corrupted youth, and that he should disappear from Czech national life. Masaryk tried to explain the scholarly and moral dimension of the debate over the Hanka manuscripts. "If it is a forgery," he said, "we have to admit it publicly. The Czech national identity must not be built on a lie—we will not be able to understand our own history if we keep company with falsifications. The dignity of the nation requires defense of the truth or rather learning the truth, and nothing more, as it is moral to courageously acknowledge a mistake that needs to be made known." On another occasion he declared: "I shall not succumb to terrorism, dishonesty, and political short-sightedness." Then he could read in return: "Go to the devil, you dirty traitor.... Don't you dare use our language any longer and foul us with your spiteful spirit and poisonous breath. Go away and stick with the enemies you have served; forget you were born of a Czech mother and walked on Czech soil. We exclude you from our national body just as we would a hideous sore. Go, run away from the Czech land before it splits to devour you." Masaryk did not "run away from the Czech land." Instead, a group of expert chemists examined the Hanka manuscripts and pronounced them forgeries. The Czech national identity did not collapse as a result, but a shadow lingered on the image of Masaryk: he was always suspected of distaste for the Czech national idea, cosmopolitan tendencies, and disrespect for ethnic solidarity.

This image of a "dissenter" was deepened by the trial of Leopold Hilsner, a Jewish apprentice accused in 1899 of the ritual murder of a young girl. During the trial, a mob bullied the judges into finding

Hilsner guilty and sentencing him to death. A higher court reversed the verdict, but a year later Hilsner was accused of a second murder and sentenced again. Clearly, every national gutter then wished to have its own Dreyfus. Masaryk, just like Zola, acted in Hilsner's defense. In several public interventions, he condemned the anti-Semitic hysteria unleashed around the trial. In reply, the Czech gutter accused him of godlessness and of acting on the instructions of Jewish circles, in whose pay they claimed he was. "True Czech" students organized a demonstration at the university to block Masaryk's lectures. He was nearly alone, for the academics chose not to support their own. But he kept repeating with great determination: "I chose to defend Hilsner because he is an innocent man. Moreover, it was a matter of dignity for the Czech nation. They call me a traitor to the nation because I could not stand the nation's shame.... What would the world think of the culture of a nation where Jews, who have lived there for centuries, were taken for cannibals?" Finally, Hilsner was acquitted. Many years later, the memory of Masaryk—the defender of Hilsner—was to prove very effective in the United States during the campaign for the independence of Czechoslovakia. That democratic society remembered Masaryk's righteousness and courage. "Wherever I went," he recalled, "the papers wrote about us favorably or at least did not criticize us. You cannot even imagine what it meant for us." In 1918, Masaryk was elected president. He kept the office until 1935. He died in November 1937. Recently, a monument to Tomáš Masaryk, the great democrat from Central Europe, was erected on Massachusetts Avenue in Washington, D.C.

VIII

Among the victims of the gutter are often people of unquestionable honesty, known for their wisdom and courage, outstanding citizens and patriots. They fall victim to cunning demagogy, blind stupidity, and cleverly set traps. It must be admitted that the organizers of the hunt certainly have a talent—they know how to tap into hidden complexes and fears, and they are skillful in manipulating emotions and utilizing rage. The politicians and feature writers of the National Democratic camp organized the witch hunts against Narutowicz and Żeromski. However, they had no monopoly on organizing the hatred of the gutter. The Jacobin and Bolshevik witch hunts were equally brutal, rotten, and bloody.

Let us return for a moment to the witch hunts against the president and the writer. Both witch hunts referred to the emotions connected with the rebirth of independent Poland: national independence was to be a panacea for all misfortunes. However, poverty has not disappeared, malefactors have not mended their ways, liars have not become truthful, and the bribe takers have not given up their lucrative business. One's labors on behalf of independence and honesty have not been rewarded, and offenses have not been punished. So the question was: Who was guilty of all that? Who was responsible? The fighters for independence—both real and phony ones—were disappointed: Why haven't those scoundrels who had stolen Poland from us and served the occupiers been sent to the gallows? Those bastards are doing all right for themselves, while simple, honest people live from hand to mouth.

How does one explain that the villainy of bribe takers and careerists did not cause Polish poverty, which is the result of many years of backwardness, economic slumps, and the dramatic problems of a young country? No, such explanations do not convince those who want to identify a perpetrator—here and now, immediately if not sooner, especially when those people are gnawed at by the frustration born of helplessness and when their bitterness turns into envy of successful people and hatred of the whole world. It is easy, then, to persuade such people that this is not the Poland they dreamed of. The propaganda of the National Democratic Party provided a simple answer: a Catholic state for the Polish nation. By that logic, the Polish Catholics have the exclusive right to elect a president, and he must be Polish and Catholic. Hence a president may be elected only by "true Poles," not by Polish citizens of German, Ukrainian, Byelorussian, or Jewish origin, and also not by those around

Piłsudski, who are a conglomeration of "Belvedervishes, defeatists, Jews, and converts," as a National Democratic journalist neatly put it. We need a "Polish majority," announced the National Democrats, enrapturing the gutter. And the gutter made that its battle cry: "They played on the lowest feelings of the broad masses: the right-wing press unleashed a campaign of hatred against him [Narutowicz], calling him a Jew," reminisces Piłsudski's wife, Aleksandra. "I was downtown and I was nearly immobilized by the crowd. On the one side, I was pushed by an old and half-deaf peasant woman who asked over and over what this was all about, on the other by a large, fat maid. The latter, red-faced and jiggling her whole body, pumped her fists and shouted: 'Away with Narutowicz! Down with the Jews!... We won't be ruled by the Jews.'" It is difficult, very difficult, to resist the mass aggression of a crowd. And it is difficult to resist this way of thinking—wicked and anti-democratic but so appealing to the mob.

IX

Years later, the eminent historian Janusz Pajewski pondered the predicament of the MPs from the Bloc of National Minorities. Had they refused to participate in voting they would have been acting against the state, undermining Polish statehood at a time when the government was trying to convince Europe to recognize our eastern borders. So, in Pajewski's opinion, they should have acted differently: "having deep insight into the situation," they should have voted equally for each presidential candidate. Had they done so, there would have been no claim that the president had been imposed by non-Polish elements; instead, their votes in favor of Narutowicz resulted in an "increase in Polish nationalism and particularly anti-Semitism."

I have no doubt that Professor Pajewski's analysis is well meant and characterized by a thorough knowledge of the reality at that time. However, I do not think his diagnosis is correct. I simply do not believe that had the minority bloc distributed its votes equally (or even thrown them to the candidate of the Right), the National Democrats would have stopped their anti-Semitic propaganda—not when even the shock of the president's assassination didn't stop it. The problem raised by Pajewski, however, has a much deeper dimension: To what extent should democracy give way to demagogy? Should Zola have kept silent, "having deep insight into the situation," been satisfied with Dreyfus's acquittal, and given up the demand for his full exoneration? Should Masaryk have let the forgery go, not stirred up the Czech gutter by defending a Jewish apprentice? In other words, is treating lies and villainy as an acceptable component of democratic debate a road to somewhere? Is it at all possible to strike a compromise with the gutter? The gutter is a significant element of public life—it can confuse people, bring them into the streets, and get them to throw clumps of mud at the president. So its existence must not be ignored. But is it all right to yield? After all, the parliamentarians of the minority bloc were choosing their president— the president of all citizens of the Polish Republic. In that case, why should they have capitulated to pressure from the anti-Semitic rabble?

These rhetorical questions do not change the reality—the crowd, egged on by the Polish gutter, actually believed that Narutowicz was only "half Polish" and that he was a "Jewish president," just as they believed that the author of *The Early Spring* was a crypto-Bolshevik. Why did they believe it so readily? Throughout the nineteenth century, Poles, defending their national identity, became used to the notion that a Pole was someone "of our own tribe," speaking our language, cultivating our own customs, and Catholic like us. And so they defended that language, those customs, and that religion when oppressed by their occupiers and facing a changing world. Faithfulness to language, customs, and religion formed a fundamental bond among all Poles.

How did a Pole perceive himself when looking in the mirror? Well, he was convinced of his centuries-old nobility and innocence. If he had ever been guilty of anything, then it was the excess of naïve idealism and kindness toward strangers. This Polish kindness had been used by foreigners to destroy Poland. And they were still using it. Otherwise, why on earth would hostile articles appear in the foreign press about Polish anti-Semitism, or about Polish ill treatment of political prisoners? Surely this must be vile slander! A Pole, by his very nature, is incapable of any ignoble deeds! So he feels even more indignant when similar things appear in Polish papers, written by Polish writers! Isn't that tangible proof that those papers are not truly Polish and the writers not true Poles? These are Polish-language papers and Polish-language writers, but they are not truly Polish! These newspapers and these writers are the most dangerous of all, for they rot the national organism from the inside; they sow discord and they tempt people into every sin. They are cunning, clever, and ruthless; they mock Polish heroism and magnanimity. And the Jews are the worst threat—a destructive element, spreading poison.

Such was the world as imagined by the Pole, the target audience for National Democratic propaganda, and that world was saturated with suspicion and fear. The climate of a witch hunt was conducive to increasing this fear, which grew to pathological proportions. The insecurity of everyday life, unemployment and poverty, fear of war and revolution, the decline of traditional authorities—all of these things contributed to the success of the Polish gutter. Fear, frustration, and confusion—all favored an outburst of blind fury. For the leaders of the National Democratic Party, the campaign against Narutowicz was an element of the fight for power and for sway over people's minds; for the crowds in the street, it was a way to relieve their fear and humiliation. Was Poland to be Polish and Catholic, or was it to be a strange republic of mongrels: "Belvedervishes and converts, Masons and Jews"? Such questions terrorized the mind and served as blackmail: Do you accede to a president "imposed by the Jews"? If so, you are not with us, the Poles! Through such blackmail, Narutowicz became a symbol of the "stranger" and an emblem of "high treason."

To point out that Narutowicz was a Polish nobleman and not a Jewish Bolshevik was of no avail—the crowd has no doubts and listens to no explanations. The crowd, swathed in its own fears and phobias, hears only one simple slogan: Away with Narutowicz! Narutowicz is a symbol of the ongoing harm, and blocking him from becoming president will surely right the historical wrong. Shouldn't the Polish nation be a host in Poland? And did generations of Poles over some 150 years suffer and fight with exceptional devotion for an independent state, so that now the president should be imposed on us by the very same peoples who once tormented and betrayed us—the Germans, Ukrainians, Jews? An abominable mockery that tries Polish patience!

X

A crowd first listens to such cries and then repeats them. Then it exaggerates, intensifies, and adds to them. A crowd already knows who the culprit is, and now it has gathered to mete out justice. A crowd is volatile, emotional, and intolerant; it gladly follows when urged to throw mud at the guilty. It is gullible—it will believe any lie, after enough repetition.

A crowd is composed of different people, but all together, gathered together, they are capable of deeds that no single participant would be capable of committing alone. In that anonymous crowd, people feel all-powerful, and simultaneously they feel they can act with impunity—as if subjected to a collective hypnosis, as if engulfed by collective madness. In a crowd, a wise man becomes mindless and cruel, and an ignoramus, a fool, and a jealous man forget their insignificance and feel just and strong with the strength of the crowd. A crowd, let's reiterate, professes crude ideas in which it sees absolute truths; it believes in a Manichean conflict between Good and Evil. A crowd does not comprehend the ambiguous, the nuanced, or the delicate—in these it perceives only weakness and deception. A crowd loves strength—the cruder and more brutal, the better. An instigated and infuriated crowd transforms itself into prosecutor, judge, and executioner. And it never feels guilty later.

A conservative hates the crowd—the crowd destroys order, breaks with traditional norms, and damages hierarchy and custom. A democrat has a problem with the crowd—he knows that a crowd took the Bastille and overturned dictatorships. So a democrat does not allow himself the right to make the crowd unambiguously anathema. Hannah Arendt expressed an opinion similar to a democrat's when she differentiated a crowd in a popular rebellion from a crowd of rabble.

Rabble, says Arendt, is a group of the declassé in which outcasts of all classes are present. A people's rebellion is characterized by the fight for freedom and real political representation, while the rabble always calls for a strong leader. The rabble hates the society that cast it out and the parliament in which it is not represented. When the rabble actually makes it into the parliament, we should add, it does everything possible to ridicule and compromise this institution. This explains the popularity of the plebiscites that will so often raise leaders of the rabble to power.

Why does the rabble listen to anti-Semites so willingly? According to Arendt, in the time of Dreyfus and Zola, Jews embodied everything that was hateful in the eyes of the rabble. Although it would be unjustified to state that the rabble hunts Jews exclusively they certainly seem to hold pride of place among its favorite victims. Therefore, anti-Semitism is usually, though not always, a telltale indicator of rabble. That is why, again, the European gutter so readily reaches for anti-Semitic language. And although Jews so often become the rabble's victims they are not the true target of gutter battles. The organizers and leaders of witch hunts are about power and money. The real fight is over the shape of the society and the state. The stakes in that game are extremely high— a victory of the rabble not only decides a change in the ruling elite but also means that the law of the rabble and the customs of the rabble will rule, and the language of the gutter will become the language of public debate.

XI

A Polish democrat remembers a great crowd in a Warsaw square in October 1956. He remembers a joyous crowd in another Warsaw square in June 1979. He remembers a dignified crowd at the Gdańsk Shipyard in August 1980. And he likes these pictures of wise courage, which have found a permanent place in our collective memory. But he also remembers that a crowd can be fickle in its opinions. Although it may believe that its actions always open up the Pearly Gates, it may cry "Hosanna!" today, only to demand "Crucify him!" tomorrow. After all, those who stormed the Bastille were nearly the same people as those who several months later murdered defenseless prisoners accused of plotting against the revolution. The history of the twentieth century made it evident to us that a crowd of people, joyful and freedom loving, can easily turn into a mob, grim and hateful. Moreover, as time passes, the spirit of the rabble and the language of the gutter make their way into the papers and onto radio and TV. In the next moment, the rabble enters the parliamentary chambers, and we hear the language of the gutter coming from a podium in the Diet. We can hear it today too.

Adam Pragier, once a well-known politician of the Polish Socialist Party, recalled Narutowicz's swearing in: "The ceremony of taking the oath was shocking in its grim terror. In the chamber, which was only half-filled, we were fully aware of being in palpable danger. But everyone was equally determined: whatever the cost, we could not allow the street anarchy instigated by the Right to gain the upper hand." But anarchy did gain the upper hand—bullets effectively determined the logic of Polish politics for years to come. The language of the gutter, that language of the brutal mob, did win. It is very difficult to oppose such a mob, just as it is difficult to put out a burning house with ink. But defied the mob must be, even if doing so means joining a lost cause. This is what Polish democrats were taught by the history of the twentieth century, by the fates of Narutowicz, Żeromski, and others who are now rightly among the Polish pantheon but who once were so badly treated by the Polish gutter.

The gutter, which hunted Narutowicz to death, transformed the political scene of the post–World War I Polish Republic into a theater of war. Two Polands faced each other, both hostile and full of hate. The camp favoring national independence, grouped around Piłsudski, became a bloc pursuing power by every available means—in 1926, it actually reached its goal, by a coup d'état. That time was marked by shameful language and abominable deeds, the abuse hurled by Piłsudski at the constitution and at opposition MPs. It was the time of the infamous "constitution—prostitution," of MPs imprisoned, beaten, and humiliated in the Brześć Fortress, of law held in contempt and elections falsified, and of criminal assaults on opposition writers—Adolf Nowaczyński, Tadeusz Dołęga-Mostowicz, and Stanisław Cywiński. Strength met strength, and wrath fought wrath. The gutter became the norm, and Polish democracy paid the price.

Tadeusz Hołówko, a politician and writer of the Belvedere (Piłsudski) camp, called the excesses of the National Democratic Party "right-wing bolshevism," while the writer Karol Irzykowski compared the practices of Piłsudski's followers in the 1930s to Soviet bolshevism. Both went over the top. The National Democrats did not have their Lenin, while Piłsudski—to cite the opinion of Herman Lieberman, a politician of the Polish Socialist Party—"is neither Mussolini nor Lenin,... he is a peculiar creation of the Polish reality. However, undoubtedly, he reflects a very dangerous hiatus in the social and political development of Poland." This is what Lieberman wrote right after the May Coup. When four years later he was beaten and humiliated in the Brześć Fortress, he certainly must have been thinking about how "dangerous" Piłsudski was.

XII

Lévi-Strauss said that people have always attempted the one and only task—the building of a society capable of living, and that, if this is true, the power that exhilarated our distant ancestors must be still within us. Our possibilities have not been exhausted yet, he insisted; we can do everything anew. What is done, and has been done badly, may be done anew. Differences in interests and opinions; conflicts, however acute;

polemics, however passionate—these are the bread and butter of democracy. Hateful slander (and the language of enemy baiting) is the nectar of the gutter. Within the democratic order, every conflict is ruled by unwritten principles: respect for the constitutional order; recognition of the common good; and the conviction that every citizen has his or her own place under the sun, and that every adversary has human dignity that must be respected. That is precisely the difference between the logic of a democratic dispute and the logic of the civil war that is unleashed by the gutter. A dispute is resolved with arguments and by choices made, while wars are resolved by slander and bullets. Therefore, saber rattling is always preceded by the language of the gutter, which poisons and depraves minds and dehumanizes the adversary, transforming him into mere trash.

Today, we encounter the language of the gutter every day—we read it in the papers; we hear it on TV and at party rallies, from the podium in Parliament, and occasionally from the pulpit. It still seems to signify little danger; it may just be a matter of politicians competing for popularity in the polls, or journalists scrambling to sell more papers. But a historian detects a very disturbing tone here: somebody accuses somebody else of "a constitutional coup d'état" just because the latter went on a trip to Moscow; somebody demands that a major political party be outlawed; somebody wants to deprive the former president of due process rights; somebody will call somebody a "pink hyena" while he himself is labeled "an agent of the Russkies"; somebody accuses the leader of Solidarity of being an informer; somebody publicly laments that free Poland was undersupplied with gallows for the members of the former regime; and somebody is going to write a contemporary history on the basis of the Security Service archives, not comprehending, the good fellow, that he thus changes national memory into a police memory.

Over and over I hear these persistent calls for hunting down traitors and spies, for vetting, and for decommunization and discrimination. I can see and hear people being humiliated by the consecutive investigatory commissions and the journalists' urge to make it to the lead in the race. They are but the pathetic bloodhounds of the wretched hunters. How rare is the pure voice of the humanist who warns against the explosion of hatred or the culture of malice. But this rare and barely audible voice is a harbinger of hope—just as it once was, in the time of Zola and Masaryk, Narutowicz and Żeromski.

XIII

Shortly before his death, Gabriel Narutowicz said to Józef Piłsudski: "You are right, this is not Europe. These people would feel better under somebody who would wring their necks and smack them in the face." I would not like anybody at any time to repeat these words of the Polish president who was hunted to death and murdered by the Polish gutter.

CHAPTER SIX

Accusers and Traitors

Dedicated to my friends who were insulted in the smear
campaigns: Tadeusz Mazowiecki in 1990, Jacek Kuroń in 1995,
and Włodzimierz Cimoszewicz in 2005.

My honest dislike of accusers and attackers dates back to the time of
the Polish People's Republic. There were witch hunts of people whom I
truly respected, often my teachers and friends. They were accused of
high treason, and those accusations were accompanied by vile abuse
and lies—lies that were usually not quite refined either. Sometimes the
accusers also tried to get at me, which at first flattered me, then amused
me, and finally bored me. The attackers had their own peculiar language: it swarmed with frightening adjectives and lofty exclamations,
while family names were used as insults. The accusers "unmasked"; they
"uncovered true faces"; they "disclosed unknown facts from the biographies" of "enemies of the nation"; they spoke of "foreign money" and
"non-Polish agendas."

The phenomenon of witch hunts is highly interesting. Witch hunts
have a long history in Poland; they have been organized on orders from
the authorities but have also been inspired by opinion makers who as-
pired to power; they have happened also in spontaneous reaction to a
statement by some daredevil brave enough to contravene a dogma considered unshakable. One precondition applied: to be the object of an
organized witch hunt, the said daredevil had to be widely respected

and seen as an authority by many groups; he had to be someone eminent and meritorious, a real obstacle to his accusers.

The witch hunt was always designed to disparage those people, to smear them and make them objects of collective hatred and contempt. Such was the meaning of the interwar attacks on Gabriel Narutowicz and Stefan Żeromski, on the one hand, and, on the other, on Wincenty Witos and Wojciech Korfanty. So, regrettably, accusers in the day of the Polish People's Republic had excellent examples to follow when they drove into defeat "wretched reactionary midgets," "agents of anti-Polish sabotage," and "cosmopolites with no homeland."

I believed, admittedly with some naiveté, that smear campaigns would become a thing of the past just like the People's Republic of Poland itself. I was completely wrong—soon the language of insinuation and slander had returned, together with the practices of intrigue and of sifting through police reports. Moreover, the same people, reaching for the same kinds of adjectives and exclamations, besmirched the dignity of the same people whose dignity they had besmirched so viciously at the time of the People's Republic.

Dr. Goebbels allegedly used to say that if we throw mud at someone long enough and systematically enough, some of it will eventually stick. In that way, the victim accused of betrayal eventually felt resentment, but the accusers who made the participation in the hunting battue their way of life would feel resentment as well. Both these resentments have survived and today dominate the campaigns inspired by documents from the archives of the Secret Police. Police snoops now issue certificates of morality; informers, once abundant among politicians and journalists, took a permanent place on the Polish scene. And that shadow will accompany us for a few years to come.

I

In 1867, the poet Cyprian Kamil Norwid wrote in a letter to Julia Jabłonowska:

It is my honor to have sent you some ephemera, Madam, as it is virtually impossible to write down all of them truthfully and humorously in the history of any people. They provide the proof that fanaticism is blindness, as we find there personages from all parties and of all possible degrees of merit, equally disgraced and disrespected. It reads quickly but hurts for a long time, and at the end one can only conclude that it's all nonsense, reflecting no civil courage whatever but draped in boasts and washed here and there with innocent blood, unwillingly shed.

Norwid attached the following addendum to the letter:

1. Rev. P. Skarga, a Jesuit, threatened with whipping by good Poles as he left the pulpit where he preached.
2. [King] John III Sobieski, proclaimed a traitor to the country by the patriotic Poles gathered then at Gołąb.
3. Prince Adam Czartoryski, described and proclaimed a bad Pole in every émigré journal but one (which he owned).
4. Adam Mickiewicz, reviled in Dresden as a bad Pole because he had not left Naples to join the insurrection and wanted nothing to do with it since he believed it could not possibly succeed.
5. Maurycy Mochnacki, reviled in the street as an agent of the Russian government, because of a manuscript which to this day nobody has seen or read.
6. Zygmunt Count Krasiński, slapped in the face by a good Pole.
7. Władysław Count Zamoyski, cudgeled by a gallant Pole in front of St. Madeline's Church in Paris.
8. General Bem, struck by two bullets fired by a good Pole, with one bullet striking his silver five-franc piece (something rarely found in that leader's pocket!).
9. Ludwik Mierosławski, slapped in the face by a heroic Pole in Paris.
10. Lord Dudley Stuart, beaten with a stick by a good Pole in London.

"Good Poles," elaborated Norwid, profess "a cosmic patriotism, that of sauerkraut and thuggish eastern accents," "delirious and unenlightened patriotism, lack of civil courage and daydreaming."

Clearly Norwid must have been bitter, hence his harsh censure. However, the list of Polish smear campaigns was quite long, and Norwid's compilation could be lengthened by many other names. Ksawery Pruszyński, himself the object of many such campaigns, said bitterly (in 1943, as an expatriate) that "there are few nations where calumny has such devastating force." He recounted that public opinion, "expressed by indignant mediocrities, condemned the May 3rd Constitution," and he listed several eminent Poles who had been "savagely slandered." "But [slander] leaves to their own devices... hundreds of mediocrities, thousands of weasels, and endless scores of riffraff." In reborn Poland, slander too was immediately reborn. Everybody and his sister were saying there was a rumor that Piłsudski "had seized the royal Polish crown," and that "a secret telephone cable linked the Belvedere Palace with the Soviet general staff." The smear campaign was "instigated by factional cabals and political splinter groups and its loudmouth and blowhards hurled the worst abuse at the greatest people." The campaign was well organized "as only Poland can organize this domestic form of terrorism and inquisition." Because of that, wrote Pruszyński, "it is necessary to keep a sharp eye both on the pack that barks and on the other pack, which urges on and directs the first."

Pruszyński's words have stuck in my memory—even now, I try to keep a sharp eye on accusers.

II

In 1951, a certain man of letters, forty-six years old, employed as a diplomat at the Polish Embassy in Paris, asked for political asylum. He was a well-known writer, probably the greatest poet of his generation. Before the war, he was connected with leftist circles in Vilnius, and then he learned the reality of the Soviet and Nazi occupation. He was not a Communist; he did not believe in the promises of Soviet propaganda. But neither did he believe that a military operation by the West would liberate Poland and, finally, he did not much miss the political system of the Second Polish Republic. The Poland set within the Soviet sphere of influence by the decisions of the Yalta Conference was for him a reality; he had some hopes for social reform; in culture, he was led by the motto that "one must save what can be saved." He called his breach with the Communist regime of his country a "suicide." He explained: "I did it at the moment when it became mandatory for writers to follow Soviet templates."

"During those five [postwar] years," the writer confessed, "I loyally served my people's homeland, trying to the best of my understanding to fulfill my duties as both a writer and a cultural attaché in the United States and France. This task was made easier by the fact that I was happy to see how Poland's semi-feudal institutions had been broken up, and how the young of working-class and peasant stock filled the universities, and how agricultural reform was introduced while Poland was changing from an agricultural into an agricultural-industrial country." The poet called his decision a "suicide" because he could not continue to write in a country where literature had to follow Soviet models. And exile? "My attitude to the Polish Diaspora," he explained, "was at best ironic: for someone who understood the dynamics of the changes happening in Poland, the disputes of parties a few members strong had all the appearance of a useless game and the very politicians looked like characters from vaudeville."

This writer's public confession was an act of honesty and despair. His compatriots in exile reacted to it with hatred and cruelty: the writer was declared a traitor to the country. Slander, which never dies, flowed fast along the gutter. The writer heard a fellow émigré's assertion that he was a fellow traveler who "for many years represented the Bolshevist government imposed on Poland as if it were a legitimate authority," and who "later on was sensible enough to remain in the West just in time," that he "drowns the truth in a flood of lies," that he "extols the current horrible reality," and that he champions "the chilly reptilian philosophy of those like Dzerzhinsky." "Can we imagine a Pole," argues the émigré compatriot, "who, if Hitler had won and established Nazism in Poland by force, would have represented that regime abroad as a cultural attaché and seriously claimed that he was serving Poland? What would we call such a man?"

Soon, voices from the domestic gutter joined in. Regrettably, the voices were those of outstanding writers. "You...impede the construction of factories, universities, and hospitals; you are an enemy of workers, the intelligentsia, and farmers.... If anything you say makes its way here, it...gives joy to the former capitalists and absolves assassins." Such were the words of one poet to another poet—the words of a poet turned a participant in the smear campaign to the poet branded a traitor. Another great poet-compatriot added: "We have found ourselves in a situation where there is no choice. There is no escape to the ivory tower, no retreat to the silence of the study. The choice for us is either/or. Let the example of Czesław Miłosz serve as a warning: Miłosz, who is trying to preserve his own ivory tower, having crossed that border, found himself in a neo-Nazi publication, on the same page with [the ally of Hitler] Vlasov."

If that was the language Antoni Słonimski and Jarosław Iwaszkiewicz used in writing about Czesław Miłosz, the poet who "chose freedom," then we can easily imagine the language of somewhat less exalted commentators. Let us call a spade a spade: it was the language of the witch hunt, a witch hunt directed by a totalitarian country skilled in utilizing the worst parts of people's characters; it was a language born of jealousy, fear, and the feeling of one's own ignobility.

So Czesław Miłosz found himself in a double bind: for the "indomitable émigrés, he was a traitor because he had once worked for the regime, while for the domestic adherents of the regime, he was a traitor because he had broken with the People's Republic in a spectacular way. Indeed, the fate of Miłosz was truly that of a man among scorpions. The situation got worse when after the publication of *The Captive Mind* he was flooded with a new wave of character assassination from Poland. He was accused of having assembled a "masterpiece of hostile propaganda" and of being "a traitor to the nation and his friends." He was branded an enemy of "Lady Art." His enemies pointed out that he had used a Lithuanian passport during the German occupation, and this was compared to being on the *Volksliste* (the list of persons in Nazi-occupied countries of German descent). They called him selfish and cowardly and said, finally, that he had slandered Poland and in so doing had "squandered his talent." Miłosz read this verse by a poet he himself esteemed highly: "And you are a deserter. And you are a traitor." So, Czesław Miłosz was "a two-way traitor"—to some, a "Bolshevik agent"; to others, "a guard dog of imperialism."

III

In the history of Polish literature, a history quite long and abounding in scandal, it would not be easy to find another writer who was subjected to such a long smear campaign, so hateful, so despicable, and so far-reaching. Admittedly, Miłosz was unruly, unconventional, and heretical—it was he who wrote that "the salt of the epoch is in heresy." He was also definitely against the dogmas of the "indomitable" diaspora, and he rejected the ritual glorification of pre–World War II Poland.

In 1932, as a young author, he wrote sarcastically about the enthusiasts of "national revolution": "Groups of young students armed with sticks and brass knuckles ran in the streets of the city shouting a very succinct slogan: 'Beat the Jew!' The thought process hiding in those narrow-minded, bigoted skulls was a complete mystery to me. It is not unlike when I try to penetrate the psychology of insects and the result is nearly the same." In 1936, he wrote of writers who eagerly embraced the class revolution: "They are so eager to sniff out treachery and class disloyalty, so tireless in parsing texts to see whether anyone happens to have written 'God' with a capital letter, that when their big editorial revision is done they have nothing left but a few books by [Communist novelist] Wanda Wasilewska.... Any attempt at independence and courage ends badly: with a prompt branding as 'fascist lackeys.'" The same year he wrote of Poland's spiritual climate: "We are led by hatred toward lies,

which have conquered this country. They are in the bray of mega-
phones, in the swaying of banners, in the mumbling over ceremonious
anniversaries: lies, nothing but lies. They are in lousy cabaret songs, in
the tail wagging of the journalists, even in the voices of children: lies,
nothing but lies."

If we add up Miłosz's skeptical attitude toward Polish politics in
the years of World War II, together with his literary excellence and his
spiritual independence, it is easy to understand that he was an ideal
candidate for the position of scapegoat in every smear campaign organized by the émigré inquisition and the domestic gutter.

IV

The accuser in a smear campaign is ruled by resentment. No self-
respecting individual participates in a battue. Anyone with respect for
his own dignity defends his views in reasoned argument; he despises
the filth of defamation. The accusers, both the great ones who are respected and honored and the second-rate ones who usually are lost in
the crowd of mediocrity and banality, reveal their latent complexes of
jealousy and hatred when they join in a smear campaign. In a totalitarian country, such a campaign is also ruled by fear: if I refuse to participate, then the powers that be may punish me. But I do not want to admit even to myself that I am ruled by fear—it is anathema to act under
the influence of fear. Therefore, I explain to myself that it is not fear
leading me but rather a profound sense of responsibility to the homeland, to the faith, and to the proletarian revolution. In addition, a smear
campaign provides an opportunity for a Napoleonic career—I may finally arise, I may shine in the limelight. At times like that, amorality
and blind fanaticism are highly praised, and crude lies and hurled
abuse become prized commodities.

The accuser is unhappy about his status in the world; he feels per-
manently undervalued, harmed, and debased. A long-hidden feeling of
humiliation and hopelessness concerning that debasement permeates

his heart. Unable to change or challenge this world, he compensates with a deeply hidden and carefully nourished dream of revenge on those whom he blames for the misery of his existence. Resentment equals spiritual self-poisoning. If I join the smear campaign, then I am ruled by jealousy of the person whose talent, courage, personal charm, and place in the sun I envy. But I cannot compete with this person, because his place is already taken. So I choose the road of depreciation: I call his talent negligible, his courage buffoonery, and his charm a talent to manipulate. But I am still devoured by a helpless jealousy—I cannot reach this man. Now the battue starts and the unattainable becomes attainable. No longer helpless, I can sling mud at this man, I can spit on him freely, and I can publicly abuse him. I no longer have to hide my jealousy, shamefaced; now I'm praised for it, as it is taken for a sign of the aroused national dignity, the righteous anger of the people, and a passionate testimony to religious faith. Now all of the loudspeakers proclaim that this weed must be pulled, this open sore must be cleansed, and this serpent must be clubbed to death!

A certain émigré writer described Miłosz as a "fellow traveler with the horrible psyche of a supporter of Bierut" [the Communist president of Poland]. Miłosz "asks that his merits be recognized. We should then recognize them in full." History seems to like ironic conclusions. Miłosz's accuser, the writer Sergiusz Piasecki, an employee of the military intelligence apparatus, had spent a few years in prison for armed robbery and criminal assault before the war. Now, transformed into an accuser, he spoke as the conscience of the Polish diaspora.

V

Émigré status has always been tainted with ambiguity. For the people in the old country, an émigré was a deserter from the battlefield or someone who had abandoned the homeland for an easy life. An émigré is someone who escapes while feeling helpless and cowardly, argued a Galician politician. "I have been an opponent of emigration from sad countries to cheerier ones," the writer Eliza Orzeszkowa stated firmly. These were not fair judgments, nor were they exceptional, and the émigrés knew it. They were also aware that they were growing farther and farther away from the reality of the old country. They created and cultivated in their own circle the mental image of a "besieged fortress," which always distorts behavior. Every difference of opinion becomes magnified, discord tends to snowball, and with them grows the susceptibility to intrigues and manipulations. The émigré community is a "pathological body, vexed and in pain," wrote the chronicler of the (nineteenth-century) Great Emigration; the poet Adam Mickiewicz spoke of "missed plans" and "hellish strife"; and Norwid observed that "the whole diaspora will constantly be caught up in wrangling that erodes its dignity and gravity and that weakens it as a whole."

The longer the separation from the home country, the greater the émigré community's helplessness will be, and the greater its helplessness, the more radical its opinions and judgments. Naturally, there have been exceptions. The leaders of some émigré hubs understood that they were ancillary to the home country: it was so with Adam Czartoryski and the Hotel Lambert; Jerzy Giedroyć and the Paris-based periodical *Kultura*; and Jan Nowak-Jeziorański and Radio Free Europe. More usually, however, the expatriates created their own patriotic code, and whoever violated it was immediately accused of treason. A culture of suspicion and pronouncements of guilt flourished. Émigrés, like fish out of water, helpless in the face of passing time and changing reality and sentenced to encroaching atrophy, felt endangered by constant provocations and betrayals, against which a shield of inviolable principles was to defend them, a moral fundamentalism as unavoidable as it was futile. Their intransigence entailed a categorical refusal to debate with those who thought differently or who proposed some sort of compromise or even reflection on the possibility of an agreement with the enemy. The enemy was the embodiment of Evil, and there cannot be any compromise with Evil—or so claimed the intransigents. However, a refusal to reflect meant a refusal to comprehend. The effort at comprehension was replaced with exalted proclamations; in that way, Czesław Miłosz was proclaimed a traitor.

These proclamations also had another source: the sense of a historical defeat (for Poland it was the Yalta Conference) and the grudge borne against all those who maintained that one could work effectively for Poland and Poles only in the old country. So everyone had the potential to become the accused. The case of Miłosz, however, was a special one: not only the "indomitable" leaders but also the émigré gutter could take revenge on a writer who so irritated with his excellence and independence. They could publicly humiliate and abuse a writer who so often said what he thought of the mentality, the morality, the reason and the political imagination of those who had "lost their home" and now created abroad a pitiable and grotesque version of the old country. Every country has its gutter; hence, the gutter of a grotesque country must be grotesque as well. But it was not exclusively grotesque, for it was also dangerous and cruel: nothing was more horrible in the Polish tradition than to be accused of treason.

Czesław Miłosz was not a traitor. What does that term really mean? A turncoat, an apostate, a dissenter, a renegade—these terms were not unambiguous, even in the nineteenth century. For some, traitors were advocates of compromise; for others, émigrés; for a third group, ultramontane, while for a fourth group yet, socialists. There was consensus only concerning those who renounced their Polish identity and called upon others to promote Russification or Germanization. For the expatriates, after 1945 all Communists were traitors, as were those who entered into agreements with them. This made even Stanisław Mikołajczyk a traitor, because he had returned to Poland in 1945 to establish an anti-Communist opposition there. For the intransigent émigrés, time had stopped on September 1, 1939; after Yalta, they were already living in a dream world and hating all those who would question it. However, a great part of Polish public opinion dared to question that world, and among the questioners was Miłosz.

Betrayal means abandoning your comrades in arms, your friends, and your homeland and going over to the enemy. Yet for Miłosz the world of the London intransigents was neither the motherland nor a group of friends. He never betrayed them because he had never belonged to them. Meanwhile, they, "trembling in the cave of shadows," vilified, accused, and impugned him. And they did impugn the honor and faith of the most eminent Polish writer of the twentieth century.

In thinking about the views of the "indomitable" émigrés in London, Juliusz Mieroszewski, *Kultura*'s chief political commentator, observed: "Our attitudes can be characterized as the psychology of a besieged town. In reference to everything, we are in a state of permanent martial law. Nothing is allowed; there is no good time for anything. Above all, nothing is permitted to change." And in a letter to Jerzy Giedroyć (May 1951), Mieroszewski commented on the attack on Miłosz in the *Dziennik Polski* [Polish Daily], which he called "the organ of émigré narrow-mindedness": "Everyone wants the right to be excellent—our gentlemen in London think that only those who have genuine dust from the Zaleszczycka Road [the route by which the Polish government retreated from Poland in World War II] on their pilgrims' cloaks are true émigrés. All others must be cut off because they do not represent the 'pure-bred' type. We are the émigré 'cadre'—Mr. Miłosz will never be one of 'ours.'"

VI

The accusations of the émigrés concealed despair, the child of defeat, and the despair of the poet Jan Lechoń when he wrote his shocking poem about Reytan and then hurled accusations and abuse at Miłosz. Nonetheless, in the shade of that despair, the spirit of the gutter was blooming, fed by the work of despicable bootlickers who sought the favor of the émigré notables and sent the American authorities reports denouncing Miłosz as a Soviet agent. Behind the accusations in Poland stood the fury that is directed against a writer who has cast off his chains. After all, that writer, as the Communists believed, was already their property; he was a diplomat who had abandoned his mission. He had simply betrayed us. He had betrayed Poland, the revolution, and the literary establishment.

In his poem about the suicide of the poet Tadeusz Borowski, Miłosz wrote: "Borowski has betrayed. He has escaped where he could. / Ahead, he saw the eastern commissaries, / Behind, the Polish reactionaries." Miłosz did not betray anybody or anything—Miłosz escaped. Francesco Guicciardini, Machiavelli's friend, used to say that there is only one way to deal with a tyrant, just as there is only one way to deal with the plague: take to your heels and run, as far away as possible.

Obviously, the Communists couldn't understand any of that; a tyrant, for them, was the Spirit of History, the Inevitable Necessity, and the Benefactor of Mankind. They felt they were the soldiers of the revolution, drivers of the engine of history, and engineers of the human soul. In other words, they were blind fanatics; narrow mental horizons (the narrowness understood as selfless devotion to an idea), ruthlessness and cruelty in human relations, and the inability to perceive reality realistically—these made up the character of a tough Bolshevik. It was these people who saw Miłosz as betraying the revolution. "There are no honest traitors!" they repeated—but there was also no possibility of an intellectual discussion with a traitor, because betrayal is not an intellectual notion. The Communists, trapped by the limits of their own discourse, reached for the vocabulary of slander and the smear campaign. The writers close to Miłosz were quite different. We have quoted Iwaszkiewicz and Słonimski, because their guilt was so instructive that we could not omit their voices. However, their actions and attitudes were motivated not only by fear of the totalitarian regime but also by a conviction that Miłosz had some sort of unwritten commitment, under which even here, in the old country, even if the price was high, one had to "save what could be saved." And it was in that particular sense that they felt betrayed. Miłosz seemed to have shared that point of view, and possibly that is why he clarified his motives so extensively.

Let us repeat: Miłosz's decision was judged in a variety of ways. But the behavior of the writers who took part in the smear campaign against him can only be described as shameful. The insinuations that Miłosz renounced his Polishness at the time of the German occupation, or that he was simply a Soviet agent, or that he "chose freedom" on the orders of his handlers were truly disgraceful. I am curious, remarked Jerzy Giedroyć, about how far one can go "in writing such abominable denunciations."

Giedroyć, the editor in chief of *Kultura*, was the person who from the very beginning courageously and consistently defended Miłosz—fortunately for Polish culture, there have always been a select few who opposed its homemade inquisitions and native gutter. Juliusz Mieroszewski stated straightforwardly, "Any fight with the Soviets must start by rejecting the Soviet method of insinuations, denunciations, and the casting of vague suspicions.... Insinuations and denunciations must not be the subject of any polemic. They can only be shrugged off as beneath contempt." Naturally, the courage and wisdom of *Kultura*'s editorial stance elicited a wave of attacks. Józef Cyrankiewicz, the premier of the Polish People's Republic, characterized *Kultura* as "a renegade center of the cosmopolitan." At the same time an émigré inquisitor declared with utter certainty that "the Paris *Kultura* was financed by the international Trotskyite organization."

How sad all of this is. Juliusz Mieroszewski argued bitterly that for both émigré and domestic accusers, Miłosz's work "is interesting as a supplement to his prospective trial. What Miłosz had seen, what he had observed, learned, and studied in people's democracies, is completely meaningless. The only important thing is whether he is guilty, or whether he has issued a public apology, or whether he acted like a swine, etc. Every émigré considers himself a judge to whom the nation, God, and the Motherland have granted the power to pronounce judgment. For those fellows, Miłosz is not an intellectual problem; he is a criminal problem."

VII

Mieroszewski was right. The witch hunt, both domestic and émigré, against Czesław Miłosz was conducted in the language of insult and slander, for such was the language of prosecutors' speeches in totalitarian countries, broadcast by megaphone through the streets, hence the qualitative difference in the result of such witch hunts—an émigré battue destroyed its victim's reputation, while a domestic hunt destroyed his reputation and sometimes killed him as well. The language of a smear campaign was not intended to persuade through arguments or to weigh arguments—it was to blame the enemy and to coerce a certain way of perceiving the world. The world is plunged in a war between Good and Evil—those who do not side with Good totally and unequivocally become allies of Evil. They may try this or that stratagem, feign neutrality, or resort to trickery, but we are able to see through the enemy and identify him. Here is a sample of this language of blackmail and fear:

> The increased frequency of demonstrating the moral poverty of a person who betrayed his country multiplies the fear of being appointed a traitor. The traitor, after all, always has the same characteristics and, above all, is devoid of all and any positive values. The traitor always acts on base instincts, craves money and luxuries, is driven by the lust for power, is cowardly and immoral, egocentric and pathologically ambitious, malignant and scheming. Finally, the traitor is venal and cares nothing about loyalty toward his country and his nation. The whole stock-in-trade was applied to Czesław Miłosz; then, in the first half of the 1950s, he paid for every transgression: for his contempt for the knights of the brass knuckles, for his criticism of Piłsudski's followers' "Strong! United! Prepared!," for his true dislike of Stalinist Communism, for his refusal to obey any orthodoxies, and for the fact that he chose freedom.

VIII

Among the insults hurled at Czesław Miłosz, perhaps the charge brought by Sergiusz Piasecki is worth a mention. Miłosz "scorned prewar Poland"—this absolutely discredited him in the eyes of the indomitable émigrés, for only a traitor could describe prewar Poland so harshly. This received notion is alive and well, even today.

Let us listen, then, to another voice, which dates to November 1939: "Here is Poland. I can see her just as you can," wrote a nineteen-year-old student of Polish language and literature at the Jagiellonian University to a friend, "but until now I was unable to see the whole truth. I was unable to find the atmosphere which could have with dignity belong to the nation of Mickiewicz, Słowacki, and Norwid, and Wyspiański ... instead, in the squares, there still gathered the traffickers, just like those whom Kasprowicz hated so much. And today, I feel ... that the nation was led astray and lied to, and its sons, just as during the partitions, were blown to the four winds. Why? So that they did not have to rot in the prisons of their homeland."

This is not Miłosz's language, but that passionate criticism makes a great impression. In this instance, "prewar Poland was scorned" by a young university student named Karol Wojtyła.

CHAPTER SEVEN

The Accusers and
the Noncivic Acts

I

In December 1965, the Polish episcopate, with Cardinal Stefan Wyszyński, the primate of Poland, and the metropolitan of Krakow, Karol Wojtyła, sent a famous letter to the German bishops. That letter, having enumerated the enormousness of Polish war damages and victims, read: "In this truly Christian spirit but also in a very human gesture, we extend our hands to you, sitting on the benches in the concluding days of the Council, and grant you our forgiveness while at the same time asking for yours" (in the popular propaganda of the time, that turn of phrase was quoted as "we forgive and ask forgiveness"). An appeal was made for reconciliation between the two nations. It was a very serious challenge to the mandatory rhetoric of hatred toward the Germans.

Let us recall some facts: Czesław Miłosz was accused, unjustly, of allying himself with the German neo-Nazis and of attempting to secure "the dominion of neo-Nazi Germany over Europe." These slanders found a favorable response: the memory of the atrocities of the German occupation was still fairly fresh and was skillfully maintained by Communist propaganda, and Poland's western border was not yet fully settled. Poles still feared German "revanchism." That fear lasted many years and provided the historical context for the pastoral letter the Polish bishops wrote their German counterparts.

The Communist regime reacted to the letter with a mass smear campaign. The bishops were accused of acting to the detriment of the Polish state, and the slogan "We shall not forget and we shall not forgive" was bandied about. Anti-German sentiment ran very deep, and public opinion was unprepared for the new tone suffusing the bishops' letter. Communist propaganda scored a hit in preying on the resentment of many Poles: the long-held, dormant sense of injury, which often turned into blind hatred, now exploded. Obviously the Germans were the target of that explosion, but through clever manipulation, another target was found, namely, all of those who had called for forgiveness and reconciliation—the bishops.

The party-owned Kraków published daily an open letter, addressed to the metropolitan of Kraków, by the employees of Solvay, the factory in which Karol Wojtyła worked during the Nazi occupation. The letter stated that "the employees were truly shocked" by the bishops' letter. They were "appalled" that Archbishop Wojtyła had helped draft it.

"The 'Letter,'" wrote the employees of Solvay,

takes a cavalier stand regarding our nation's vital interests. The Polish episcopate has never been authorized to represent the citizens of Poland in matters that clearly fall within the purview of other authorities. The bishops should be aware that only the government of the People's Republic of Poland is authorized to speak on behalf of the Polish nation. We are not even asking whether His Excellency has forgotten about Auschwitz, where thousands of Polish priests—among others—died at the hands of German executioners, or whether His Excellency has forgotten the children forcibly relocated from Zamość and the horrific conditions of that expulsion, as well as other brutal means extirpating life. It is impossible to forget. Therefore, we state that the license in formulating the "Letter," which includes, among other passages, mention of the alleged guilt of Poles with respect to Germans, is offensive to our national identity. The Germans have nothing to forgive us for, as the direct blame for starting the Second World War and for the savage course it took lies exclusively with German imperialism and fascism, whose heir is the German Federal Republic.

Further on, the letter's authors express their "profound disappointment with the Archbishop's non-civic act." The letter concludes: "We staunchly protest against the views and acts expressed by a segment of the Polish Episcopate...in the 'Letter.'"

II

So what could a reader learn from the Solvay employees' letter to Archbishop Karol Wojtyła? Well, a reader learned that those who guarded the memory of Poland's wartime devastation took a stand against those who did not choose to remember that harm, and that the guardians of memory staunchly defended the image of Poland as an innocent victim against those who wished to ask forgiveness from the "successors" to German fascism. Hence, if you, dear reader, do not join us in our indignation, then you have already forgotten the horrors of Auschwitz, the tragedy of the children of Zamość, and the genocidal annihilation of Poles by Germans. It also means that you are asking the heirs to the murderers for forgiveness and that you do not remember that it was Germans who started World War II and are responsible for its savagery. This form of blackmail often proved effective. In this case, the consequence was that the right of Polish bishops to voice their "arrogant" opinions concerning "the vital interests" of Poland was revoked. And that was exactly the purpose of the regime's propaganda—to discredit the episcopate in the eyes of public opinion. The episcopate was the only sovereign national institution in a nonsovereign country. The bishops had to be silenced—the right to speak was to belong only to the Communist authorities.

The campaign against the bishops meant to consolidate resentment of Germany, while the fear of Germany paralyzed social opposition to the authorities. Even people who truly resented the Communist authorities gave in to the pressure. After 1945, those people lost all hope and took shelter in their "spiritual hideouts," as the Reverend Józef Tischner once put it. In those redoubts they secreted their individuality, together with their scars, their helpless angers, and their suppressed sense of injustice. They felt wronged by the German Nazis, by the Soviet Bolsheviks, and by the Polish Communists. These traumas were authentic and deep, but they did not make up a coherent worldview—they were just like injuries inflicted on different parts of the body: the arm, the leg, and the head. The campaign against the "Pastoral Letter" opened up one of those wounds, and the reaction was a furious cry of hurt; hidden fear had been transformed into noisy aggression. "What right," asked a furious man from his hideout, "do the bishops have to offer forgiveness on my behalf? Who gave them the right to ask Germans for forgiveness?"

Many years later, a well-known writer recalled her reaction: "I survived three years in German concentration camps. The Germans killed my father and I lost a few other people in the war. I understood that as a Christian I should forgive. But to ask for forgiveness...?" These were the voices of genuine pain. But the tone of the campaign was set by cunning manipulators and skillful accusers. They got the gutter moving and made it explode with wild slanders and street uproar. The cry "Let Rome take back its cardinal!" expressed the Communists' fury against Cardinal Wyszyński, and their hatred of him. This attack was to be a punishment for the "noncivic act" which, according to the accusers' allegations, was the bishops' first step on the road to "high treason."

I feel compelled here to quote a passage from my own book *The Church and the Left*, written in 1976. I wrote there:

> For I myself participated in this ignominious spectacle, though the very thought of it makes me blush with shame. I am embarrassed by my own stupidity, though, of course, stupidity is no justification. Why did I do this? Why did I decide to run that interview with Professor Grzybowski in *Argumenty*, the journal I was working for at the time? In response to my question, and in the context of a general propaganda assault on the Church, Grzybowski gave a very critical assessment of the past and present of the Church. I myself felt fully irreproachable. After all, no one had forced me to do this piece, or even tried to talk me into doing it. What guided my hand was not weakness of character but rather the absurd conviction that I was speaking out in a just cause. It was one thing, I thought, to have conflicts with the Party, conflicts that I had already had. My disagreements

with the Church I saw as something entirely different. That my contribution was not a debate but an assault, which I spoke not in my own voice but, *nolens volens*, in the voice of a propagandist in an unjust cause—of all this I was unaware. Even though I knew the episcopate's position only from the biased accounts and the out-of-context quotations I saw in the official press, I considered its position to be nothing more than a defense of the 'trenches of the Holy Trinity'...I make no attempt to justify my actions, for nothing can justify participation in organized lies. It is not the motives but the consequences of our actions that are most important.[1]

This rather extensive self-quotation thirty years ago is a reminder that it is worth considering the beam in one's own eye before starting to expose the mote in somebody else's. Well, I felt ashamed, and that shame is still within me. Because of it, thirty years ago I publicly evaluated my own conduct and have never again participated in any campaign against anyone.

III

The primate of Poland was accused of entering on a path that led to treason and, similarly, the archbishop of Kraków was accused of an offense against national sentiments. The archbishop responded with a letter to the workers. Citing his work in the Solvay factory during the German occupation, he called it "the best education in life." He wrote, "As I read your letter, I realized with pain that it was not only a grave public accusation against me personally but also something of a judgment passed in absentia." This "charge against me and other Polish bishops" was reached without real knowledge of the matter. "In the letter," the archbishop explains, "the Polish bishops included first of all a long and strongly worded recitation of all the harm our nation has suffered at Germany's hands throughout history, and in particular in the years of the recent terrible occupation. The German bishops fully

1. Adam Michnik, *The Church and the Left*, edited, translated, and with an introduction by David Ost (Chicago: University of Chicago Press, 1993), pp. 87–8.

accept these charges, first asking God Himself for forgiveness and then asking us to forgive their nation's transgressions. The two letters need to be compared carefully in order to assess how, against the background of their request, our request for forgiveness is evangelically proportionate. With respect to human relations, especially over a long period of time, it can never be the case that we cannot find reasons for mutual forgiveness." Later, the archbishop recalls the passages of the "Pastoral Letter" regarding the national border on the rivers Odra/Oder and Nysa/Neisse and along the western territories. The omission of these issues in the letter of the workers must have led to the "unfair judgment."

The archbishop concluded:

> I am replying to your letter first of all as a person who has been wronged. I was wronged because I was accused and publicly slandered without an attempt at thoroughly learning the facts or the vital motives. When we worked together during the occupation, we had many things in common— above all, respect for man, his conscience, his personality, and his social dignity. This is what I learned to a great measure from the workers of Solvay, yet I cannot detect that basic principle in your open letter.
>
> It gives me great pain to write and publish this. I must reiterate that not only do I have a right to defend my good name, but also those whom I serve as a shepherd and as archbishop of Kraków have a right to be served by a person of good name. And I have no other agenda but an interest in the truth and the decency of our public life.

IV

The archbishop of Kraków responded to the language of a witch hunt with the language of dialogue. This dialogue had a double intention: it was meant to shape new Polish–German relations and also to shape new Polish–Polish relations. The collective consciousness of public opinion in Germany and Poland constituted the main obstacle to Polish–German dialogue. In the Polish–Polish dialogue, the chief obstacle was the attitude of the Communist authorities, who thought the Polish state was their exclusive property.

The leadership of the Polish United Workers' Party (PZPR) pronounced the following: "Polish bishops, asking authorization from no one, were the first to forgive those who reduced our country to ruins and rubble, who blighted it with death camps, who murdered 6 million Poles, and who reduced our capital to ashes. They forgave them at a time when international public opinion in a collective protest rejected the setting of a statute of limitations for Nazi crimes." The party's attitude comprised a double rejection of dialogue, both Polish–German and Polish–Polish. The language of the ruling Communists was that of a permanent monologue. The bishops set off against it a different worldview and a different language.

Their letter was preceded by an extensive study by the archbishop of Wrocław, Bolesław Kominek, who, alongside Archbishop Wojtyła, belonged to the informal team preparing the "Letter." The text, "A Dialog between Germany and Poland? Thoughts and Conclusions," explains well the genesis of the letter and the motives behind it. Archbishop Kominek points out the diversity of German public opinion: on the one hand there were voices obstinately repeating old formulas about the 1937 borders, but on the other hand there were those friendly to Poland, searching for dialogue and reconciliation. Dialogue was a "key notion." For Archbishop Kominek, it meant the opposite of a war of words: "indeed, they are separated by an utter, nearly metaphysical gap." Aggression through words "is an expression of evil in man—it lays the ground for war." It kindles demonic passions, and one result had been Nazism. Therefore, "man should never contribute to spreading the flames of discord but instead should try to put them out, for they do not serve peace nor do they build bridges between the nations."

Only dialogue can build bridges between nations and people, although doing so is not always possible—in 1945, Polish–German relations, through no fault of Poland, were like "molten iron." The archbishop argued, "It was not Poland that invaded Nazi Germany and laid waste to the German land, or that wanted to annihilate the German nation—as they wanted to do with us." Dialogue became possible when "here and there good qualities were noticed in the opponent." Dialogue is difficult: "On the one side and on the other, there remain many people who perceive any kind of dialog as betrayal"; for these people, hostility and tension are "necessities of life." The basic condition for dialogue is "good will ... and honest intentions, without hidden agendas, so that the dialog is not abused and the partner is not exploited." Those who choose the path of dialogue risk a lot, for they undertake pioneering work, put themselves in jeopardy, and may face "personal sacrifice." "The first apostles of peace," argued Archbishop Kominek, "will probably be attacked by both sides and even slandered. [Still] ... without sacrifice there can be no progress."

According to Pope Paul VI, the archbishop continued, patience with your neighbor, farsightedness, prudence, and mutual trust are the necessary conditions in dialogue. Dialogue should start with what unites— common values and goals. Great traumas, still unhealed, should be set aside at first, in a "tactical and cautious" manner; if that proves impossible, then they should be treated "delicately." Each participant in a dialogue should demonstrate his respect not only for his own nation but also for the partner's. Both sides must overcome arrogance and inferiority complexes; they result from traumas—the elusive feelings that are always present in a dialogue. "Obviously, one should not glorify one's own nation, which is never made up exclusively of angels. One should not perceive one's own nation as an absolute value." The idea of a dialogue presupposes shared responsibility, which is often difficult to accept and uncomfortable. The bitter past hovers continuously over a dialogue. The problem of collective responsibility is so complex that "we can never manage to deal with it," according to the archbishop. Moreover, both sides have some percentage of guilt, and both nations share blame. If a given nation feels itself chosen to the degree that it considers itself completely innocent, then it is no longer "a chosen nation" but a simple group of Pharisees.

Archbishop Kominek's argument illustrates well the axiological horizon of Polish bishops in the last days of Vatican II, toward the end of

1965. It was the spirit of the Polish *aggiornamento*—of opening up, of dialogue, of crossing chalk circles, and of forgiveness and reconciliation. The "Letter" became a priceless link in the long Polish democratic tradition; it rejected revenge and hatred and taught dignity and tolerance. Should not these latter two fix the framing of today's language of Polish–German dialogue? And should not the memory of the campaign against the bishops serve as a constant warning against the use of lies and insinuations in Polish–Polish dialogue?

The Reverend Professor Jan Krucina remembers that moment today: "When Archbishop Kominek was on his way back to Poland from Germany after the 'Letter' was published, I went to pick him up at the border. The customs officers in Zebrzydowice stripped him of his clothes and took away all his books. I asked him whether the formula of reconciliation in the 'Letter' could not have been articulated differently, since society was not prepared for it and since there was an imbalance of guilt between Germans and Poles. To that the Archbishop said, 'You make me sad, Father! I am surprised that you do not see that the Gospel is not partial'" (*Gość Niedzielny*, September 18, 2005).

Peculiar is the fate of Polish debates, and even more so that of Polish witch hunts. Today we remember with pride the courage and imagination of the Polish bishops who, because of the "Letter," so noble in its message and so wise in its farsightedness, were subjected to such an aggressive and intensive smear campaign. Two attitudes clashed during that campaign—on one side, that of a vengeful accusation, and, on the other, that of a dialogue. For anticlerical members of the intelligentsia, the "Letter" came as a great surprise, for it contradicted the stereotype of the monologous Church as known since the Second Polish Republic. That very moment became a turning point for many; it marked a time when the lay intelligentsia revised their stereotype.

Who were the people on the side of dialogue? What were their aspirations? The person of dialogue attempts to transform the enemy into an opponent and the opponent into a partner. An opponent is for him one who presents challenge, who wants and asks to be understood. The person of dialogue believes that dialogue is the only way to be understood by others. So he makes an effort to look at the world through his opponent's viewpoint, to "change hats with him," and to "step into his shoes." After all, the key sentence in the Polish bishops' letter read: "Poland's western border, on the Odra/Oder and Nysa/Neisse, is for Germans, as we well understand, a truly bitter fruit of the last war and of its mass destruction, just as is the suffering of millions of German refugees and displaced persons." Up until that point, no one had been able to look at German suffering through German eyes as honestly as that. It must have been difficult; but the person of dialogue believes in patience and goodwill, which will help dispel prejudices, and, in persuasion, which will allow the revision of stereotypes. He does not shy away from defending his own arguments and is not afraid of the truth, but, invariably, he puts respect for human dignity first. He believes in the possibility of a meeting with his adversary at which not only do opposing arguments, views, and judgments fly but at which certain equality is also binding—each partner accepts that the dignity of the other is of immeasurable value. This presupposes the ability to strike a compromise, whenever possible, the readiness to admit that one is not in possession of the sole and complete, and the willingness to accept somebody else's reasoning and to change one's own attitudes.

The person of dialogue is aware that at such a meeting he becomes somebody slightly different than before. He also knows that dialogue is not synonymous with compromise but, rather, is a method of coexistence in a pluralistic society. When the language of dialogue dies out, the yapping of the witch hunt and the language of attack grow much louder. The person of dialogue is well aware that a meeting and a conversation will not make the wolf share a residence with the lamb, will not make the panther and the goat lie down together, and will not make the calf and the lion graze together. Nevertheless, he is also aware that if the human need for dignity and justice makes dialogue possible, then the human inclination toward fanaticism and cruelty makes it necessary.

It is so, though the price to pay may be the mockery and contempt of those who sneer at dialogue and despise the people of dialogue.

V

The Solvay workers' letter probably was written at the regional headquarters of the Polish United Workers' Party—the archbishop of Kraków could have had no doubts about that. However, he actually addressed the reply to all Poles who did not understand the real sense of the bishops' "Pastoral Letter" and who repeated, sometimes in good faith, the accusations of official propaganda. Therefore, though he was replying to the bishops' accusers, he assumed the goodwill of his readers and treated the Solvay workers as if they were ill informed but not ill intentioned. He warned them against "blind" trust in propaganda and explained the real content of the "Letter." Above all, he invoked the universal right to defend the truth; he also reiterated that human dignity must be respected. He was talking to people who were lied to every day and whose dignity was violated every day. Finally, he clearly termed the smear campaign "a false accusation and a libel." That extraordinary text also contains a passage about the meaning of granting forgiveness in the Gospels: forgiveness is always necessary in human relations; nobody can treat himself as the embodiment of innocence.

In 1951, replying to his émigré attackers, Czesław Miłosz wrote of Poland's eternal "petty hatred"; answering his critics from back home, he wrote that "if in following orders from above, you rescind the right to free speech in Poland, you are bound to experience such catastrophes as the flight of a citizen who is capable of speaking for himself and others."

In 1965 Karol Wojtyła's letter to the employees of Solvay spoke of "slander" and of "respecting the person and his conscience." But at the same time, infused as that letter is with the spirit of dialogue, we also find in it a categorical rejection of the hatchet job. The hatchet job cannot allow for dialogue. The hatchet job must be called by its real name.

How unusual are Polish vicissitudes: the archbishop of Kraków, accused of a "noncivic act," was elected pope in October 1978; the poet accused of treason was honored with a Nobel Prize in October 1980. Twice, free Poland enjoyed a great celebration.

VI

In 1989 everything became normal, or so it seemed; things fell into their rightful place. People left their hiding places, the Communists gave up power, and censorship was abolished. The attackers grew quiet and meeker. Nobody dared deny that John Paul II was the most influential authority in all of Polish history. Czesław Miłosz triumphantly received the honors that were his due and was revered as the "pride and glory" of Poles, the writer who "made Poland's name famous in the world"; he was called the Kochanowski or Mickiewicz of our times. It did not last long. Together with new conflicts, new attackers appeared, supported by a large group of veterans of the previous campaigns.

Here is what an accuser of 1985 looked like: he despised everything and everybody: the Church, the Catholic press, people who thought for themselves, and especially writers. He attacked people directly, using their names, and, among others, he went after Miłosz. The famous verse by Miłosz—"You who wronged a simple man"—the verse that is engraved on a monument in Gdańsk, was in his view only "a lying, anti-socialist poem." He equipped his hatred, as every Communist psychopath should, with ideological instruments. The enemies were not only opponents of the system, they were a stupid mass of bigots and crazies. "Only the left is enlightened—in other words, only we are, while our adversaries are dim-witted fools who don't have a thought in their heads and who indulge in outmoded rituals."

Here is another accuser, this one easygoing. He says:

The opponents of socialism in Poland have lost, the world has collapsed around them, so it is not worth fighting them personally; it is enough to show them they have wound up on the garbage heap of history. They are fairly intelligent and they can even write, but what does that matter when they are simply ridiculous in their opposition and stubbornness? They mouth off about their various hobbyhorses, but that is no longer of any importance, because the future does not belong to them but to us. After all, they have no vision, they are unable to formulate any program, and they have no clue about the current political reality because in their rage and fanaticism they are unable to see it clearly. In short, this is the rambling of those who have suffered a defeat.

Michał Głowiński, eminent critic and scholar of literature, from whose books I have borrowed both depictions of attackers, observed a few years ago that in the era of Communism, writers were accused of "serving the bourgeoisie, of ideological immaturity, and of yielding to foreign formalist models"—such was the vocabulary of those campaigns. Today, even graduates of the Stalinist school of criticism have forgotten that. It is grotesque and deplorable, says Głowiński, "that a critic who started his long career with thunderous socialist realist publications, who for years was a member of the Communist Party, and for quite some time its militant and beneficiary, finds in the biography of a consistently anti-communist writer...some youthful episode to confirm that that writer was also a communist and therefore should be condemned." It thus appears that for an attacker it is easier to switch to a new witch hunt leader than to set aside the very custom of hurling abuse; the almighty feelings of resentment and hatred, and the grudge against the world, never stopped ruling his heart.

A new category of accusers has appeared; many of them were recently among the victims. They still suffer from the trauma of those years, and they retain the memory of how they once had no hope in the face of humiliation. Now the time has come for their revenge, especially if they felt marginalized or believed they had not been sufficiently compensated for their former opposition to the dictatorship. The same could be said of those accusers who claim to have connections with the Catholic Church. As the Reverend Józef Tischner asked: "Will the opponent whom we today humiliate, accuse, assault with suspicions, and publicly disparage come to us tomorrow to accept baptism from our hands?... Often, those with a cross hanging from their necks 'bear false witness against their neighbors,' and treat the very thought of forgiving their enemies as a betrayal of 'the only just cause.'"

Józef Tischner was among the most sensitive observers of the smear campaigns of the new era. "It is out of resentment," he wrote, "that a 'Catholic' attacks moral authorities because they are 'lay' authorities. Petty people have taken out a lease on morality and with its help they sling mud at those who proved that the grape is not sour. It is an old truth: even the smallest gesture of freedom is an insult to those who have warmed their bodies by the hearth of slavery. Today, we can observe the fruits of yesterday's offense."

So the smear campaigns are back, together with the customs typical of the attackers. There were quite a few such campaigns: against the people of the democratic opposition, who were accused of youthful connections with Communism, and against the Solidarity leader accused of informing. There were campaigns connected to the demands for lustration and decommunization and to the poet who had been honored with the Nobel Prize for Literature. There were also campaigns against Jacek Kuroń and the Committee for the Defense of Workers, and campaigns connected to the revelation of the truth about the massacre of the Jews of Jedwabne. It seems, however, that the symbolic crown of the hate campaigns of the last fifteen years was the new attack on Czesław Miłosz.

VII

In 1991 a right-wing literary magazine proclaimed Miłosz a completely anachronistic writer because of his axiological—humanistic and liberal—attachments. A few years later, these objections by the "pimple-faced" young of the Third Polish Republic were formulated by one of their representatives.[2] He accused Miłosz of betraying his Polishness, of rejecting Poland and her newfound independence and freedom. The new "pimple-faced" set Miłosz's world of values against the national radicalism of the poets grouped around the underground magazine *Sztuka i Naród* [Art and Nation] during World War II and placed those values in the milieu of the Konfederacja Narodu [Confederation of the Nation], the wartime successor of the ONR-Falanga, a Polish variant of fascism. Miłosz, according to the new "pimple faces," had his day—it ran from 1930 to 1980—but for a long time now had been part of the archival junk whose trademark was "the betrayal of Polishness." Subsequent attacks were no less brutal either. "Actually, it is sweet to belong to the past," commented Miłosz in his letter to poet and Catholic writer Marek Skwarnicki, "if today is like theirs."

In another letter to Skwarnicki, Miłosz commented on a statement made by the young editor of another right-wing magazine who said that his ideal was the program of *Sztuka i Naród*. He bitterly wrote:

> Does collective memory want to remember nothing and learn nothing? Is heroic legend forever to substitute for thought? The *Sztuka i Naród* group had a fascist program. Full stop. They were a part of Bolesław Piasecki's Confederation of the Nation, who saw as ideal systems the Italy of Mussolini, the Spain of Franco, and the Portugal of Salazar. The young poets of that group, noble and courageous, wrote songs for the "Striking Battalion," that is, the military arm of the leader.
>
> Thanks to her volatile history, Poland did not find herself in the camp to which the mentality of these young ones would have predestined her, just like the Croats under the banner of Ante Pavelić. It is said they would have grown out of that ideology, had they survived. But has Bolesław Piasecki? As he was a totalitarian, he remained a totalitarian, simply changing his rhetoric slightly.... The Polish soul invariably turns toward the Right, as if it had a built-in magnetic needle pointing in that direction.... The experience of this century, and here I refer mostly to the inter-war period, is

2. The "pimple-faced" was a derogatory term for the generation of Stalinist poets, ardent believers in Communism.

sufficient to conclude that Polish culture grows barren when right-wing thought takes over. Whoever thinks, then, that turning right serves the Nation with a capital N chooses the road that leads to its paralysis.... Must we remind everyone that the prewar alliance between the Church and the National Democrats pushed away creative and inquisitive people and that it produced a gulf: on one side, the world of literature and art, or the so-called intellectuals, etc., and on the other, bigots and nationalist excess.

Sixty years ago, when watching National Democrat students armed with sticks, Miłosz said that "the thought process concealed in those narrow-minded, bigoted skulls was a complete mystery" to him. And it remained such a mystery to the end of his days.

VIII

Czesław Miłosz died on August 14, 2004. A daily of a nationalist–Catholic orientation said good-bye to the poet with a very peculiar tone: "Before the war, he was a communist sympathizer, and after the war he was a communist diplomat for a few years. He was in favor of making Poland a 17th Soviet republic. It is worth a mention that in 1945 he publicly proposed that the Bible not be published in the Polish People's Republic. He claimed it was a cruel, bloody, and depressing book. On the pages of *Tygodnik Powszechny* he attacked Father Maksymilian M. Kolbe. He disparaged the journals *Mały Dziennik* [Little Daily] and *Rycerz Niepokalanej* [The Knight of Holy Virgin], published by Saint Maksymilian, calling them anti-Semitic."

Every single word here is a lie—it is a chronicler's duty to emphasize this. But it is not our ambition to refute the lies of the attackers, which provide precious information entirely about themselves. What is important here is the spirit of the attackers—the spirit of accusation and humiliation, of slander and the gutter. Two days later, the same daily published an interview with one of the accusers, "The Anti-Polish Face of Czesław Miłosz." Miłosz's enemy proclaimed that the poet's main activity had been slandering Poland, the Church, and the Catholic religion.

What was even worse, Miłosz was not a Pole but "a cosmopolitan Lithu-anian, so the burial of the writer at the Skałka [Crypt for Worthy Poles] in Kraków 'would be a scandal.'" "There are still enough sensible people among us," claimed the accuser, "to prevent this mocker of Polishness from finding a place among eminent patriots."

In turn, a group of Miłosz's parliamentary enemies stated that the idea of burying the poet at the Skałka was "a mockery not only of the national pantheon but also of Miłosz, who treated with contempt and hostility the work of the great Poles buried at the Skałka." A "Social–Patriotic Protest Committee" was established to lobby against the prof-anation of the National Pantheon; that group's spokesman declared: "We still have enough national dignity to defend this place" against Miłosz, whose work "is filled with hatred of everything Polish." The public, with few exceptions, fell silent, deafened by the attackers' bayings. Finally, just a day before the scheduled funeral, someone said: "Enough! A tele-gram with condolences from John Paul II has arrived from Rome."

Czesław Miłosz was buried at the Skałka.

The gutter fell silent. We will never know how many of the accusers considered the pope's telegram another "noncivic act."

IX

Right after Miłosz's death, listening to the baying of the witch hunt, I reached for the poet's poem "My Faithful Mother Tongue." This is what I found:

> Faithful mother tongue,
> I have been serving you.
> Every night, I used to set before you little bowls of colors
> so you could have your birch, your cricket, your finch
> as preserved in my memory.
> This lasted many years.
> You were my native land; I lacked any other.
> I believed that you would also be a messenger

between me and some good people
even if they were few, twenty, ten
or not born, as yet.

Now, I confess my doubt.
There are moments when it seems to me I have squandered my life.
For you are a tongue of the debased,
of the unreasonable, hating themselves
even more than they hate other nations,
a tongue of informers,
a tongue of the confused,
ill with their own innocence.

But without you, who am I?
Only a scholar in a distant country,
a success, without fears and humiliations.
Yes, who am I without you?
Just a philosopher, like everyone else.[3]

Perhaps it is a pity that nobody read this poem at the poet's grave.

X

What did those people have in common—the Great Priest who became pope and the Great Poet who was honored with the Nobel Prize? Undoubtedly, much divided them, but I think they were united by some image of the motherland.

Czesław Miłosz said over and over that he was a child of the Grand Duchy of Lithuania, which was a component of the Polish Republic of many nations and cultures, religions and languages. On the other hand, John Paul II wrote that the Polish idea of the fatherland had evolved from the "purely Polish" idea of the Piast dynasty to the idea of the Jagiellon dynasty. John Paul II wrote:

3. Czesław Miłosz, *The Collected Poems*, trans. Czesław Miłosz and Robert Pinsky (New York: Ecco Press, 1988), p. 216.

For over five centuries, it was the Polishness of the Jagiellon epoch which allowed for the creation of the Polish Republic of many nations, many cultures, and many religions. All Poles carried in themselves this religious and national diversity. I personally come from the region of Małopolska [Little Poland], ... and here, in Małopolska, perhaps most of all in Kraków, one could feel the proximity of Vilna, Lvov, and the East. The presence of Jews was also a very significant ethnic element in Poland. I remember that Jews composed at least one third of my classmates in my primary school in Wadowice.... I was friends with some of them. What really struck me about them was their Polish patriotism. So Polishness in essence is multiplicity and pluralism and not narrowness and insularity. It seems to me, however, that in our time, the "Jagiellonian" dimension of Polishness that I mentioned earlier regrettably stopped being evident.

In this perfectly clear disquisition, the word "regrettably" is of utmost importance—a word that would not have been uttered by any of the Polish attackers who hurled accusations of treason in consecutive epochs, from the campaign against Narutowicz to the vilification of Miłosz's memory. And the reason is that the little word "regrettably" denotes a longing for a precious ethos laden with virtue.

When pondering the notion of patriotism, John Paul II emphasized that "one absolutely must avoid one particular danger, namely that it does not degenerate into nationalism. In that respect, the twentieth century provided us with extremely telling experiences, not only in themselves but also in their dramatic consequences. How can we free ourselves from that risk? I think patriotism is a proper medium. For it is characteristic of nationalism that it recognizes the good of one's own nation only and it strives for that good while disregarding the rights of others. Patriotism, on the other hand, as a love of the fatherland, accords to all other nations the same rights as to its own; hence it is a road leading to orderly social love."

Czesław Miłosz rarely used the word "patriotism," but his whole oeuvre was devoted to the defense of Poland against oppression under foreign rule as well as the defense of Poland against her own vices: intolerance, megalomania, and nationalism. The Great Priest and the Great

Poet also had one more thing in common—a sense of tolerance and the wisdom of the heart. John Paul II quoted Sigismund August, the king of the (Jagiellonian) Polish Republic of many nations: "I am not the king of your conscience"; both the Pope and the Poet always refused to treat people like dirt, for both knew only too well the taste of the smear. Karol Wojtyła wrote once: "Freedom must be constantly won, it cannot be simply possessed! It comes as a gift but is maintained through struggle." Both struggled throughout their lives to save and preserve the gift of freedom; both were free people.

Karol Wojtyła pondered, "Where does the generational division lie between those who have underpaid and those forced to overpay?" Who are those forced to overpay? Obviously they were the ones who struggled, suffered, and died fighting for "what the enemy had forcibly seized." But I think they are also the ones who demanded a better Poland, free of intolerance and iniquity, and the mud was slung at them in thanks. If patriotism is to be understood as faithfulness to the community of fates shared by generations, then it must be faithfulness to those "forced to overpay"—the victims of smear campaigns, defamed and sometimes killed by our own domestic gutter.

XI

History is not a cloth woven by innocent hands, Lord Acton seems to have said. We shall never free ourselves from the gutter—passions and madness and resentment and fanaticism will always accompany us. We need to understand their nature and muster the courage to protest. When faced with a collective protest, the accusers grow silent. The death of Czesław Miłosz was followed by baying, which was silenced by the voice of John Paul II. The death of John Paul II was followed by silence from the accusers: the infamous lovers of revenge, the impudent parliamentarians, and the specialists in denunciation grew silent.

Can we detect an indestructible ray of hope in that silence?

CHAPTER EIGHT

A Wound upon Adam Mickiewicz's Brow

I

In *Forefathers' Eve*, Adam Mickiewicz says while many wounds had been inflicted upon him by enemies, wounds that "soaked his breast with blood," "the wound upon his brow" was of a different character:

> The Woman: He had one wound upon his brow,
> A single wound and very small:
> It seemed a drop of black, I vow.[1]

> The Wizard: That is the sorest wound of all:
> I saw it, I examined it;
> That wound he did himself commit.[2]

Konrad (the protagonist of *Forefathers' Eve*) "did himself commit" the wound—but why? Historians of literature were inclined to connect the wound with Konrad's suicide attempt. Others saw it as a result of arrogance and egocentrism, as allegedly proven by the impudent apostrophes he directed to God and the insolence with which he placed

---

1. Harold B. Segel, ed., *Polish Romantic Drama* (Ithaca, NY: Cornell University Press, 1977), p. 174.
2. Ibid., p. 176.

himself above the national community. Professor Stanisław Pigoń was of a different opinion. In his essay "The Wound upon Konrad's Brow," he wrote: "The most likely guess is that it happened as a result of a trial. He inflicted it on himself at a portentous moment of confusion and amid a profound internal conflict with no solution; it was an act of prostration and despair. He himself considered it the equivalent of suicide—if not a physical suicide, then a psychological and moral one."[3]

Was Pigoń's reasoning correct? We shall probably never find out. If we agree, however, that a literary work lives its own life and that we, the readers, assign new meanings to it and relate it to our own experiences, then we are permitted to accept the interpretations offered by Pigoń. He included this essay in the last book, *Wiązanka krytyczno-literacka* [A Critical-Literary Potpourri], which was published in the fall of 1968, while he was still alive. As he wrote to the publishing house, he had added the essay "at the very last moment, after much deliberation." It was a memorable year for my generation. Adam Mickiewicz's play was taken off the stage of the National Theater and again entered the history of Poland.

II

Ryszard Krynicki wrote about that episode at the time:

> Perhaps we were just children with no experience;
> we were only aware they forced us to believe in lies
> and we did not really know what we wanted,
> apart from respect for human rights and truths,
> when we gathered in a small square
> near the monument to our great poet,
> who spent his youth in an enslaved country
> and the rest of his life in exile;
> we smoked cigarettes, and we burned papers full of lies;
> we smoked cigarettes though they poisoned our bodies,

3. Stanisław Pigoń, *Zawsze o Nim* [Always about Him] (Warsaw, 1998) p. 244.

and we burned the papers because they poisoned our minds:
we read the Constitution and the Declaration of the Rights of Man
and, really, we didn't know that the rights of man
may turn out inconsistent with the interest of a citizen,
and, really, we didn't know that so many combat vehicles can be sent
against the defenseless,
against us, who were just children
armed only with ideas that we learned in school
and were told to unlearn by the same school,
armed with the ideas of the poet, around whose monument
we gathered,
and, really, we didn't know that all those ideas
can be wiped out easily
with blackmailing speeches, provocative
articles,
a ruthless attack of the sated and arrogant violence,
and lie piled on lie.[4]

Once again the word was made flesh; the Philomaths (the student association at Vilnius University) poured out onto the Polish streets. They were promptly arrested and interrogated. Many were expelled from their homeland. The wound on Konrad's forehead bled again.

III

On November 25, 1967, the National Theater in Warsaw hosted the premiere of *Forefathers' Eve* by Adam Mickiewicz, directed by Kazimierz Dejmek. After four days, Dejmek was informed by the director general of the Ministry of Culture and Art that there were "objections of a political nature" concerning the play. He received orders "to stage the play only once a week, to sell no more than one hundred tickets to students (and then only at full price), and to note the audience reaction in the production notes."

4. Ryszard Krynicki, *Organizm zbiorowy* [Common Organism] (Kraków) 1975.

On January 3, 1968, Dejmek was informed that the play could be performed only three times in February, and only twice in each subsequent month; it would close entirely after the summer break. On January 16, Dejmek was informed that the last performance of *Forefathers' Eve* would take place on the thirtieth of the month.

During and after the last performance, there were demonstrations by college students. The eminent theater historian, Professor Zbigniew Raszewski, who witnessed the events, noted in his *Diary*:

> January 30, 1968, evening. Tonight at 7:30 p.m. the eleventh and final performance of *Forefathers' Eve* at the National Theater.... A teeming, dense and loud crowd in the foyer.... We are going to the second floor. The first floor is packed wall to wall. The balcony is so crowded that it is impossible to get through.... More and more students get in without tickets.... It's nearly 8 p.m.—stuffy and crowded but the atmosphere is solemnly cheerful, the way it might be before a procession or a parade. Eventually a crowd of students floods the whole first floor, clearly without tickets, and those who have reserved seats follow them. All the seats are taken. The staircase, which links the stage with the auditorium in the National Theater, is entirely occupied by students, boys and girls alike. Some of them are simply squatting on the edge of the stage. When the lights dim, the students lie down so that they do not block the view for those on the ground floor. Other youngsters stand near the walls or crowd the balconies. Many boys are sitting on the balcony railing.... The first act goes by in an atmosphere of attentive concentration, broken only by long-drawn-out applause after the rites and the two parts of the Great Improvisation. The second act is similar.... The third act in its entirety gets what amounts to an accompaniment: spontaneous applause, long-lasting, fervent, frequently mixed with jeering laughter or shouts. At solemn moments, everyone grows quiet, and deep silence prevails; but in the next instant, waves of emotion course through the audience and intermittently short murmurs, whispers, and giggles are heard, mingled with great cascades of applause and shouting. After the words of the Master of Ceremonies:
>
>> A man long prisoned sees and hears too much—
>> Our governors have views, deep aims and such
>> As must be hidden (Segal, p. 134)

—come prolonged jeering laughter, applause and shouts....
And here are samples of other bits.

WYSOCKI: They're on its surface. We're a lava field, [new wave of applause,
nods of approval]
With surface cold and dirty, hard, congealed;
But here are fires beneath, no years can end;
Let's spit on this foul crust, and then descend [Segal, p. 139], [drawn-
out applause and shouting].

. . .

SENATOR: When have we sought more carefully for taints?
Willing confessions, evidence, complaints [Segal, pp. 140–41] [applause,
overall merriment, and loud chuckling from the students on the
staircase].

. . .

RUSSIAN OFFICER: No wonder that they curse us here:
A generation has now passed,
And still from Moscow every year
A sewer-stream of rogues runs fast [Segal, p. 159] [drawn-out applause].

...The curtain falls. A standing ovation starts, passionate, ostentatious,
and ardent. Everyone is on their feet. The clapping seems to reach its peak,
but then Holoubek [the lead actor] appears on the stage and the noise
grows by many decibels. Now, the students change their repertoire. At first,
we do not quite understand what they are shouting, but after a while we
realize that on every floor they are chanting in unison: "Free—dom with—
out cen—sor—ship! Free—dom with—out cen—sor—ship!" They keep at
it for a long time.... In the street, we see some two hundred students with
a banner that reads: "We demand more performances of Forefathers' Eve."
They start chanting: "We want Mic—kie—wicz! Mic—kie—wicz!"[5]

I remember well that performance and that demonstration, which
later on the same evening moved to the Mickiewicz monument on

5. Zbigniew Raszewski, *Raptularz 1967/1968* [Diary 1967/1968] (Warsaw 1993). For
page numbers for Mickiewicz quotes, see Segal, op. cit.

Krakowskie Przedmieście. The slogan "Freedom without censorship!" was most probably Karol Modzelewski's invention, and it signified that whoever curbs democratic rights also censors the Polish tradition of independence and freedom. In chanting that slogan, I felt an almost physical fire beneath me—a fire that the passage of years could not extinguish that interior flame of Polish freedom, which was piercing the hard and foul crust of a regime that resembled the czarist. Again—even if only for a while—we were free. And then the militia started to arrest and book those who had joined the street demonstration. And the magistrate punished them for "disorderly conduct."

IV

Polish writers took a stand in defense of *Forefathers' Eve* and the students. At the extraordinary meeting of the Polish Writers' Association, a resolution was passed demanding that the play return to the stage and that the repressions end. The vote was preceded by a dramatic debate in which some respected writers took the floor. Paweł Jasienica said, memorably, "Mickiewicz's *Forefathers' Eve* is a bit like the Wawel Cathedral. Privately, one can consider it a piece of architectural kitsch, but no one has the right to touch even a single stone."

Equally interesting are other accounts written right after the events. Zygmunt Mycielski wrote in his diary on February 15, 1968: "They have taken *Forefathers' Eve* off the stage of the National Theater. So I reached for the text again. I read it, deeply moved and riveted. . . . *Forefathers' Eve* is horrifying. And today the small-mindedness is horrifying that takes it off the stage." Andrzej Kijowski noted in his "Journal": "I would not like to be an acknowledged prophet. Whatever Minister [of Culture] Motyka has done in the past or will do in the future, he will always remain the minister on whose watch *Forefathers' Eve* was taken out of the repertoire of the National Theater. The very same applies to the Polish Writers' Association, and particularly to its board. It was during our term or in our lives as a literary generation that a blow was dealt to the prestige of Polish culture.... You are afraid of the real Mickiewicz, who is closest to us because he denounces conservatism, servility, the collapse of national aspirations, and unfaithfulness to tradition."

V

The Vilnius Philomaths, jailed in 1823, were sentenced after a rather oppressive inquiry to a relatively lenient punishment for their acts, which had "contributed to the spread of unreasonable Polish national-ism." Upon leaving prison, they were forced to sign this oath: "I shall never disclose or describe to anyone what the commission inquired about or what answers I gave to its questions, subject to legal penalties for disclosing secrets; in addition, I shall never belong to any society estab-lished without government permission but rather I shall inform the proper authorities, in accordance with the loyalty of a faithful subject, if I learn that such a banned society has been formed." On April 20, 1824, Adam Mickiewicz signed this declaration of loyalty and cooperation. "In other words," Pigoń comments, "the signer committed himself to act as an informer for the Tsarist political police."

"Obviously," Pigoń continues, "the majority of the signers treated the documents as a repugnant necessity and as a promise that, having been extorted from them, did not in reality commit them to anything. Signing was just like stepping through a puddle in order to get to the next portion of dry path. But Mickiewicz with his deeply ethical nature undoubtedly felt otherwise. The poet must have been horrified at the trap he was in. The monstrous plan of the inquisitor Novosiltsev was to force friends to debase themselves and inform on others; it must have left him feeling of disgust and self-contempt at being a committed col-laborator of 'the servants of the police.' That was the commitment made by the poet; he had done a deal with the political devil." "The incurable wound upon Konrad's brow, which 'he did himself inflict,' may have been" the poet's admission of guilt (Pigoń, op. cit., pp. 244–49). The "wound on Konrad's brow" would reappear on Polish foreheads for the next two centuries, and it would come to haunt Poland. It would become one of the cursed Polish problems—almost every one of us will bear this wound, which bleeds afresh in every generation.

Zygmunt Mycielski noted on March 10, 1968: "What a strange country it is, where the figure of a poet appears like a specter in the streets! Horses' hooves, batons pummeling young people, and a fight against the national aspirations expressed in poetry—do these attest to the life of a nation? What kind of mindless country is that? It is ruled by people who aren't even aware that they are playing out the next scene of the very same play they took off the stage. So, here they are, right in front of me in the streets, the scenes from part V of *Forefathers' Eve.*"

Those who joined the protests of March 1968 also received punishments that were relatively light, at least when compared to the verdicts of Stalinist courts. But we all came out of prison wounded.

VI

"The fate of Mickiewicz is the fate of Poland," claims Jarosław Marek Rymkiewicz; "it is the fate of the Poles; it is a paradigm of the fate of Poles and Poland."[6] Mickiewicz's *Forefathers' Eve*, in the opinion of Ryszard Przybylski, is "a mysterious roadside boulder on which, at times of dread and misfortune, the stymied Poles beat their heads."[7] Rymkiewicz and Przybylski are right. The life and work of Mickiewicz return over and over and give us pause. That holds true even today, when in debates on literature and history, on politics and people's fates, the so-called cognitive perspective seems to dominate what I call the worldview of the "lustrator." The lustrator is the new hero of our times. He combines the fanatical zeal of an inquisitor with the cold cynicism of an incisive investigative officer. His philosophy is simple: just give me

6. Jarosław Marek Rymkiewicz, *Mickiewicz czyli wszystko* [Mickiewicz, or Everything] (Warsaw, 1999).

7. Ryszard Przybylski, *Słowo i milczenie bohatera Polaków* [Word and Silence of the Hero of Poles] (Warsaw, 1993).

a man and I will find something to accuse him of. The lustrator knows perfectly well that almost no one, himself included, was exactly a saint in those less-than-saintly times. But it is better to be a lustrator than to be the one who is lustrated.

The lustrator examines the past of the one who is lustrated and searches for blots and ambiguities. Unlike Professor Pigoń, he does not believe in the existence of "deeply ethical natures." He examines a writer's works to prepare an indictment on the basis of the weakest, least successful, or most frankly conformist pieces. By this means, Stanisław Trembecki is reduced to the condition of a czarist lickspittle, Henryk Sienkiewicz collects censure for his bad book *Wiry* [Whirlpools], Konstanty Ildefons Gałczyński is remembered for the anti-Semitic attitudes he briefly held, and Stanisław Jerzy Lec is branded a Soviet collaborator. "From a small seed of truth [the lustrator] produces a crop of lies." He researches the biographies of the examined in a special way—he knows better. To top off his findings, he searches the police archives and adduces the reports and denunciations therein. He diligently checks every bit of dirt dug up on the subject of the examined, whether by the Ochrana, the KGB, or the Secret Police. Was the inspected secretly an informer? Or at least a candidate for an informer? Or was he simply an operational contact? Let us examine history with the eye of a lustrator; let us lustrate Adam Mickiewicz and the wound on Konrad's brow.

In 1948, a conference was held at the Belvedere devoted to the staging of *Forefathers' Eve* done by Leon Schiller, with the participation of (Poland's president) Bolesław Bierut. As Mieczysław Jastrun recounted twenty years later, Schiller thought that *Forefathers' Eve* was a "fragmentary drama," "passages of which could be moved around in order to strengthen it." Given the current political situation, the point was to tone down the piece's anti-czarist sentiments because these, in the view of the Communist regime, might have been understood by the audience as being hostile to Russia. Schiller proposed that it would be "easy" to add "a scene in which Mickiewicz addresses the crowd in Milan in

1848, or to depict Princess Wołkońska's salon, where Decembrists could gather and speak more freely than in its Warsaw counterpart."

Jastrun protested against the attempt to return Mickiewicz to the "path of righteousness." "It seemed an impossibility to me," he recalled; "it would have been a cardinal sin committed against this great writer. The work is a vision of the fate of the Polish nation." Therefore, this fate cannot be examined properly without understanding all the circumstances of the time.

It does not seem that the words by Jastrun, Mickiewicz's biographer, poet, and essayist, would have convinced the Great Lustrator. Leon Schiller was a great artist of the theater and, obviously, had no intention of lustrating anybody. However, at that time, this is what his ideas meant.

VII

Here is the process of lustration.

The Great Lustrator reaches for the examined writer's books. Having completed his reading, he declares that the "truth must be spoken, however sharp its sting; that charm must be destroyed which for so long has protected him against just charges; the true face of Mr. Mickiewicz must be finally disclosed to show what he was in reality."

Let us reach for a piece by the writer under examination: "Konrad Vallenrod." The second edition, dated 1829, appeared with a special preface that was nothing but a loyal obeisance to the Russian czar. In it we read:

> This is the third consecutive piece I have published in the capital of the Monarch who out of all the kings on this earth counts the most peoples and languages as his own. Being also a Father to us all, He ensures the free ownership of landed property but also, what is more precious, the possession of moral and mental goods. He not only allows His subjects to keep their existing faith, customs, and language, but also orders that those which have been lost, and the fading remnants of past ages, be preserved as the heritage of generations to come. Thanks to His generous support, scholars

will undertake intensive field studies to research and preserve Finnish monuments; scholarly associations, honored by His patronage, teach and maintain the old language of the Letts, the Lithuanian brothers. May the name of the Father of so many nations be praised equally in all languages!

These words, the Great Lustrator would say, do not even require commentary; this shameless praise of a despot, the enemy of the Polish nation, calls for absolute condemnation. And he would add that the work itself invites censure because it idealizes lies and betrayal. Historical documents may serve here as witnesses. The witness, the Reverend Jan Koźmian, testified, "The poem 'Konrad Vallenrod,' so rich in noble ideas and charming images...was made up of the most damaging notions. The poet idealized in it lies and betrayals committed for the country's benefit; thus borrowing a most deceptive beauty of beneficial deeds to serve the vile doctrine of evil means," through which "the notion of simple virtue has been greatly harmed for the nation." In addition, Koźmian emphasized that "the idea of that dynamic heroism had not appeared in Poland first, [but] Mickiewicz just reworked Cooper's 'spy' to some extent." James Fenimore Cooper was an American writer, hence Mickiewicz's evil is obviously American in origin.

Another witness, the professor of literature, Stanisław Cywiński, described *Forefathers' Eve* as propaganda for a type of patriotism foreign to the "life of the Polish nation" and full of perverse and immoral ideas attributable to "Mickiewicz's assimilation to the Russian environment." Other witnesses point out that "Konrad Vallenrod" is a pamphlet of the Carbonari, which nurtures the deadly psychology of the conspirator. The witness Kajetan Koźmian, a well-known and respected poet, testified: "Nobody ever before dreamed of making a rhyme that unites a madman and a drunk, and that, embellishing this figure even more (contrary to history), also makes him a shameful traitor and presents him as a Lithuanian in order to show how nobly the Lithuanians love their homeland. It simply boggles the imagination what those eastern minds can concoct.... No imaginative power can excuse treason by making it seem a virtue." The greatest writers of the epoch, quite unexpectedly and incidentally, may become allies of the Great Lustrator. Finally, Zygmunt Krasiński revealed that "Vallenrodism is simply Jewishness. Once I met the author, I realized that both the man and the idea come straight from the Jews." And, he elaborated, "Mickiewicz is a perfect Jew! His mother was Jewish and she converted before marrying his father." In this very manner, the Great Lustrator gathered a large body of evidence. Though the testimonies varied, and though sometimes they even contradicted each other, they were nevertheless all damaging. Only damaging testimony is of any interest to the Lustrator.

VIII

But Mickiewicz was examined in so many different ways! One evening in 1929, the amateur theater of the Polish workers' club in Kiev held a recitation of Mickiewicz's poems. The reaction was immediate. The fundamentalist Marxists and Leninists who were present protested so loudly that the frightened theater manager came on stage to apologize to the deeply wounded Polish Bolsheviks. *The Soviet Tribune*, a Bolshevik paper published in Polish, raged: "Now, when the clergy and the bourgeoisie are building a united front, the workers' club sponsors Vallenrodist propaganda, presenting Mickiewicz's clerical/patriotic works." A few years later, *Forefathers' Eve* was staged in Warsaw. Antoni Słonimski wrote in his review, "Probably no other country in the world has a national mystery play that can speak such a lively emotional language." And then he added sarcastically:

> The enormous inspiration contained in *Forefathers' Eve* is a national treasure, but it is a somewhat troublesome treasure. The young person or statesman thinking "nationally" has to look at this great rapture with a cool and suspicious eye. Which side is he to take in the eternal argument between Mrs. Rollison and Novosiltsev? The phrase "raison d'état" must be closer to him than the despairing cry of Rollison's mother. Who knows, maybe eventually a courageous person will call this great national poem an instance of "rancid idealism" or "aesthetic pretension." Whose side is this poetry on

today, when it challenges to a duel of hearts those who fight with their brains?... This poet will appear over and over as a ghost at memorials to dead ancestors, and he will be a ghost not easily satisfied or repulsed. The ashes of Mickiewicz are not the dead dust of the past, and the dust is not even really dust but dynamite.

That dynamite never stopped blowing up. It has been doing so since Nikolay Nikolayevich Novosiltsev prepared a report for the Russian czar, expressing his opinion of Poles and their patriotism in general, and of Mickiewicz's works in particular.

Wrote the lustrator Novosiltsev:

In the land that was once Poland, the Pole was left to be a Pole. He is able to cherish his language and the customs and habits of his forefathers, while remaining a dutiful subject of the current monarchs. If his patriotism does not exceed these limits, no offense is committed.... But the matter takes on an entirely different cast when such patriotism is linked with dreams of a future independent Poland, and when the works of Polish writers are meant to plant such thoughts in their compatriots' souls; then they certainly violate the duty of fealty, tearing their hearts away from their real homeland and attaching them to some non-existent future nation. If we consider works of this nature harmful or even immoral, then what shall we say of works that, dressed in the alluring beauty of poetry, teach hidden animosity, false loyalty, and the laying of vile plots to betray compatriots labeled "foreign" because they belong to another tribe. Mickiewicz's "Konrad Vallenrod" is such a poem.... It is in Mickiewicz that these make-believe patriots see a representative of their secret schemes; as they praise and admire his works, they spread their own feelings to others.... "Vallenrod" deals with "the strongest emotions of the human heart; it espouses the most cunning treachery and relentless hatred, presenting them as the noblest virtues of magnanimous patriotism.[8]

Novosiltsev criticized the decision by the censor Basil Anastasevitch to allow "Vallenrod's publication in the Russian Empire, with the stricture that just one verse should be removed. The verse in question read, 'You are a slave, and betrayal is the slave's only weapon.'" The Russian

8. Bartłomiej Szyndler, *Mikołaj Nowosilcow (1762-1838)* (Warsaw, 2004).

censor paid for his liberality with his job; this was an exemplary demonstration of effective lustrating.

IX

"Konrad Vallenrod" was not the only work to incriminate Mickiewicz
in his examination. The aforementioned Reverend Jan Koźmian charged
that in his "Ode to the Youth," Mickiewicz did not "mention the homeland at all," the poem being permeated with a "cosmopolitanism that
leads astray"; so, he said, the poem was more a "Masonic or Carbonari
hymn than the song of a Polish Christian patriot." On the other hand,
Zygmunt Miłkowski (Teodor Tomasz Jeż), a writer who founded the
National League Party (and was also a contemporary of Mickiewicz's),
called the poem "To a Polish Mother" "Mickiewicz's greatest sin against
patriotism," because it discouraged Poles from "not only taking up arms
but even from listening to their forefathers' tales of the nation's history."
The poem, according to Miłkowski, deprived one of "any hope whatsoever of escaping enslavement by Moscow." So the conclusion of the
Great Lustrator must be that "Konrad Vallenrod" actually incited Poles
to collaboration and treason.

Facts from the biography of the lustrated Mickiewicz support this
diagnosis. The lustrator is even merciful enough to disregard the examinee's somewhat exotic and scandalous erotic life. However, the lustrator
cannot possibly disregard the evidence making it clear that during his
stay in Moscow, Mickiewicz was guilty of fraternizing, disgracefully,
with Muscovites; it is well known that he reveled with them many a
time. Jan Czeczott, Mickiewicz's old friend and a philomath, thought
that it was scandalous to maintain any social relations with Russians—
such was the rule for keeping up with "Polish faith." According to Professor Józef Kallenbach, Czeczott "bitterly condemned Mickiewicz for
visiting Russian homes and accepting invitations to balls, dinners, etc.,
for he perceived this behavior as violating the love of the motherland."
The news that Mickiewicz "[was] having a good time among friendly

Russians touched him to the quick."[9] Mickiewicz's friendly relations with a Russian woman were an unacceptable breach of the rules; Juliusz Kleiner wrote that Czeczott admonished Mickiewicz, in the spirit of the Old Testament, to "go away from that foreign woman."

Mickiewicz considered "reveling" with Russians "trivial" and called Czeczott's objections a sign of "true pettifoggery." "My dear Jan!" he wrote, "how can such trifles be linked or related to this high and noble feeling? Are dinners, dances, and singing supposed to offend [Poland] this divine lover? ... Trust me; it is possible to dance, play, and sing without misbehaving." The Great Lustrator would ask rhetorically, "Are these words not an open display of contempt for the accepted custom and a treason?" Moreover, Czeczott could not swallow Mickiewicz's decision to remove the dedication present in the first Vilnius edition of 1827 from the reissue of his volume of *Poemsy*, dated 1829. The original dedication read, "I dedicate this to Jan Czeczott, Tomasz Zan, Józef Jeżewski, and Franciszek Malewski, my dear friends, in memory of the happy days of youth I spent with them." Mickiewicz withdrew this dedication to his friends when they became exiles in the czarist empire. The lustrator, morally offended, would ask: Is one allowed to pay such a price to the Russian czar merely to get a book published?

There was more: in January 1829, Mickiewicz wrote a letter to General Aleksander Benkendorf, the chief of the gendarmerie, in which he complained that he "deserved no punishment." He argued that his "conduct was exemplary" and assured General Benkendorf that he "could be trusted [with a passport]." Then, on June 12, 1829, having already left Russia, he wrote to Tadeusz Bulkharin, a "Moscow-fied Pole," who was also an agent of the Secret Police: "I received a message from Warsaw about the coronation [of czar Nicholas I as a king of Poland] with enthusiastic descriptions of feasts and celebrations. How could I not be there? I share the happiness of my compatriots from afar. ..."

9. Józef Kallenbach, *Adam Mickiewicz* (Kraków, 1897).

I am also reporting to you that our Emperor is currently being received with much enthusiasm in Berlin; everyone says that he was very pleased with his reception in Warsaw, and the Empress graciously mentioned the heartfelt elation with which she was received by the inhabitants of the Polish capital." Are these words, addressed to the czarist agent, not sufficient proof that Mickiewicz was on Moscow's payroll? After all, we know that he had left Russia as a result of his courtship of a very influential lady, disloyal behavior that was unbecoming to a Polish patriot.

Is this not enough to reveal the true face of Mickiewicz?

X

"No," the Great Lustrator will say, "that is not yet enough. Adam Mickiewicz avoided participating in the Polish uprising of 1830." Maurycy Gosławski, a poet who did not dodge his insurgent duties, wrote a well-known poem at the time: "To Adam Mickiewicz, Staying in Rome at the Time of the National War." The poem begins with an epigraph from "Konrad Vallenrod." Gosławski wrote:

> Awakened by the echoes of the news,
> Hurry—abandon faraway Rome,
> Hurry—for should we prove victorious,
> With no merit you'd be ashamed to breathe the Polish air.
> But should we perish in the ruins, again,
> O, Bard! Then in the time of pain
> You'd be unworthy to share a grave with those who, glorious,
> Shared the effort and shed their blood!

In other words, while the nation took up arms, Mickiewicz spent his time in Italy wooing aristocratic Russian ladies and, later, in Greater Poland (outside the Russian partition), seducing Polish women.

Romantic poets dreamed of participating in noble insurrections. Byron, dying in a Greek city besieged by Turks, became the idol of that epoch. So it is easy to understand Gosławski addressing his verses to this poet-bard. Nevertheless, considering the nineteenth century as a whole, it seems that the charge of nonparticipation could be made against Mickiewicz only by Mickiewicz himself.

It has not yet been ascertained who—Leonard Chodźko or Ludwik Nabielak—made the famous statement that "the Word was made Flesh, and Vallenrod the Belvedere";[10] it is obvious, however, that the cadets who started the insurrection were inspired by Mickiewicz's poem. General Dezydery Chłapowski noted some years later: "The mind that concocted 'Vallenrod' cannot be pure. As soon as I read 'Vallenrod,' some twenty years ago, I felt revulsion toward Mickiewicz, and that revulsion grew in 1831, when everyone was fighting while, before my very eyes, he spent four months in debauchery with a loose woman. Perhaps he mended his ways; may God forgive him, but people are not as merciful."

Kajetan Koźmian confessed: "I know Mickiewicz's talent, which is particularly clear in 'Farys,' but I hate him as the author of 'Vallenrod,' the master and corrupter of youth, the reformer and abandoner of all principle." "Those were such good times," reminisces Koźmian, when "Ode to the Youth did not yet exist, and neither did 'Vallenrod' or a thousand other pieces of Lithuanian rubbish, and when this evil genius still slept in his cradle; this—so to speak—Satan of literature and morality, this Antichrist of our education, this wicked spirit was still in his cradle and his arrogance and conceit rocked him through his light ballads.... [W]ith his 'Vallenrod' in hand, by way of an extraordinary miracle, he secured for himself the chair of Slavic literature in Paris, where he sullied and trampled truth, morality, virtue, and religion, and was relegated to the lunatic asylum only by virtue of the common sense of the French." Koźmian called Mickiewicz "this deceiver who, cloaked in patriotism and love of nation, in league with wicked troublemakers, used a new form of literature to impose on youthful minds and hearts a whole

10. This expression meant that the 1831 attack by young Polish insurgents on the seat of czarist power in Warsaw was an act of treason inspired by Mickiewicz's "Konrad Vallenrod."

moral order of emotions, imagination, and taste, and led this country into destruction and chaos out of which only God himself (and not immediately at that) can lead it, with the words "Fiat lux." Koźmian summed up Mickiewicz's conduct as that of a person who, with the charm of his verse, incited his fellow countrymen to spill blood, but for himself chose exile.

The words of Kajetan Koźmian would provide an excellent climax for the summation of the Great Lustrator's speech for the prosecution. The verdict is rather obvious: guilty.

XI

On March 8, 1968, a rally was held in the courtyard of Warsaw University demanding that performances of *Forefathers' Eve* resume at the National Theater. Soon afterward, similar rallies were held at every large university in every town that had one. The Communist authorities reacted to the students' demands first by publishing a series of lies in the press and by imprisoning many of the demonstrators. Then, on March 19, there was a huge party meeting at Congress Hall in Warsaw, where Władysław Gomułka, the secretary general of the Central Committee of the Polish United Workers' Party, took the floor:

> Why has *Forefathers' Eve* in Dejmek's adaptation been taken off the stage of the National Theatre?... The anti-tsarist edge of *Forefathers' Eve* cannot be transformed, in the name of abstract freedom and artistic license, into an anti-Soviet weapon. The attempt to deploy Mickiewicz's poetry, born of young people's patriotic struggle against the tsarist oppression, to slander the Polish People's Republic, is nothing but a political fraud, for it distorts the most profound, democratic, and progressive sense of Mickiewicz's works. Mickiewicz has never carried the banner of reaction and never will.... Today, when the alliance with the Soviet Union and the reborn socialist Russian nation is and will remain fundamental to the security, sovereignty and development of Poland, it is our duty—without distorting history in any way, for there is no need to do so—to uproot from our minds the remnants of old and long-vanished differences, and not to harden and aggravate them. Such is the imperative of patriotism and internationalism—the two qualities that form the most

beautiful tradition of the Polish nation and of the Polish working class. Mickiewicz was and will remain a patriot and internationalist of his times. We shall never agree to make him a rallying point of anti-Soviet demonstrations.[11]

Even today, forty years later, one gets goose bumps when reading this rubbish, spoken by the dictator of Poland at the time, rubbish accompanied by savage attacks on eminent writers, on émigrés, and on the muzzled, repressed, and imprisoned people. What Gomułka said about the protesters was more or less what Novosiltsev had said about Mickiewicz and the Philomaths; Novosiltsev had analyzed "Konrad Vallenrod," while Gomułka criticized the staging of *Forefathers' Eve*. Dictators right up to the present day have always had problems with Mickiewicz.

It is all so sad and so pitiful.

Then, in March 1968, while I was incarcerated in the Warsaw prison, I read Gomułka's speech. Over and over I wondered how it was possible. Gomułka, to me, was not an average person—he was a Polish Communist, not a Soviet; he was a man courageous enough to oppose Stalin; he had been imprisoned during Stalinist times and had never given in under interrogation. And now the very same man was speaking in the language of a police constable, a spiritual simpleton, and an unscrupulous liar. I then thought: Are the seeds of evil always present in the mentality of Communism's adherents? Does hunger for power make a scoundrel of everyone?

I was sure of only one thing: Adam Mickiewicz certainly deserved a different literary critic and a different defender.

XII

In order to defend Mickiewicz before the Great Lustrator, one must believe that the author of *Forefathers' Eve* actually needs that defense. It would be extremely difficult today to find, even among the most convinced adherents of the lustrating worldview, any historian or critic

11. Władysław Gomułka, *Przemówienia 1968* [Speeches, 1968] (Warsaw, 1969).

brave enough to prepare an indictment charging Mickiewicz with dirty-
ing "the snow-white robe of Poland." Again, we are talking about the
present, but during the poet's lifetime, as Professor Maria Janion reminds
us, Mickiewicz "more than once fell victim to a frighteningly ruthless
smear campaign. One contemporary correspondent would even have denied him the right to join émigré circles, 'for he never fought for the Fatherland, never hummed a song for her during battle, but rather has now de-
parted not only from the Church and Roman Catholic Poland, but also
from reason itself.' So he was a complete stranger in every possible sense....
The Polish democratic inquisition was just that dangerous."[12]

One should keep in mind Professor Janion's caustic remarks when
observing the behavior of today's examiners. The lustrating mind-set is
a parody of Marxism and Leninism, or dialectical materialism or historical dialectics. Marxists-Leninists, among them Gomułka, searched
for the reasons for human behavior in material interests, while lustrators, or followers of "detective materialism," looked in police archives
for the truths that rule human behavior. So for a Great Lustrator the
matter would be entirely plain: the life and works of Mickiewicz were
forever tainted by the pledge of cooperation he made in 1825. And that is
clearly sheer nonsense.

Mickiewicz's biographers have always had a problem—the poet has
been a national icon, a legend, and a mythical ideal for Poles; any cloud
over Mickiewicz's biography was like a cloud over the idea and ideals of
Poland. So the poet's biographers reinterpreted some facts, disregarded
others, and kept completely silent about others still. Zygmunt Krasiński
wrote after Mickiewicz's death: "For my generation, he was milk and
honey, and bile, and spiritual blood." Sunlight, however, can be perceived only where there are clouds, and brightness only where there is
darkness. In Mickiewicz's biography, there appears both the sunlight of
genius and the clouds of the fate of one enslaved by the czars' empire.

---

12. Maria Janion, *Życie pośmiertne Konrada Wallenroda* [Posthumous Life of Konrad
Wallenrod] (Warsaw, 1990).

In Polish history, there has been the brightness of heroism and the love of freedom, but there has also been the darkness of enslavement, compromise, and capitulation. That is why an analysis of Mickiewicz's life and work is like a look into the depths of the Polish heritage.

Thus it is not sufficient to state the obvious: that a declaration of loyalty signed under duress is painful and humiliating but not disgraceful; that "Ode to Youth" and "To a Polish Mother" are neither depraved nor anti-patriotic but, rather, are masterpieces of Polish writing; that "Konrad Vallenrod" is a magnificent achievement of Polish culture and not the result of American, Russian, or Jewish inspiration; that the accusations against this work say little about the work itself but speak volumes about its critics; that the charge of "fraternization" with Muscovites, analyzed by Professor Janion, grew out of patriotic orthodoxy, whose cruel and uncompromising nature manifested itself as simple xenophobia; and that, as Professor Alina Witkowska has put it, that charge sprang from a narrow-mindedness and spiritual shallowness that transformed the ideal of a fatherland into idolatry of Poland. As for the charges related to the poet's nonparticipation in the 1831 uprising—a revolt in whose success he did not believe—they can be attributed only to bad faith and the absurd conviction that shooting a gun always serves the homeland better than creating its culture.

Repeating the obvious is not sufficient for me. After all, the charges against Mickiewicz are exactly those that Poles leveled against each other throughout the nineteenth century, and then throughout the era of the People's Republic; they still haunt us today, like a specter rising from the archives of the Secret Police. We have always been faced with a dilemma: What may one actually sign for the police, and what should one never sign? Should one become a conspirator, or should one act within the law and pay the price for that compromise? Should one emigrate or remain in the country? Where is the border between a devious game played against the enemy, on the one hand, and compromise, on the other? At different times, we have answered these questions differently. And often we were wrong.

XIII

A mere trifle prompted the investigation of the Philomaths. On May 3, 1823, a few students from a Vilnius gymnasium wrote on a blackboard "Long live the May 3 Constitution!" This set off inquiries, house searches, interrogations, detentions, and the first denunciations. Later, as a result of the statements of those detained, came the first wave of arrests. During the night of November 4, 1823, Mickiewicz was arrested as well. He was kept in the Basilian Monastery. The young men, unprepared for the rigors of prison, were threatened, blackmailed, and brought to the brink of physical and mental exhaustion. In that manner, the interrogators extracted from them further information about the secret meetings of the Lovers of Virtue (another student group), the Philaret Society.

Mickiewicz was interrogated on December 1, 1823. What follows is the account of a historian:

> The poet was interrogated by the state counselor, police superintendent Piotr Shilkhov, and the counselor of the province, Wincenty Ławrynowicz, who asked him three questions. The first one regarded the data of the defendant; the second concerned his means of support. Coming to the third question, the interrogators informed Mickiewicz first that they already knew he was a member of the Philomaths and also of the Philarets, so he would be expected to disclose "with utter honesty" everything he knew about those organizations, to remember who the other members were, and, obviously, to name them.
>
> Mickiewicz denied being a member of the Philomaths and stated that throughout its existence he had been away from Vilnius, vacationing in Kovno. He also denied being a member of the Philaret Society. He admitted that he had heard of both organizations' from university colleagues who were Philarets and whom he occasionally visited. Then he testified that Tomasz Zan was the president of the Philaret Society and that he himself had been invited to participate in the meetings held at the lodgings of Odyniec and Czeczott, where poems were read. He also took part in a breakfast the Philarets gave on the occasion of Zan's birthday, and urged by those present, he presented him a ring with the inscription "With friendship for merit" and then improvised some poems.

Besides Zan, he named other friends whom he had seen at picnics, or whom, he had heard, were members. The following statement was attached to the signed deposition:

To these truthful statements, I should add that although I was not an active member of the Philaret Society, I shall never stop regretting that by my foolhardiness in having become involved in the meetings of this Society, I incurred the interest of the authorities; I also solemnly promise that in [the] future I shall live in accordance with the beneficial lesson this mistake has taught me.[13]

On December 16, the investigative commission rejected numerous pleas to free those being held, among them Mickiewicz. With respect to him, the commission stated that although he did not admit to being a member of the Philarets, the twelve members of that organization had testified that he was among them. "For this reason he must be confronted with the witnesses face to face, and therefore the commission finds it impossible to free those persons." On February 12, 1824, as related by Bartłomiej Szyndler, Novosiltsev's biographer, the investigative commission arranged a confrontation between the Philomaths' president, Józef Jeżowski, and Mickiewicz, who was brought in from prison. Jeżowski denied being a member of the Philaret Society. At the confrontation, Mickiewicz stated that he "had heard that Jeżowski was a Philaret but had no evidence to prove it."

Mickiewicz was interrogated again on April 20 in relation to the Knowledge Lovers, or Philomaths, whose existence had been revealed during the interrogation of Franciszek Malewski. "Mickiewicz recounted the history of the Society from 1817 to 1819 in great detail; on behalf of its members, he detailed the organization's goals and projects, described its structure, and cited the themes discussed at certain meetings. He stressed that the Philomaths had never breached the 'boundaries of duty and propriety' and that they felt 'the most sincere gratitude toward the Monarch for the benefits provided our nation'; nor had they ever violated

13. Juliusz Kleiner, *Mickiewicz* (Lublin, 1948).

'the duty of respect and obedience to the Government.'" Once again, he denied being a member of the Philaret Society. Subsequent confrontations brought out nothing new. Sometime later, on a guarantee of good behavior given by university professor Joachim Lelewel, Mickiewicz was released. It was then that he signed the declaration described by Stanisław Pigoń.

The poet described the atmosphere of the interrogation in a distilled form in the third part of *Forefathers' Eve*. It is here that we read about one of the prisoners:

> He was alive, but tortured to the hilt
> Because as yet he'd not confessed his guilt;
> For many nights they had not let him rest;
> Had fed him on salt fish, all drink suppressed;
> Dosed him with opium, with ghosts beset,
> Tickled his soles and armpits to a sweat—
> But soon men spoke of others, jailed for a plot;
> His wife lamented, but the rest forgot.
>   At last, by night, they rang at his wife's door:
> An officer, a gendarme, and one more—
> Himself at last. They bade him take a pen
> And sign himself as safe returned again.
> They took his signature, and with a threat—
> "If you betray!..." And grimly off they set. (pp. 135–36)

... to which the poet could only mutter, through clenched teeth: You scoundrels, you bastards!

The hell with you!

XIV

One hundred and forty-four years later, in March 1968, we were woken early by a banging on the door. Detentions began as early as the eighth of that month, because the rally at the university had been called for that day. A copy of *Forefathers' Eve* lay on my bedside table then. It was the right moment for me to read it carefully; before then, I had barely thumbed through it for my high school exit exams, which was exactly what I'd done with all the rest of the books on the curriculum. *Forefathers' Eve* read then, in 1968, dazzled me, and this sense of enchantment has accompanied me throughout my life since. And I shall always retain the memory of the secret policeman who (during the search of my apartment) went through Mickiewicz's book, undoubtedly looking for coded messages or leaflets—he was doing it with pronounced revulsion and fear, as if what he held was the worst and most illegal anti-Soviet pamphlet.

Later, in prison, I returned to *Forefathers' Eve* many a time. I repeated many passages in my mind, and especially this one, which served as a consolation:

> Prisoners are glad to tell of bondage past:
> I thought that he'd be glad to talk at last,
> And bring to light from earth and tyrant gloom
> His tale, and Poland's heroes' daily doom.
> For Poland lives and blossoms in the dark—
> Siberian mines and torture-dungeons stark. (p. 137)

And I silently recited "To My Russian Friends," repeating to myself that our nation is like "a lava field."

There, in prison on Rakowiecka Street, *Forefathers' Eve*, a story about Vilnius students imprisoned for the sake of their dream of freedom, served as a spiritual support and a source of internal strength. It helped us realize our place in the long chain of Polish generations, all of which had to serve an apprenticeship in "fortresses and prisons."

I shall also remember forever the goddamned interrogations, during which people were broken down with intimidation, slander, blackmail, solitary confinement, and taunts. I shall never forget the punishment cells—we called them the "hard beds"—where the cold would wake you from your sleep on the bare planks; the phony smuggled messages; how we were set against one another; the psychological pressure used to extract confessions, the cruel derision, and the reek of anti-Semitism in the tirades of the interrogators; the extorted statements; and my own

helpless rage at this barred and vicious world, in which every conversation was a trap. Just as their counterparts had once done to the Philomaths,
our interrogators forced us to be evasive, to pronounce half-truths and
lies, to commit ourselves—in the words of Professor Witkowska—to the
ambiguity of open and covert acts. It is easy to make a mistake at such
moments. Like many of the Philomaths before us, many of us did make
mistakes.[14]

But these were extraordinary people who had the courage to stand
up against the dictatorship. No lustrator is even worthy to tie his
shoelaces—so he weaves a noose for them out of old police reports. That
is why the wound on Konrad's brow is not only a wound on Adam Mickiewicz's brow—as Professor Stanisław Pigoń would have it—but also a
wound on every Polish brow. A refusal to see that is plain Pharisaism.

XV

Pharisaism is not in short supply among us today. Before our very eyes,
we see swarms of eleventh-hour anti-Communists, underground conspirators, Konrads and Kordians, and Catos and moralists who poke
through literary works, life histories, and police archives, who are relentless in tracking down compromisers and traitors. They are a new breed
of the great and small lustrators so helpful to the fatherland—the in-
quisitors without blemish, mindlessly cruel and infected with suspicion. Ryszard Przybylski, analyzing the character of Konrad from *Forefathers' Eve*, remarks that "throughout Polish history of the nineteenth
and twentieth centuries and up to the present day, there has been a
parade of patriotic buffoons, who use their love of the nation to claim
an imaginary uniqueness and to justify their unwarranted ambition and
their especially vile arrogance.... Thus Mickiewicz has revealed one of
the most disgraceful diseases of the Polish soul."

14. Alina Witkowska, *Mickiewicz: słowo i czyn* [Mickiewicz: Word and Deed]
(Warsaw, 1975).

How well we understand the path Mickiewicz took—we, like him, a generation "born in slavery and swaddled in chains." First there was the impulse of contrariness, the policy of refusing consent that led him and his Philomath friends. Those young students founded rather innocent organizations to discuss ideas, share their knowledge of the world, and cultivate good national traditions. How many of us went through similar initiations—forming study groups, reading books together, sharing our dreams of freedom.... The punishment was swift and cruel—house searches, interrogations, imprisonment. The tyranny effectively defended its all-encompassing power. In order to elude it, many attempted to outsmart their interrogators and found themselves in uncomfortable and ambiguous predicaments. It was then that these young people confronted the question: How can we live with dignity and resist effectively and at the same time be a slave of the empire, "free by the grace of Moscow"? Mickiewicz provided the answer in "Konrad Vallenrod." If you cannot be a lion, be a fox, he repeated, citing Machiavelli; cunning is the only weapon of a slave. Many years later, Mickiewicz would add: "I duped the despot by crawling like a snake." After all, that exactly was the essence of Vallenrodism—"duping the despot."

History provides few answers to the question of how to deal with a tyrant. One can choose the road of conspiracy or of insurrection, like Walerian Łukasiński or Piotr Wysocki. But only a few follow that path, so we glorify them as examples of extreme courage and pay homage to them as national heroes. Conspiracy, however, has the inevitable logic of great risk—conspiracies are searched out, infiltrated, and prone to betrayal and denunciation, while conspirators wind up in prison and often break down, scarred by the experience for the rest of their lives. Another way is simply to flee the tyrant, the farther the better; this is the path followed by hundreds of Polish emigrants. Finally, there remains some form of adjustment that is neither collaboration nor betrayal but a permanent choice about what seems to be possible in the concrete circumstances of enslavement. The consciousness of Polish elites from before 1830, both in Warsaw and in Vilnius, was dominated by such thinking, as exemplified by dozens of accounts.

Princes Adam Czartoryski and Ksawery Drucki-Lubecki, Joachim Lelewel and Jan Śniadecki, and the brothers Wincenty and Bonawentura Niemojowskis all worked toward important Polish goals within the confines of the Russian empire. The dilemma such people face is familiar to us, for instance, from the history of the Christian denominations. Christians would often ask themselves: Is it permissible to profess the holy articles of faith in a veiled, oblique way for fear of the long arm of the Inquisition? Is it the duty of true Christians to accept fully all possible sacrifices that may be called for on account of their professed beliefs, including torture and burning at the stake? Or, may they leave the country of persecution in order to practice their religion freely in a tolerant land? Is not the practice of the Pharisee Nicodemus who, fearing persecution, visited Jesus at night—in other words, the formal acceptance of binding rites while one simultaneously believes in and, among intimates, professes different principles—a permanent result of every ideological tyranny? One needs a lot of imagination and wisdom of the heart to assess the conduct of such people; one must enjoy the condition of being without sin if one is to cast the first stone at them.

The process of examining Adam Mickiewicz, conducted here as a sheer exercise, demonstrates the wretchedness of the lustrating mind. As if sensing what might happen, Mickiewicz addressed the Poles:

> Search not continually in the past for errors and sins.... Exclaim not: "Lo, in this man is such a blemish, I must point it out; lo, this man hath committed such and such a transgression." Be assured that men will be found whose duty it will be to dig up these blemishes, and judges to whom judgment shall belong, and a hangman who shall punish.... For be gentle toward others, but stern toward yourselves. And with what judgment ye judge others, ye shall yourselves be judged.... That he who very sternly condemneth his neighbor for some error, either for timidity..., he himself shall surely fall into this error and shall be judged by others.... If thou sayest of someone unjustly:

"He is a traitor"; or if thou sayest unjustly: "He is a spy"; then be sure that of thee others are saying the same thing also in the same moment.[15]

XVI

Let us finally have a closer look at this seeker-out of other people's mistakes and sins, faults, and wrongdoings, who is so lenient toward himself and so strict toward others, this true hunter of traitors and spies. Let us examine the Great Lustrator.

The Great Lustrator is absolutely certain that he possesses the absolute truth. He, once and for all, has broken away from that spiritually suspect condition in which the world appears contingent, chaotic, and uncertain. The world of a lustrator is stable and well organized, so he always has the last word, and he cannot possibly lose because his defeat would spell ruin for the whole axiology of lustration. If ever he fails—in a debate or at trial—the failure is not caused by his error but is rather a fruit of a conspiracy by the "anti-lustration forces," for the Great Lustrator is the essence of truth and justice.

How does he perceive himself? Well, he is energetic and resolute, determined and honest, and intelligent and perspicacious. Among his other qualities are nonconformism and courage, which allow him to survive the brutal attacks of the "anti-lustration forces." Equipped with amazing intuition, and psychologically astute, he can easily penetrate the examinee's psyche. Finally, he is the embodiment of character integrity, strengthened by his unblemished past, which allows him to judge other people's transgressions in an exemplary and a just manner. The Great Lustrator knows only too well that the examinees' world is engulfed by evil, which must be rooted out, and evil is advocated by evil people, who must be exposed. Yes, indeed, they must be exposed, barred from exerting any influence, punished, and preferably annihilated. After

15. "The Books of the Polish Pilgrims," from *Poems by Adam Mickiewicz*, trans. various, ed. George Rapall Noyes (New York: Herald Square Press, 1944), pp. 391–95.

all, those people, those bad apples with their hidden agendas, are responsible for the ubiquity of filth and sin in public life.

Filth and sin fascinate the Great Lustrator. He deals only with decline, weakness, and moments of uncertainty, fear, and confusion but never with spiritual power, disinterestedness, nobility, courage, loyalty, or faithfulness. For the Great Lustrator, who lives in a climate and culture of suspicion, the latter are only calculation and masquerade. Every single human being is suspect, much like every single human act. His psyche, no matter how staunchly he denies it, is rooted in the conviction that human nature is soiled and hypocritical and that man is egoistic and malicious, evil and cowardly, because instinct itself drives him to violence, venality, and betrayal. This is why the spiritual world of the Great Lustrator is so poor and barren—he simply does not see any beauty in the life around him. Instead, he sniffs out informer after informer.

The Great Lustrator is never satisfied with what is commonly known. So what that the villainy of the era was overt, so what that denunciations were not published anonymously, so what that prosecutors and judges obligingly failed to use pseudonyms? The Great Lustrator is not satisfied with skimming the surface of the problem. He needs to dig deeper to ascertain the essence of the matter. He searches for it in police archives, and there he finds the key to absolute truth—the one and only truth, the truest truth of all, which leaves no doubt whatsoever. Reports and denunciations from police files have something in common with pornography; blushing like a fourteen-year-old looking at porn, the Great Lustrator studies those denunciations and does not even see that a truly satanic temptation is slowly growing within him. For the devil, according to one philosopher, "is arrogance of spirit, unsmiling certainty, and a truth that is never doubted." The devil is grim, and so is the Great Lustrator. They both deal in dirt and know where they are going; they are heading for precisely where they came from: from the dirt, through the dirt, searching for dirt.

The Great Lustrator knows that the enemy is constantly active, cunning, and persistent. Therefore, one must be highly alert to every protest against the process of examination and note every single criticism of it, for all such criticisms, in essence, support dirt and sin. In view of that, "the enemy must be actively uncovered," his past must be fully known, and what is secret must be exposed. The Great Lustrator would say: "To meet our standards, Adam Mickiewicz had to be not only a great poet but also an exemplary father, a good husband, a patriot, a totally progressive man, and so on, and so forth. But have any of us read books that discuss how many members of the opposition were, for example, drunks? And that news obviously comes from the archives of the Ministry of Internal Affairs. The archives also include information about who cheated on their spouses. Has anyone researched this behavior, written about it, published a scholarly monograph on it?" The Great Lustrator will fill those gaps, giving thorough consideration to what kind of patriot Mickiewicz was and also to how many people from the democratic opposition drank vodka and behaved licentiously. For it is here, in the police files and in reports by informers, that the key can be found to the real nature of Mickiewicz and the members of the opposition; that is the key to understanding.

The Great Lustrator has the soul of a tracker, and he prides himself on that. He is ruthless; he believes that the end justifies the means, and that for the sake of saving all humanity, it is permissible to trample the human dignity of individual examinees. Hence, his lustrating categories grow endlessly more radical, and so does his appetite: a scrap of a document here, a copy of a report there, and a portion of a denunciation somewhere else—everything, in other words, nothing, is sufficient for the Great Lustrator to formulate public accusations against people whom he might consider suspect. For him, a simple conversation is no longer a dialogue between free people but an interrogation, conducted for the purpose of examination. He will never believe that to treat people this way is simply grotesque. The Great Lustrator is absolutely convinced of his impeccability. He works diligently to justify this conviction: some information he simply disregards, distorts, embellishes, or misrepresents; sometimes he simply creates his own information and treats his own suppositions as empirically proven facts. This is a piece of cake for him, because an atmosphere of psychological intimidation and mutual mistrust is conducive to his wonderful self-perception. Every associate and every informer confirm the necessity of the lustration.

The Great Lustrator, powerful though he is, nevertheless has his superiors. So uncompromising and strict toward the examinees, he has to be flexible and obliging toward his bosses. They, after all, dictate who should be examined and who should be spared the process of examination. The Great Lustrator would never admit it, but at the bottom of his heart he knows only too well that the process of examination is used to discredit the political enemies of his superiors. Therefore, when examining the life histories of dissidents or those under suspicion, he remembers that he is helping to create a world in which people become lustrators, denouncers, and hunters of others for their own benefit. The Great Lustrator combines in himself the megalomaniac, because of the fear he evokes in some people, and the lackey, because he himself must still fear certain people.

After all, the existence of covert agents is the precondition of the Great Lustrator's existence, his material status, his prestige, and his power over people. Just as the Grand Inquisitor created heretics to justify the existence of the Holy Inquisition, so the Great Lustrator creates ever more suspected informers, for without them, he would be nothing.

XVII

The Great Lustrator wields a powerful weapon: the fear he evokes. That fear makes a potential examinee meek and obedient, eager to fulfill the wishes of the examining authority: blackmail is an excellent means of persuasion. Blackmail is also a great way to deflect criticism of the lustrators—if you oppose the process of examination, then you must wish to conceal the identities of informers, who will surely be blackmailed by the spy agencies of a neighboring superpower. So if you oppose the examinations, you endanger the sovereignty of the Polish state. This kind of logic, simple as a mathematical equation, gives moral power to the Great Lustrator. He knows very well that examinees do not take the straight and narrow path, so it is not easy to catch them red-handed. One must therefore apply the most effective method: accuse them all and let God recognize his own. In that way, the Great Lustrator slowly sinks into an atmosphere of concealment and obliqueness, and into the world of snoops' denunciations and police reports. In such a world it is very difficult to comprehend that dire situations exist in which "the border between good and bad may be hair thin." When examining human behavior in such situations, the Great Lustrator may follow every jot and title of the law but at the same time violate its spirit. He equates recklessness and momentary weakness with betrayal, venality, and spying. The mission of the Great Lustrator is not to find the guilty but to smear the accused and to finish them off.

The process of examination, started on the principle that "the truth will set you free," instead offers only that miserable sliver of truth present in police archives. The former political police functionary becomes the ultimate source, the "police truth," which is so different from human truth. It is he who verifies whether the Adam Mickiewicz really was an agent, as the police file records. Lustration is the product of a twisted mind, for through it human fates are once again entrusted to the Security Service. Lustration was intended to provide moral cleansing for a society contaminated by long years of tyranny, but instead it led to a permanent witch hunt, the pursuit of victim after victim from the police archives. The process of examination has become a tool of the struggle for power and a way to eliminate people who are inconvenient for the authorities or the lustrators. It has become a means of degrading public life.

It does not follow, obviously, that critical reflection on Polish history should be suspended or that we should simply accept that there have never been examples of vile behavior, wicked provocation, and the ignominious service of informing. Too many such things occurred, and this important collective experience needs to be discussed and considered carefully. This is exactly why we should focus on the mechanisms and on acts and not on people who were entrapped by the Secret Police. Analyzing a disease is not the same as hunting down human sins and human beings.

Obviously shabby conduct ought to be stigmatized, betrayal ought to be called by name, and crimes ought to be punished. Of course, all citizens have a right to learn about the people who poisoned their lives—the informers, spies, provocateurs, and traitors. This does not mean, however, that we should consent to the games organized by the Great Lustrator. The difference between these obvious truths and those games is exactly that between a theological debate and the persecution of heretics, or between the procedures of law enforcement, which prosecutes offenders, and the inquisitor's interrogations, during which heretics and witches are put to torture.

There exists the opinion that the process of examination may be compared to the work of the Evangelists who, after all, exposed and described the betrayal by Judas, the denials by Simon Peter, and even the Apostles' dozing off in Gethsemane. I do not think such a comparison is valid. The Evangelists tell their own truth about Christ and the Apostles. In their stories, they do not omit painful or even embarrassing facts. But the very same story would have looked very different if it had been told by Pilate's police spies or by informers for the Pharisees, or even by Judas himself. The Great Lustrator does not believe in the Evangelists' accounts—he trusts only denunciations by Judas.

Informers have always existed; they exist even today. There were informers in the conspiracy of 1863. There were informers in the Combat Organization of the Polish Socialist Party. There were informers in the Home Army. There were informers in the Catholic Church. But no sensible scholar has ever arrived at the notion that he should document the history of the Home Army or the Catholic Church solely on the basis of informers' denunciations or police reports. Moreover, even if such a history were to be written, it would tell us more about those who examined the Catholic Church than it would about the Church. Have we not read enough articles about the Home Army or the Catholic

Church that are based on information drawn from the Security Service files of the previous, not so glorious regime?

At times, it seems as if the Great Lustrator were a brand-new hero for our times. He is sometimes a prosecutor, sometimes a judge. He may also be a journalist, a historian, or a politician. Invariably, though, in every single incarnation, he has something in him of the mentality of those who passed the verdict on Socrates, forced Galileo to recant, burned at the stake Jan Hus and Giordano Bruno, and set up the guillotine in Paris during the revolution. Those were the people who, magnifying glass in hand, tracked down any deviation from orthodoxy and hunted heretics in every epoch, all the while claiming that they were merely in pursuit of foreign intelligence agents and the minions of ousted regimes. Those minions, as is nearly always the case, proved necessary to the hunters of the new era. After all, they and only they could serve as prosecution witnesses against the victims of yesteryear.

Sometimes I cannot suppress the feeling that the Great Lustrator knows nothing, although he feels that he knows everything better than anyone else. He relives the spirit of war, and in war one kills one's enemies. However, the logic of annihilating one's enemies, when applied under conditions of social peace (however fragile) and democracy (however faulty and imperfect), leads to the destruction of peace and democracy. That is why the Great Lustrator and his behavior are simply dangerous. He arouses my fear—I will keep an eye on him.

XVIII

Soon after 1945, in *Tygodnik Powszechny*, Stefan Kisielewski told a funny story. In the 1930s, in the courtyard of Warsaw University, Kisielewski was having a serious political argument with a fellow student. "He was a National Democrat and I was a follower of Piłsudski," Kisielewski said. "Agitated, if not enraged, I was yelling at him from very close up, hanging on to his lapels and occasionally sprinkling him with spit (regrettably, I am unable to unlearn the unfortunate habit of sprinkling people when

I get very angry). A crowd of fellow students gathered around us, listening to the argument. My opponent heard out all my arguments with stoic composure; finally, once I had had my say, or shout, and had fallen silent, he took out a hanky, wiped off his face, and calmly pronounced these words to me: 'You have bad breath!'" This is more or less what a debate with the Great Lustrator looks like—in reply to your arguments he takes out a file on you that comprises denunciations and police reports. Denunciations tend to be more interesting than arguments; the former are in great demand today and simply sell better.

Let us, however, remain faithful to argument. Let us set the passion of the Great Lustrator against the gentle wisdom of the Forgiving Man. As Stefan Kisielewski wrote:

> The Forgiving Man feels comfortable among a diversity of phenomena, forms, concepts, and views. The Forgiving Man considers diversity a priceless treasure in his life. He tries to understand everything and everyone, because understanding is the necessary attribute of a man who considers diversity a treasure and not a threat. Forgiveness without understanding is only a form of indifference. The Forgiving Man, though believing in one truth, is still able to see elements of truth, even traces of truth, in various views, even in those that look most at odds with his own. The Forgiving Man, respecting all views and demanding basically that their proponents be granted the right to profess them, is often bound to engage in a fight against some of them. In such a case, should he be certain of his own truth, he ought to fight as effectively as possible—but always without anger. The Forgiving Man, having brought the opponent to his knees, extends a hand to help him up. If the opponent is still strong enough to bring him in turn to his knees, the Forgiving Man, accepting his mistake, should not be surprised or angry, nor should he regret his action, for the mistake totally annihilating the enemy would have been a hundredfold greater and more dangerous than the error of extending his hand to the enemy prematurely.[16]

The Forgiving Man is aware that as long as people exist, there will be various understandings of the truth and people will give different

16. Stefan Kisielewski, *Rzeczy małe* [Miniatures] (Warsaw, 1998).

evidence for their truths. So the Forgiving Man knows that "though he fights uncompromisingly for truth, in his heart he must be forgiving of human untruth. A person can be a tamer of human beings but never their judge."

Kisielewski's last commandment may be the most difficult—it is extremely difficult to be forgiving of the Great Lustrator. Still, and I stubbornly repeat this to myself, for the sake of the future, we must learn to forgive the Great Lustrator—preferably when he has been tamed.

History has never spared Poland; the devil himself might have written her script. It is full of partitions, occupations, last-ditch schemes, unsuccessful uprisings, expulsions and betrayals, deportations to Siberia, the gallows, cowardice, corruption, villains and traitors galore, multitudes of con men and troublemakers, and just as many noble failings and despicable betrayals. How many times have Mickiewicz's prophetic verses proven true in Polish history?

> One day an unknown spy will challenge him,
> A perjured court his adversary be,
> The jousting-field, a secret dungeon grim;
> A powerful foe the verdict will decree.
>
> And for the vanquished man as monument
> The gallows tree will rear its sullen height;
> For glory—but a woman's tears, soon spent,
> And fellow patriots' whispered words by night.[17]

Today, it is entirely up to us whether we choose our compatriots' whispered words by night or the examination of our compatriots by night.

Meanwhile, the wound on Konrad's brow is bleeding still.

17. Ibid., p. 238. This translation by Jewell Parish and G. R. Noyes. First published in 1925.

PART III

The Complex
Polish-Jewish Matters

CHAPTER NINE

The Kielce Pogrom

Two Examinations of Conscience

In memory of Stanisław Musiał, SJ

In the report prepared by the Kielce Curia and delivered by Bishop Czesław Kaczmarek to the U.S. ambassador in Warsaw, Arthur Bliss-Lane, two statements are worthy of mention. They read as follows:

> The Kielce events, regardless of their background, regardless of the fact that they were provoked, and regardless of the fact that the authorities could have prevented them but did not want to, were nevertheless a crime that blemished Polish society. It was known that certain of Poland's enemies would try to attack her because of that crime. Any honest Polish government, like any government in the world, would consider it a duty to present the Kielce events as carefully as possible and to report all extenuating circumstances. For these undoubtedly existed; after all, the people who killed in Kielce were not professional murderers.

Another passage gives us the following account of the crowd murdering Jews: "When a deed is committed in a fit of passion, guilt is always mitigated, particularly when the criminal is one of a crowd of transgressors, and when he is agitated by the crowd or in some way incited by it."

What can be said of those statements? "Instead of haggling and excusing ourselves," wrote Jan Błoński in his famous essay "The Poor Poles Look at the Ghetto," "we ought first to consider ourselves, our own sin or weakness." A comparison of these two attitudes seems to illustrate quite well the differences between various understandings of what an examination of conscience by Polish Catholics should consist of.

I

Jan Błoński published his memorable essay in *Tygodnik Powszechny*, the weekly of the Catholic intelligentsia (in nr.2, 1987), which with admirable courage and consistency had opposed anti-Semitic stereotypes for decades. In August 1945, at the very beginning of its existence and just after the Kraków pogrom of August 11, that very same *Tygodnik Powszechny* published this revealing declaration: "Numerous statements by the Holy See as well as those by representatives of the Church hierarchy unambiguously point to the fact that anti-Semitism cannot be reconciled with a Catholic outlook on life. Anti-Semitism is racism; it is a conviction that there exists a natural inequality or even animosity between races; anti-Semitism is hatred. The Church teaches that all people are equal before God.... A decline in moral standards, mob rule, and crime—these are the painfully obvious effects of five years of war and occupation. Particularly in view of...the gruesome extermination of the Jewish people by Germany, of which every Christian must think with the deepest empathy, the Kraków events evoke deep sorrow." And *Tygodnik Powszechny* has remained faithful to this declaration throughout the sixty years of its existence.

Jan Błoński's essay was an obvious reflection of that way of thinking: the clear admission of guilt when the crime actually happened, and the clear truth telling that liberates and heals. Yet the essay, one of the most noble and beautiful texts ever written in the Polish language, evoked much resistance in public opinion. I too was among those who thought that it was not the best time for Błoński to tell the painful truth. I thought that a society struggling with the sense of humiliation and abasement in the grim days of martial law should not—at that particular time—be obliged to critically review the past with its heavily dramatic baggage of Polish–Jewish relations. And I was wrong. On several later occasions, when I participated in Polish–Jewish debates—in New York, Chicago, Los Angeles, Toronto, Melbourne, and Paris—and represented polemically the Polish point of view, I had came to understand that Błoński's wise and insightful essay had become a turning point in those relations, that it served to "[clean] the contaminated land." That very essay also initiated a manifest new way of thinking and writing about anti-Semitism; it broke the decades-long chain of hypocrisy and silence caused by the Communist dictatorship and censorship. Polish public opinion spoke in the language of a free people and proved able to tackle a serious examination of conscience.

The process of arriving at the truth is often understood in different ways. Case in point: one proponent of the "new historical policy" notes that it is "impossible, by virtue of its very nature, to apply the category of national interest" to the position articulated by Błoński. This is quite an amazing judgment; isn't the drive to arrive at the truth of one's own history, which for decades had been falsified by the Communist dictatorship, an elementary condition of the national interest? Another defender of the national dignity against repentance and the "ritual breast-beating" says: "Today, it is fashionable to loudly beat one's own breast over anti-Semitism." I cannot hear this "pounding"—only occasionally do I read bitter words of truth; still, I cannot resist the impression that our defender of "dignity and pride" would much rather beat someone else's breast for someone else's faults.

Recently I read of a developing "retreat from history," the result of a "political process of rewriting the past—a practice in which, for various reasons, both the post-Communists and a part of the former opposition, led by those around *Gazeta Wyborcza*, have a vested interest." It is the Left and the liberals, we read, who "are in the forefront of this fad for revelations." One could ask: What is improper about revealing lies? The authors of the cited quotations are prominent members of the ruling party in Poland today; this provokes the sad reflection that dishonest insinuation is again replacing factual argument, as easily as it did during the Communist dictatorship. It was then, after all, that accusations of "national nihilism" or "contempt for Polish tradition" were employed against the political opposition with no pretense of decency whatsoever, or moderation, or sense.

After 1989, a process began of clearing out the lies now ingrained in the national consciousness. There was a filling in of the blanks in historical research encompassing all the events that had been censored, sentenced to oblivion, during the dictatorship: the Molotov-Ribbentrop Pact; the Soviet invasion of September 17, 1939; the Katyń massacre; the Warsaw Uprising; the persecution of the Catholic Church; Polish–Ukrainian relations; Polish–Jewish relations—quite simply, the whole of Poland's heritage. That is why today we can speak freely about the most difficult questions, including the tragic fate of the Jewish population in Poland after World War II.

II

That fate is undoubtedly one of the most tragic and complicated matters in the contemporary history of Poland. And it was not a Polish–Jewish conflict; it was a Polish–Communist conflict, of which Jews often became victims.

In considering the postwar period, we find a clash of two different, sometimes opposing memories. Two monologues are being spoken here, and they usually do not turn into a dialogue. There is no lack of generalization in those monologues, generalization that falsifies the reality; there is no lack of unjust accusations based on each side's complete misunderstanding of the other. Two ways of thinking clash here—two ways of remembering and passing judgment on the other group, each group proclaiming its own innocence and nurturing its own "triumphalism of suffering." As an understatement, one can say that this state of affairs did not promote empathy toward the neighbor, the antagonist, the Other.

In short, the Holocaust was the most important experience for Jews, while for Poles that experience was the loss of freedom and sovereignty.

For Jews, the entrance of the Red Army into Poland meant the end of the "time of the gas chambers," while for Poles it marked the beginning of the new wave of repressions and foreign domination. After 1945, the basic problem for Jews was still survival; the basic problem for Poles was the new enslavement. Jews lived in fear of the anti-Semitic excesses that had shadowed them even as the war was ending; Poles lived in fear of the Communist security apparatus, which from the beginning was a constant threat to them. At a time of dread, the presence of the Russian Security Service meant, for Jews, hope of rescue, while the appearance of those same functionaries was, for Poles, dread itself. Jews feared anti-Semitic pogroms; Poles were under the impression that the Communist authorities had arranged for a permanent pogrom against them.

Krystyna Kersten, an eminent expert on the matter, wrote, "There was this stereotype plaguing the Polish psyche: Jews—power—endangerment of things Polish; while Jews perceived the following chain: underground army—right wing—anti-Semitism—grave danger to Jews." In Jewish eyes, the Kielce pogrom was an outbreak of brutality by a mob poisoned with the traditional anti-Semitism of the Polish right. For Poles, the pogrom was a Communist provocation meant to sully, in the eyes of the democratic West, the image of a Poland fighting for freedom.

There is no hard evidence that the Kielce pogrom was the result of a purposeful provocation by the security apparatus or other Soviet agencies. There is no doubt, however, that immediately after the fraudulent national referendum, the Communists used the Kielce pogrom for propaganda reasons, to divert attention from the falsification of the results and to shame the anti-Communist opposition. There is also no doubt that the anti-Semitism raging then resulted in acts of aggression against Jews. It is also a fact that the totalitarian Communist authorities of that time enjoyed the support of Jewish institutions, though one might debate to what degree these institutions were representative of the Jewish people.

One should also keep in mind that the Kielce pogrom, although it was the most infamous of the time, was regrettably not the only one. It was a period of widespread violence and of a bloody battle between the Communist authorities and the armed underground; it was a period of chaos, savagery, and lawlessness. The ugly and comprehensive Nazi propaganda campaign had stigmatized Jews and dehumanized them. The practice of Nazi terror made the robbery and murder of Jews part of everyday reality. It also practiced the principle of "divide and rule" by confining Jews in ghettoes and encouraging and rewarding people who blackmailed hidden Jews as well as those Poles who hid them. A Jew ceased to be a neighbor; a Jew became something not unlike vermin that needed to be exterminated.

Finally, as noted by New York historian John Micgiel in his introduction to the recent edition of Bishop Kaczmarek's report, anti-Semitism drew mainly on the fact that many people lived in houses or apartments that had belonged to Polish Jews before the war. Fear that the legal owners might return aroused in them a hostility bordering on anti-Semitism. Jews were to be no more. But they returned. Not very often, and not many of them, but some did.

III

Bożena Szaynok, author of a book on the Kielce pogrom, reports that after the war some three hundred Jews returned to Kielce, which before the war had had nearly 25,000 Jewish inhabitants. According to data from May 1946, 163 Jews lived in Kielce, mainly in two houses at Planty Street, in the center of the city.

The course of events during the pogrom has been described several times. Everything started with allegations by a young boy, Henryk Błaszczyk, that he had been kidnapped for the purpose of ritual murder. An enraged mob, supported by policemen and military troops, attacked a house on Planty Street, where Jews lived and which was the seat of the Jewish Committee, to search for Polish children whom Jews had imprisoned in the cellars for use in ritual murders. Once the mob forced its way into the Planty Street house, Jews were dragged out of their apartments, beaten up, robbed, and murdered over the course of many hours. Whether by omission or intentionally, none of the institutions responsible for law and order in the city did more than watch passively. Forty people died in the pogrom and eighty were beaten up, injured, or even crippled. These are the indisputable facts—the rest is a matter of interpretation, speculation, and conjecture.

One such interpretation is provided in the memorandum quoted earlier, given by Bishop Czesław Kaczmarek, coadjutor of the Kielce diocese, to the U.S. ambassador, Arthur Bliss-Lane. According to Bishop Kaczmarek's biographer, Jan Śledzianowski, in July 1946 the bishop called a special commission, led by Father Professor Mieczysław Żywczyński, to study the circumstances of the pogrom. In delivering its report to the ambassador, Bishop Kaczmarek assumed responsibility for its content and conclusions. This substantial document on the "Kielce events" should be read in the context of the Communist authorities' propaganda campaign.

From the very beginning, Communist propaganda accused the anti-Communist opposition of organizing the pogrom. The press wrote that the pogrom mob had been led by General Anders's soldiers; this was soon proved to be a lie. On July 6, 1946, Władysław Gomułka, the secretary general of the Polish Workers' Party (PPR, later PZPR), clearly identified the murderers in a speech addressed to the activists of the PPR and the Polish Socialist Party (PPS): "The Polish Peasant Party (PSL) and the National Armed Forces (NSZ), having been defeated in the people's referendum, seek to gain victory by throwing the country into the turmoil of anarchy....The glaring proof of this is the Jewish pogrom in Kielce....Polish fascists, the very same people who are so enthusiastic when seeing Mr. Mikołajczyk and who are greeted in return by his lordly smile of satisfaction, have managed to outdo their Nazi masters in anti-Semitic madness." The proclamation by the Kielce organizations of the PPR and PPS also put blame on the Polish clergy.

IV

Bishop Kaczmarek's report was made on September 1, 1946, that is, after a series of propaganda publications and show trials whose course resembled the Stalinist trials of which the main point was the exemplary punishment of scapegoats and the equally diligent cover-up of circumstances that might compromise the representatives of the authorities. The most sensational trials consistently ignored the role played by the police, the military, and the security apparatus. So, justifiably rejecting the version of events offered in government propaganda, the Kaczmarek document presents the bishop's assessment. We read here:

> Poles do not have a reputation as sadists.... Kielce had never before experienced any anti-Jewish riots; the population is peaceful—after all, it is Catholic—and the murderers, according to the charges in the criminal indictment, were not the unemployed or the embittered poor; rather, they were members of the petty bourgeoisie, people who didn't have much money but who weren't paupers.... So why did it happen at all? There can be only one possible answer—because the mob hated Jews. This hatred may have caused them to believe the boy's allegations, so that his story became the last drop, bringing about the overflow of their hatred in dramatic and drastic form. Obviously, one does not hate people who are indifferent toward one or who are harmless; one hates one's enemies or those who appear to be enemies for what, from the mob's point of view, are concrete, clear, and obvious reasons. In Kielce the sources of hatred were of two different types.... After the mass murders of Jews by German authorities in Poland, and thus in Kielce, there was no hostility to Jews and no anti-Semitism. Everyone sympathized with Jews, even their sworn enemies. Many Jews were saved by Poles, for without Polish help none would have survived. They were saved, although those helping Jews risked harsh punishment, including the death sentence. Such was the situation in 1944 and at the beginning of 1945. Once the Red Army enters and the Communist government controls all of Poland, that state of affairs dramatically changes. Hostility toward Jews appears, and it spreads quickly throughout Polish society, including Kielce. Jews are disliked or even hated everywhere in Poland. This is undeniable. Jews are disliked not only by Poles who belong

to no political party or belong to the opposition, but also by many official members of government-sponsored parties.

The reasons for this dislike are commonly known and they have nothing to do with racial matters. Jews in Poland are the main proponents of the communist system, which Poland does not want and which has been forced on Poles against their will. In addition, every Jew has either a good job or unlimited possibilities for such a job in trade and industry. There are many Jews in the government ministries, in foreign missions, in factories, in offices, and in the military—and invariably they occupy important managerial positions. They run the government press, they control the strict censorship in Poland, they run the security agencies, and they make arrests. Even apart from their spreading of communism, they behave insensitively, particularly toward people who do not share their communist ideology. They are often arrogant and brutal. Many of them are not even from Poland. Newcomers from Russia, they barely speak Polish and know even less about Polish issues. For all these reasons, one could say that Jews themselves are responsible for the lion's share of people's hatred of them. The average Pole (whether or not he is justified in this) thinks that the only true and sincere adherents of communism in Poland are mainly Jews, and that the majority of communist Poles—again, this is a matter of popular belief—are people who have a vested interest, people who have no ideology but rather are communists only for the sake of advantage....

Besides, the masses in Kielce were also influenced by another factor, which may be characterized as indirect. A few months before July 4, 1946, there were rumors in Kielce that children of both sexes had been disappearing.... The general public speculated that the perpetrators were Jews and that they ritually murdered the children. The parents' complaints agitated people, particularly uneducated people, against the Jews. The undisputed fact of the children's disappearances enraged even many members of the intelligentsia. Some of them, for example, informed the author of this report that Jews were administering blood transfusions and then killing the very victims whose blood was drawn.

The facts described here have been reported to the police. They responded with complete indifference, neither beginning investigation nor disputing the information they received. This inaction by the police authorities persuaded the general public that Jews could do whatever they pleased in Poland, that they could act with impunity.

The author of the report wonders why a small boy would run away from home and then make up a story about being kidnapped. Was he put up to doing this? And, if so, by whom? Rejecting, and logically at that, the idea that this was a provocation by the anti-Communist opposition, the author of the report ponders the question of whether the provocateurs could have been Jews. Would Jews bring down a pogrom on themselves? Wouldn't that be absurd? asks the author of the report. And then he says:

> Before answering this question, one must mention two closely related phenomena. First of all, it is a fact that European Jews want to pressure the government of Great Britain to rule the Palestine supreme. The recent Jewish terrorist attack on the King David hotel in Jerusalem, in which many Jews allegedly perished, is a telling instance of that pressure. Second, in order to obtain permission to leave for Palestine, Jews in some European countries attempt to prove that they are persecuted. Poland is among the ranks of those countries and Jews, particularly those from Russia, dislike Poland because it refuses to accept the imposed communist system. For all these reasons, it is not impossible that a Jew may have induced Henryk Błaszczyk to tell a story such as his account of being kidnapped ... in anticipation that the mob, already angry with Jews, would engage in violent excesses, which could later be turned to many different ends.

Replying to the charges against the Catholic Church, the report's author said:

> The teachings of the Church, which preaches that all men are brothers and that one must not kill or harm anybody, [are] perfectly clear. The Church condemns extreme nationalism and the class struggle. The conduct of priests has never strayed from that. The best proof of that is provided by the government press, which, despite the closest scrutiny, has not been able to find even a single anti-Semitic address by a bishop or to name one Catholic priest who would encourage people to attack and beat up Jews. The government press attacks Cardinal Hlond with one voice for the interview he gave foreign journalists on the Kielce events, but it has never printed the whole interview, choosing instead to quote certain sentences out of context or simply to misquote them. The primate of Poland presented a brief but

accurate sketch of the Kielce events. He clearly stated that Jews are disliked in Poland because they occupy the highest government positions and are attempting to impose communism. Against this background, the Kielce events become more comprehensible, although Cardinal Hlond perceives them as lamentable and the Church as a whole, in his opinion, condemns them as murder. One should grieve for Jews who die in Poland's political violence, but one should also grieve for Poles, who also die in this manner, and who do so in much greater numbers. Cardinal Hlond's statement is so true that the Polish government press has never dared to publish it in its entirety. We can see that it must have infuriated the press—this is evidenced by the vicious press attacks on the Polish primate, who is revered by 90 percent of Poles....

The official press demands a joint address by the Episcopate of Poland denouncing anti-Semitism. This is a paradoxical demand and an affront to the dignity of the Church. In addition, it cannot be done, and not only for fundamental reasons. The great majority of Jews in Poland enthusiastically participate in spreading communism, work in the infamous security services, make arrests, torture and kill prisoners—so they face the hostility of a society that does not want communism and is weary of Gestapo methods. And now the Church, in accordance with the wishes of the official press, is to ceremonially declare that society's aversion is unjustified, that the conduct of Jews is blameless, and that it is the Poles who are guilty for resenting them.

That is the true meaning of the demands made in the government press. It is passed over that the Church every day promulgates brotherly love, which forbids anti-Semitism, that it readily and honestly extends its hand to Jews of goodwill, and that it sternly prohibits attacks on Jews (the Kielce murders, after all, were cited in the Kielce Curia's July 11 address as an outrageous crime, worthy of "complete and unconditional condemnation"). Nevertheless it is demanded that the Church publicly and officially state that Poles and Catholics bear Jews no ill will. It seems to be demanded that the Church accept the system of terror currently reigning in Poland.

In the report's conclusion, we read:

The analysis of the events and of witnesses' accounts leads us to the following conclusions: communist activism by Jews elicited the hatred of the general public in Poland. The actual disappearances of children in Kielce, attributed to Jews, did not trigger that hatred but greatly intensified it. A certain communist–Jewish element, in conjunction with the security service they controlled, used the situation to incite a pogrom, which would later be cited as proof that Jews needed to emigrate to a country of their own, as proof that Polish society is permeated with anti-Semitism and fascism, and, finally, as proof of how reactionary the Church is, since it incited the murderers.

V

I think these extensive quotations from the memorandum were indispensable if we are to understand the thought process, the axiology, and the spiritual condition of Bishop Czesław Kaczmarek and possibly of a large segment of the clergy. Bishop Kaczmarek was undoubtedly right when he accused the Communists of lying and dishonesty—they wanted to make the Kielce tragedy into a weapon in their fight against the anti-Communist opposition. So the memorandum's argument about the manipulative character of the perpetrators' trial is surely correct: "Among the murderers at 7 Planty Street there were policemen, soldiers, workers, and a mob that had assembled at random. Arrests were made exclusively among the last category: to charge policemen and workers, who were members of the PPR, would have made it impossible to claim that only Catholics had killed. It would also have made it impossible to attack the Catholic Church, General Anders's soldiers, and the PSL."

These indisputable statements, however, do not explain how a Polish bishop in 1946 could prepare a report so full of anti-Semitic stereotypes. And the completely clear and unambiguous conclusion does nothing to dispel the tone of anti-Semitism: "Any kind of anti-Semitism is unethical and degrading to a human being." After all, this statement was addressed to the American ambassador and not to Polish public opinion.

For the sake of thoroughness, here is the account of Jechiel Alpert, once a resident of Kielce, who witnessed the pogrom and was deposed in Israel in August 1967. In the period 1945–1946, Alpert was an active member of the Jewish Committee in Kielce. In December 1945, when unknown perpetrators threw several grenades into a Jewish Center, Alpert and the president of the religious congregation paid a visit to Bishop Kaczmarek. "We spent about an hour with him," recalled Alpert. "I said I had come to ask him to exert some influence over his clergy, who in turn would convey it to the general public, to make them understand that the handful of remaining Jews should not be further persecuted. He smiled and said: 'Strange you should come to me with that. Surely, you read the papers and know that we have no influence whatsoever. How can I affect those souls, when I myself have no say at all.'

"And he said that with such irony. Then he continued: 'You know, Jews are such talented merchants, gifted doctors and lawyers. Poland is devastated; it needs a lot of help. Why don't Jews do what they are good at instead of dealing in politics? Can you imagine what it looks like when a priest comes to some government ministry and a Jewess sits there, from only God knows where, and treats our clergy with such superiority and insolence? What kind of impression does that make?'"

Alpert was asked: "Did the bishop promise to help?"

He replied: "Just a diplomatic 'I'll see what I can do.' But one could see nothing would come of it."

Thus was the conversation between Bishop Kaczmarek and Jechiel Alpert, a Jew who miraculously survived the Holocaust, on the eve of the Kielce pogrom.

VI

There is no sense in trying to correct all the contradictions, inconsistencies, falsehoods, or even obvious absurdities in Bishop Kaczmarek's report. At the foundation of this peculiar text, which is filled with understandable and justifiable protests against the Communist terror, lie two intertwined anti-Semitic stereotypes: the stereotype of "Jewish Communists" and the conviction that there exists a world-wide Jewish conspiracy. Only thus could one link the activities of Zionists trying to establish a Jewish state with the actions of the Stalinist security apparatus in

Poland. I do not think that it is necessary to convince anyone today that such reasoning is as absurd as it is anti-Semitic. Yet it was not easy for me to make that statement, because I vividly remember the later fate of Bishop Kaczmarek: his imprisonment by the Communists; the Stalinist trial; the disgraceful, draconian sentence. The bishop openly opposed the Communist system and became one of its victims. So common decency requires one to be reserved in expressing one's criticism; such is the imperative of memory and respect to those who were brave enough to oppose the totalitarian dictatorship and who paid a high price for doing so.

Finally, one needs to appreciate the extremely difficult situation of the Church for which it was enormously hard to speak in the same voice as the propagandists of the Communist regime. That regime violated human rights and civil liberties on a daily basis and aimed to establish a Soviet-style totalitarian dictatorship in which Catholic bishops had a place only in prisons or labor camps. One must never forget this.

However, it is difficult not to recall the dramatic, despairing speech that Rabbi Kahane gave at the funeral of the victims of the Kielce pogrom: "The number of tragic graves is increased today by one—that is, by the grave of those murdered in a revived Poland: the Jews of Kielce. These were people who had miraculously escaped dying at the Nazis' hands.... It is not our intent to analyze now who organized that shameless pogrom. But there is one thing I wish to say in this solemn moment, before the victims of the Kielce pogrom. There exists in Poland one category of people, one entity that could have prevented it.... That is the clergy, the officials of the Catholic Church in Poland.... The priests of the Polish people!... Upon leaving here, can you say with a clear conscience: 'Our hands have not shed this blood; our eyes have not seen it.' Does 'Thou shalt not kill' not apply in the case of Jews?"

The words of Cardinal August Hlond, the primate of Poland, for whom a Poland ruled by Communists was not an independent Poland, provided an answer of sorts. In his statement to the foreign press, the primate said: "The Catholic Church has always ... condemned all murder, whether committed ... against Poles or Jews, in Kielce or anywhere else in the Polish Republic." In addition, he said: "At the time of the exterminatory German occupation, Poles, although themselves persecuted, protected, hid, and saved Jews, risking their own lives. Many a Jew in Poland owes his life to Poles and Polish priests. These good relations have deteriorated, and it is the Jews who to a large degree are responsible. They occupy leading positions in the life of the state and are attempting to impose a political system unwelcome to most of our nation. This is a harmful game, for it breeds dangerous tensions. Regrettably, many Jews die in fatally violent political clashes, but so do even more Poles."

Cardinal Hlond's declaration overflows with awkward, misleading, and unjust turns of phrase. How can the cardinal's vague and euphemistic "these good relations deteriorated" be squared with Bishop Kaczmarek's categorical statement that "Jews are disliked or even hated throughout Poland"? How can one blame the entire Jewish community for the deeds of Communists bearing Jewish names? How can one compare Polish–Jewish relations to "fatally violent political clashes"? And, finally, how can we comprehend the cardinal's total silence, his failure to make any declaration, concerning the absurd accusations of "ritual murders"? All of that is only a painful surprise.

However, the words of Cardinal Hlond—once again, they are unjust and misleading—provoke another question that needs to be asked: Shouldn't Rabbi Kahane, who was fully aware of the Polish reality in 1946, have publicly appealed to the Jewish community to avoid collaboration with the forcibly imposed Communist regime, and, in particular, with the security apparatus, which for Poles was simply the apparatus of oppression? Shouldn't the rabbi have condemned the violations of human rights, the persecution of Home Army supporters, the harsh censorship, and the falsified results of the national referendum? Didn't the commandment "Thou shalt not kill" apply to the Polish patriots who were murdered by the security apparatus? And finally, shouldn't Rabbi Kahane have supported the proposal by the PSL to send a parliamentary commission to Kielce to investigate all of the circumstances of the pogrom?

Public opinion in Poland—largely contaminated by anti-Semitic stereotypes—never heard such a declaration from Rabbi Kahane or any major Jewish organizations. That silence was also significant. Wasn't the defensive and self-exculpatory attitude of Bishop Kaczmarek quite natural and understandable then? Many people thought so then and think so to this very day.

VII

However, that document, when read today, is simply shocking. It illustrates the profoundly anti-Semitic stereotypes ingrained in certain segments of the clergy. It points out how completely insensitive and indifferent those people were to the fate of the handful of Jews who had survived Hitler's hell, and how utterly they failed to comprehend that the pogrom—even had it been provoked—sealed the Holocaust and tore away Polish values by their roots. And, finally, how blameless must the shepherd have thought himself, since he did not feel at all responsible for his flock's uncritical belief in the absurd rumors of "ritual murders."

Concluding his introduction to the text of the "Memorandum," John Micgiel writes that we do not know how the U.S. government reacted to the document. If indeed there was no reaction, then we should be pleased that this document drowned in the great sea of Washington archives. Otherwise it would have inevitably have become irrefutable evidence of and a basic supporting argument for the thesis that Polish society and the Polish clergy were anti-Semitic. For many, it would have been a satisfying proof.

VIII

However, during that dreadful time, July 1946, the Polish Catholic Church and the Polish clergy also showed a different face. Here it is:

To the whole citizenry of the city of Częstochowa and of
Kielce Province,

Kielce was the scene of a mass murder of Polish nationals of Jewish
extraction. More than forty Jews were murdered, as well as two Poles.
They had lived through the hell of the German occupation, witnessed the
slaying and suffering of their loved ones, and themselves avoided death at
the hands of the occupiers, not without the assistance of the Christian
Polish population. Those morally and actually guilty of this murder have
trampled on human dignity; they have committed a terrible violation of
the Christian commandment to love one's neighbor and the universal
principle that "thou shalt not kill."

Nothing, nothing whatsoever can possibly justify the Kielce crime,
which deserves wrath both human and divine, and whose background and
causes can be found in criminal fanaticism and inexcusable ignorance. The
fanaticism of certain persons, who, for the purposes of perpetrating a crime,
invoked notions from the distant Middle Ages and beliefs foreign to a
Christian society and its principles of co-existence of all citizens regardless
of nationality or religion, they preyed on the ignorance of others to commit
murder. Both those who were fanatic and those ignorant ought to be
unconditionally and without exception condemned as criminals by any
understanding of divine and human law. Leaving the first category to the
justice of the courts, we deplore the others for having allowed themselves to
be provoked into participating in a crime that has produced turmoil within
our country and besmirched the good name of the Pole abroad.

The Kielce crime has been unequivocally condemned by all whose
hearts beat as one with love for their neighbor, with attachment to the
inviolable beliefs and customs of our fathers and grandfathers, and with
honest, pure human feeling. Therefore, as representatives of Częstochowa
society, trusting in that society, with steadfast faith in its humane
consciousness and its adherence to Christian and moral principles, we
hereby state and make an appeal as follows:

All assertions of the reality of ritual murders are lies. No member of Christian society in Kielce, or anywhere else in Poland, has been harmed by Jews
for ritual or religious purposes. We do not know of a single case in which a
Christian child has been abducted by Jews. All news and rumors to that
effect are either deliberately concocted by criminals, or come from confused people who do not know any better and aim at provoking a crime.

Criminals and confused people ought to receive a fair trial or merciful piety, but they ought not to be heeded and followed by society at large. Therefore, we appeal to all inhabitants of the city of Częstochowa and Kielce Province, without exception, and to people of goodwill in particular, not to listen to criminal tales and rumors, to verify such stories and rumors at the source, to correct them in their immediate environment, and to oppose by all available means the possibility of further injustices beginning against the Jewish population.

We trust that responsible citizens of the city of Częstochowa and Kielce Province, bound by the principles of Christian morality, will not be led by incitements to murder and will never debase themselves by raising a hand against a fellow citizen only because he is of a different religion or nationality.

Bishop Teodor Kubina
(Signed also by the Częstochowa
city and county officials
Dr. T. J. Wolański, J. Kaźmierczak,
and K. Zajda, and the president
of the county council, S. Rękas.)

IX

The appeal of Bishop Teodor Kubina is one of the most wonderful instances of spiritual witness in the history of the Catholic Church in Poland. The uncompromising tone of the Nazarene is clearly audible, and the radicalism of the evangelical principle "Let your 'Yes' be 'Yes,' and your 'No,' 'No.'" Faced with the terror and shame of the pogrom, Bishop Kubina said yes to the truth and love of one's neighbor; he said no to crime, lies, and hatred. He said it upon hearing that forty people met their Holocaust a year after the final defeat of Hitler. Those who had managed to elude Treblinka and Auschwitz were slain by a Polish mob. So those simple but clear and noble words had to be said publicly, even if they caused a scandal. Perhaps, one may suppose, for Bishop Kubina that kind of scandal was the essence of the evangelical message. Wasn't the Sermon on the Mount itself a scandal? One may also suppose, therefore, that the appeal of Bishop Kubina, evidence of the spiritual greatness of the Catholic Church in Poland, would always remain with us and be remembered as an example.

However, the episcopate, at its plenary conference, "required the bishops to refrain from taking an individual stand on any and every event in the country, in order to avoid creating a situation like that after the Kielce events . . . when the ordinary of one diocese . . . participates in the issuance of an appeal the content and intention of which other bishops find impossible to accept because of the fundamental theoretical and canonical assumptions of the Catholic Church."

The majority of bishops—one may suppose—found Bishop Kubina's stand "impossible to accept." According to a historian, other bishops understood Bishop Kubina's appeal as "indirect approval of the authorities' attitude toward the pogrom." In my opinion this reading was completely unjustified. Communist propaganda, in the language of a savage witch hunt, blamed the pogrom on the anti-Communist underground and the PSL, while in Bishop Kubina's appeal there were no such lies. It was full of grief for the murdered and it warned against lies and fanatical hatred. Nevertheless, the way of thinking apparent in the declaration of Cardinal Hlond and Bishop Kaczmarek won. And it held sway for a long time. The Kielce pogrom did not become a matter for moral reflection; instead, it was buried in collective oblivion for thirty-five years, as if wiped away by a national amnesia.

X

However, after thirty-five years, the subject of the Kielce pogrom has returned. It has returned owing to the activists of Kielce Solidarity, who in July 1981 paid homage to the victims. It has returned because of the well-known article by Krystyna Kersten in *Tygodnik Solidarność* (Solidarity Weekly) in December 1981. And after that it returned regularly; there appeared films and books, all the way up to 1996, and the memorable observances of the fiftieth anniversary. Prime Minister Włodzimierz Cimoszewicz participated in these. Poland's national memory has spat out its gag, and normal conversation among Poles about the past has become possible again.

I think that consideration of the two faces of the Catholic Church is an important component of such a conversation. Both faces were revealed in 1946, right after the Kielce pogrom. Let us call them the face of Bishop Kaczmarek and the face of Bishop Kubina.

In his attitude toward anti-Semitism, Bishop Kubina did not exactly stand out from the majority of bishops of prewar Poland. Ronald Modras, a professor of theology at the Catholic University of St. Louis, has written: "The [Polish] bishops obviously could not conceive of Poles and Jews working together to resolve Poland's social and economic difficulties. A 1936 pastoral letter of Bishop Teodor Kubina explained why: the world was divided into the rival camps of Christ and Antichrist. Christians must embrace the battle cry 'Rule over us, O Christ!' They must counteract the materialistic capitalists and communists who had embraced the 'Jewish' battle cry: 'We do not want Christ to rule over us.'"[1] This does not strike one as a particularly refined theology.

Obviously Bishops Kaczmarek and Kubina were not separated by their attitude toward the dogmas of their faith. Neither did they differ in their attitudes toward Communism. When assessing the postwar situation, Bishop Kubina said in January 1946: "The fight to determine the new face of the earth, this new world, has already begun. Two compact camps participate in this fight: the materialist camp, which wants to build a new world without God, and the Christian camp, which wants to base the new world on God. The Combat between them must necessarily occur, for each is a negation of the other in its fundamental assumptions and in its views of the world and life." Such was the shared opinion of all the bishops.

So, while not differing in their fundamental assessment of Communism or "Jewish" materialism, the two bishops differed in their reactions to the Kielce pogrom. Why was that? We can only resort to hypotheses.

---

1. Ronald Modras, *The Catholic Church and Anti-Semitism: Poland, 1933–1939* (op. cit.), p. 352.

By comparing the bishops' language, we can easily identify the differences. The report of Bishop Kaczmarek speaks with the voice of a politician of the Church—he wants to defend and exculpate his Polish flock in the face of brutal accusations by the Communists and unjust charges in the foreign press. Bishop Kubina, on the other hand, speaks in the voice of a shepherd warning his flock against the evil that exists in themselves, against the sin of vehement hatred, which leads, as in Kielce, to mayhem and murder.

In the history of the Church two traditions have always existed: the teacher's office—the pastoral tradition; and the evangelical office—the prophetic tradition. The voice of Bishop Kaczmarek was the voice of a pastor deeply concerned for the institution of the Church, for its standing, and in defense of the teacher's office, as well as for the chances of that institution's continuing to function in the world where hostility and hatred were spreading like the plague. Bishop Kubina, on the other hand, spoke with the voice of the messianic tradition; he spoke with the voice of a prophet who does not care about his own safety but is appalled by the misfortune of others, and who wants to ease the pain of the victims and stay the hand of the potential torturers.

What was the reality of the Kielce pogrom and of the Communist terror for Bishop Kaczmarek? He perceived them from the perspective of the teaching office of the Church, the office that was molding the tradition of an institution that ruled its people's hearts and minds "forever." By virtue of this institution, during an interregnum, the primate functioned as interrex. Is it any surprise, then, that the period of dictatorial Communist authority was for the people of the Church just an interregnum? The Church as an institution has been shaped by the articles of faith and the history of the apostolic mission understood as the Christianization of pagans and the fight against the heresies of the Reformation, against the libertarian spirit of the Enlightenment, against the liberalism of the positivists, against socialist anti-clericalism, and against the specter of the atheistic and sanguinary Bolshevik revolution. Another element in the history of the Church in Poland was the tradition

of the Catholic Pole who survived because of his religion and who pre-
served his national identity while he was in constant conflict with Prot-
estant Germanization and Orthodox Russification. Catholic Poles, raised
on the writing of Roman Dmowski and his followers, were steeped in
anti-Semitic resentments and believed that Jews were the primary
threat. The most exalted shepherds of the Church hardly ever explained
to their flock that this was not so.

What is more, in 1946, the most exalted shepherd believed that the
whole Polish nation hated Jews because the latter were identified with
the Communist authorities. One may suppose that he himself shared
that sentiment. In addition, he felt himself to be entirely in the right—
for he was defending the Church, that is, defending supreme values
against the absolute anti-value, the unmitigated evil of godless Communism. This exalted shepherd formulated his opinions in full awareness that the Polish nation and the Catholic Church were on the precipice of Bolshevism, having been driven there by Soviet rifle butts. So
the Kielce pogrom was, in the eyes of the exalted shepherd, a provocation organized by the enemies as a step in the process of making Poland
a Bolshevist state, one more act that would enslave the nation and annihilate the Church. It was as if he saw the face of a Jewish functionary
of the Office of Public Security, a man who humiliates Polish patriots, a
man who debases, tortures, and murders them.

XI

Bishop Teodor Kubina saw the faces of the Jews murdered in the pogrom. Was he occupied in painful reverie by the meaning of the Church's
existence—the Church as the betrothed of Christ, the guide leading
humanity to salvation, the Church with the power and the ability to
define sin and virtue? Did he remind himself that the Church, that
giver of intangible goods in a material world, did not exist of its own
volition? That its purpose was not to propagate the hope of its own
eternal existence but rather the hope for the coming of the Kingdom of

God? Did he think of Jesus who stood up for the rejected and oppressed, for the hopeless, and for those in hell on this earth? The very same Jesus who said: "Whatever you did for one of the least of these brothers of mine, you did for me"?

When looking into the faces of the murdered Jewish women, men, and children, did he see some reflection of the One who "suffered under Pontius Pilate"? Did he see traces of that suffering, of those tears, of the torture of Crucifixion? Or, perhaps, full of pity for those slain people, did he remind himself that Jesus was a Jew? Or that those referred to in the commandment to love one's neighbor are not only close friends but also strangers, the helpless and the friendless? Or that the murder of Jews in Kielce—not far removed in time from Auschwitz—even if it had been provoked—was really the mob's vote of no confidence in the Poland of Christian tradition and Christian tolerance?

Whatever his reasons, Bishop Teodor Kubina offered uncompromising Christian witness.

XII

Bishop Kubina chose not to mince his words; he spoke bluntly of "murdered Jews" who "had lived through the hell of the German occupation" and who had "witnessed the slaying and suffering of their nearest and dearest." Bishop Kaczmarek put it differently: he simply reminded people that "all men are brothers and one must not kill or harm anybody." Similarly, Archbishop Hlond said that "the Catholic Church has always condemned all murder, wherever committed."

The proclamation of the Kielce Curia, "To all Reverend Parish Priests of the Kielce Diocese," read in churches with no further comment, speaks in a general way of "incidents" that "snuffed out the lives of many people." Later in the text we read that "the act of deliberate murder is an outrageous crime, and as such it is worthy of total and unconditional condemnation. The act is even more reprehensible because youths and adolescents witnessed it." In conclusion, the Curia "appeals to the Catholic people of the Kielce Diocese to remain calm and composed, and to appreciate the seriousness of the matter—this is in its own interest, as well as the interest of the nation. No Catholic should allow himself to be deluded by anyone who incites similar actions." Nowhere does the proclamation mention that there had been an anti-Jewish pogrom spurred by the rumor that a Christian child had been kidnapped for the purpose of ritual murder. It was just that some people had killed some other people, for no apparent reason.

I cannot help but wonder: Wasn't the situation of the Jews in 1946, right after the Holocaust, somewhat unique? Hadn't they been singled out and sentenced to death by the anti-Semitic regime of the Third Reich? Didn't they see in the faces of the brutal mob the familiar features of those who had sentenced them to death by betraying them to the Gestapo? So wasn't the trivialization of this murder—the murder of Jews who had escaped from the clutches of the Nazis and from those who denounced Jews to Nazis—perceived as another slap in the face, another insult?

During Hitler's Holocaust and in later pogroms, weren't Jews murdered on a completely different basis than in any other nation? Didn't they suffer all that they suffered simply because they were Jews? Wasn't silence about the events of the Holocaust, and the obliteration of the differences among people's fates, an attempt to strip Jews of their claim to their own incomparable tragedy?

But at the same time, while Jews were denied their claim of particular suffering in the Holocaust, a special responsibility and sense of guilt were imposed on them for Communism and its crimes. Isn't that a dreadful absurdity and a terrible injustice?

And, finally, isn't it absurd that this harm should be done to survivors of the Holocaust, and then pushed away to the very bottom of the collective subconscious—with disastrous consequences for the thinking and the conscience of all those who are willing, even today, to repeat the formulas of Cardinal August Hlond and Bishop Czesław Kaczmarek? Isn't it high time to reach for the witness of Bishop Teodor Kubina?

XIII

Certainly that time has not yet arrived for everyone. Just a few years ago, the editor of a conservative Catholic paper, while lamenting that no detailed research has been conducted on the participation of Jews in the Communist Party apparatus, made a point worth quoting:

> Public opinion was constantly surprised by the news of murderous squadrons of the AK [Home Army] and the NSZ [National Armed Forces] liquidating defenseless Jews. Interestingly, those victims of the armed underground, before they were executed, were not Jews—they were officers of the NKVD and torturers working for the UB [Office of Public Security]. When they were alive, they were communists, because—as journalists from the opposing camp write (while insisting on the irrelevance of the nationality of many officers of the UB and the PPR [Polish Workers' Party] activists), "A Jew who became a communist stopped being a Jew. However, when he was shot, precisely in his capacity as a communist torturer, the leftist press automatically saw him as the victim of an execution with ethnic overtones."

How should one reply? By saying that there were no security officers among the victims of the Kielce pogrom? By reminding one's interlocutor that armed security agents did not fall victim to pogroms? The editor I quote cannot have read Bishop Kaczmarek's report, but his method of trivializing the tragedy of the Holocaust survivors is a good illustration of that harm pushed away into the collective subconscious of contemporary homegrown anti-Semites. Over and over, hypocritically, in bad faith, they repeat: "These were not anti-Semites—they were only anti-communists fighting against Jewish communists."

In a recently published article, a historian who is also a columnist for another conservative paper characterized the arguments regarding the Jedwabne massacre as a debate "which is to transform the remnants of our historical consciousness into a community of shame." This very same journalist, commenting on Aleksander Smolar's well-known essay of twenty years ago about Polish–Jewish relations, "Taboo and Innocence," wrote: "Smolar bemoaned the fact that after the war the right in Poland experienced no crisis of its world-view." But, said the journalist, the Polish Right, "in view of its consistent resistance to both the invaders of September 1939," had never lost its "moral legitimacy."

I had to read this sentence at least three times, wondering whether I understood its meaning. What on earth? Shouldn't the experience of the Holocaust lead one to conclude that anti-Semitism has criminal consequences? Shouldn't it induce one to reflect on the rich and manifold homegrown contributions of rightist groups to the dissemination of anti-Semitic ideology? Shouldn't the people who with a club and a razor introduced the "ghetto bench" to Polish universities examine their own life and intellectual affiliations? Shouldn't the authors of anti-Semitic books, articles, and leaflets—keeping in mind the images of the burning ghetto—think carefully about what they contributed to, even unconsciously, when they incited contempt and hatred of Jews?

Is the "community of pride" to be based on such hypocrisy, as advocated by the heralds of the "new historical politics"? Weren't four decades of Communist lies about history enough? Should we return to mendacious boasting? Is that the way to overcome what one politician of the current ruling party called the "crisis of Polonism"? "The Muse of history is gentle, learned, and unassuming," wrote Leszek Kołakowski, "but when neglected and deserted, she takes her revenge: she blinds those who scorn her."

XIV

Rabbi Kahane, speaking at the funeral of the victims of the Kielce pogrom, appealed to the Polish bishops: "We turn to you in the face of this new tragedy so that your weighty, dignified words might soften hearts of stone." But the hearts of Polish bishops were not made of stone. They were full of pain, suffering, and sympathy for the hunted soldiers of the Home Army, for the activists of the Polish Peasant Party, for those deported to the interior of the Soviet Union, for the victims of the Katyń massacre and the Gulag, and for the sixteen leaders of the underground who, taken in by the "word of honor of a Soviet officer," were then removed to Moscow and sentenced to death following a disgraceful sham trial. Their hearts were full of sympathy for those lied to and forced to lie, those humiliated and blackmailed, and those imprisoned, tortured, and murdered. One may rest assured of it—the hearts of the bishops cared tenderly for that suffering. The bishops must have reflected many a time on "the hearts of stone" of those who silently tolerated the violation of Poland, and sometimes even justified it or supported it with false accusations. Rabbi Kahane—let's reiterate the point—did not appeal to Jewish society to condemn that violation and never condemned it himself.

I think there exists a phenomenon that I would call the "egotism of suffering." Pain is always egotistic, for we experience our own suffering and that of our family or our friends egotistically. Collective suffering is also egotistic, in terms of the pain inflicted on all those with whom we join in the community of historical fate, remembrance, inherited values, and in the community of meaning and of faith in our immortal fatherland. We feel this pain together with the others who are part of our own spiritual fatherland. And when that fatherland of ours is subjugated, when its memory is uprooted and its values trampled, when our nation is being murdered, then—filled with our own pain—we do not consider the misfortune of others but, rather, expect them to suffer with us.

Usually they do not suffer with us—it does not work that way. After all, they have their own "egotism of suffering," their own trampled-on community, and their own grievance against the world for not suffering with them. We then become bitter, and our bitterness breeds dislike for them, while they are overcome by similar bitterness and aversion. There is the hostility a Jew feels for a Pole, because the latter did not experience the Holocaust as a Jew did. And there is the hostility a Pole feels for a Jew because the latter does not share his pain at Poland's violation by the Communists. Locked in the fortresses of our own memories and suffering, we do not even notice how aversion and pain mutate into hatred and vengefulness.

A prominent Hungarian writer, an insightful chronicler of those years and an observer of people paralyzed by war and fearful of the specter of Bolshevism, noted: "With its scorching and putrid breath, hatred burst out of people and against people, as if someone careless had inadvertently lifted the lid of a hellish burning cauldron. Hatred? But why? Because the other has survived. Because he has not suffered as I have. Because the one who suffered has not instantaneously received moral compensation. Hatred, because nothing is sufficient and all punishment and satisfaction fall short. Because there exists no condemnation commensurate with the world's cruelty."

Immersed in the "egotism of suffering," loyal to our own community, we do not want to suffer another's pain, nor can we. Bishop Kaczmarek's report illustrates that inability to feel another's suffering. And his report makes clear why the episcopate shared his point of view and not Bishop Kubina's. Yes, Bishop Kaczmarek's point of view was based on falsehood, but it was a falsehood widely believed by those around him during a time of chaos and terror. Yes, it was unjust, but its roots could be found in the patriotic and courageous opposition to Poland's Sovietization, and that was then the highest priority for the opponents of Communism. Krystyna Kersten rightly observed that the Church faced a "choice worthy of the devil": either to participate in the Communist propaganda campaign after the Kielce pogrom, or to become a target of attack as "co-conspirators—even if only morally—in the crime." How can we possibly be surprised by the bishops' mistrustfulness and caution?

XV

However, one conviction expressed in Bishop Kaczmarek's report remains a shock: the belief that, since "the great majority of Jews in Poland participate enthusiastically in spreading communism, work in the infamous Security Agencies, make arrests, and torture and kill prisoners," then "for fundamental reasons" the Church cannot condemn anti-

Semitism. For the "dislike of Jews is justified," and "Poles and Catholics bear a justified grudge against them." A clearer illustration of anti-Semitic thinking in postwar Poland would be hard to find. It is sufficient, then, to equate Jews with "secret police torturers" in order to cleanse one's conscience of the sin of anti-Semitism. This defensive strategy allows one to transfer the weight of sin onto the Jews by making them the real instigators of the Kielce pogrom. Despite its noble intentions, the shepherd's defense of the flock is transformed into a discourse of hatred for the victims and a complete exoneration of the guilty. Yet, as Leszek Kołakowski says, our experience of evil is, above all, the experience of feeling the evil in ourselves, and to experience our own evil is to experience guilt. Without the ability to experience guilt, we cannot be fully human. Without it, the experience of evil deserts us and, a fortiori, so does the very difference between good and evil. The indisputable evil—especially right after the Holocaust—was to make the hatred of Jews ordinary and to excuse anti-Semitism as a form of anti-Communism. That evil went undetected in the summer of 1946 by the shepherd of the Kielce flock.

Years went by and the time of the pontificate of John Paul II arrived. It was this pope who, in a series of magnificent, magnanimous gestures, cleared the path to a new way of thinking about anti-Semitism. The spirit of that pontificate permeated the pastoral letter issued by Poland's bishops on the twenty-fifth anniversary of the declaration "Nostra aetate." In this letter, read in January 1991, the bishops wrote: "We particularly lament those Catholics who in any way have contributed to the death of Jews.... Even if only a single Christian could have helped but either did not extend a helping hand to a Jew in danger, or contributed to his death—we are compelled to beg our Jewish sisters and brothers for forgiveness.... We sincerely regret all incidents of anti-Semitism at whatever time and by whomever perpetrated on Polish soil."

Having quoted these beautiful and noble words, let us repeat: Bishop Teodor Kubina was the first.

XVI

The remarks just quoted do not, obviously, foreclose the questions about the ambiguous relations between the Jewish community and Soviet Communism. The traditional Jewish community was naturally anti-Bolshevist, for it could not accept a system that repressed and destroyed Jewish religious life and erased all forms of market economy and private ownership. On the other hand, however, the Jewish community perceived the Stalinist Soviet Union as a country that fought against the Nazi Reich and every day of that fight improved the odds of survival for remaining Jews murdered according to the "final solution." Is Jewish ambivalence really so surprising?

Another problem was the "evil of Communism" perpetrated by the Communists of Jewish extraction, with Jewish names. Such people in 1946 were not rare. To describe and condemn their abhorrent crimes is a normal part of squaring accounts with the heritage of the totalitarian dictatorship. It is worth remembering that such examinations were often made by critics of Communism who bore Jewish names and who made themselves vulnerable to virulent anti-Semitic propaganda from the Communist side. Anti-Semitism could appear in the guise of Communism or anti-Communism, but it invariably had the same characteristic feature—it evoked the stereotype of a hostile, demonic, and despicable Jew, who was to be blamed for all the evils of this world.

When thinking about those years, those people, and their intellectual failures, it is necessary, I think, to make the effort to understand their experience, to empathize with them, and to look at the world through the eyes of the Different One, the Other—to see the Polish drama of enslavement through Jewish eyes, and to see the Jewish drama of the Holocaust through Polish eyes. Then, it was impossible; today, it is essential.

In view of the aforementioned, the more we reverence the stand taken by Bishop Kubina, the more remarkable it becomes in its purity. The words of his message offer mercy to the weak and encourage the persecuted—the two most fundamental human values. At the grave of the pogrom's victims, Bishop Kubina expressed a few basic truths, though it was extremely difficult to state them then: One must not torment and kill people just because they are Jews; "Jewish ritual murder" is a despicable fabrication by anti-Semites; and anti-Semitism leads to crime. Bishop Kubina knew, or perhaps he just sensed with the wisdom of his heart, that one cannot react to a pogrom by searching for excuses for those who became beasts.

In Bishop Kaczmarek's report we read that those participating in the pogrom were "peaceful people," "Catholics," "representatives of the petty bourgeoisie, people who didn't have much money but who weren't paupers." Certainly that was so—these people were not pathological killers. Nevertheless, if those "peaceful Catholics" hated Jews so much that they killed them because of their belief in ritual murder and because of their own resistance to Communism, then every man of public influence, every teacher or writer, politician or priest, was obligated to ask his conscience: Have I done everything possible to prevent the crime hatched in the depraved minds of those "peaceful Catholics"? Have I warned them against such thinking often enough and explicitly enough? Am I really completely without guilt?

Even if in those years anti-Semitism produced pogroms as a form of anti-Communism and patriotism, which cannot be ruled out, then that patriotism was a degenerate form worthy only of comparison with the "patriotism" of those who believed that Hitler was solving the "Jewish problem" for Poles and that they themselves were doing Poland a favor by blackmailing and denouncing Jews in hiding on the Aryan side.

Bishop Kubina totally rejected this degenerate patriotism. In doing so, he became a voice of the Church warning against the "patriotism of anti-Semites." It was the voice of a priest taking a stand against evil when it cost a great deal to do so. After all, it had often happened before the injured felt themselves alone and deserted by God, and the Church stood in their defense, in memory of Jesus, eternally calling out from the cross.

At such a moment, Bishop Teodor Kubina did not want to repeat the actions of Pontius Pilate.

CHAPTER TEN

The Shock of Jedwabne

Did Poles collaborate with Germans to murder Jews? It is indeed difficult to find a stereotype more absurd and more false. There was no Polish family that would not have been injured by the Nazism of Germany and the Communism of the USSR. These two totalitarian dictatorships claimed the lives of three million Poles and three million citizens categorized by the Nazis as Polish Jews. Poland was the first country to categorically reject Hitler's demands and the first country to oppose Nazi aggression militarily. The Polish people never produced a Quisling and no military unit bearing the Polish standard ever fought on the side of the Third Reich. Poles, attacked by two totalitarian regimes as a result of the Molotov-Ribbentrop Pact, fought from the first to the last day on the side of the anti-Nazi coalition. Poland developed a broad resistance and a military underground and carried out extensive anti-Nazi sabotage. The prime minister of Great Britain honored the Poles for their participation in the Battle of Britain, and the president of the United States called Poles an inspiration to the world. None of this, however, prevented the former or the latter from entering into the Yalta pact with Stalin, a pact of which Poland was a victim. The country fell into Stalin's clutches. The heroes of the resistance were sent to Soviet gulags and Polish Communist prisons as enemies of Stalinist Communism.

All of these elements came together to form the Polish historical self-image: Poland was a guiltless and noble victim of hostile oppression and foreign conspiracy.

After the war, when in free countries there came a time of reflection on the experience of Nazism and the Holocaust, Poland was subjected to the Stalinist terror, which for many years effectively blocked any debate on the past, the Holocaust, and anti-Semitism. The anti-Semitic tradition was deeply rooted in Poland. In the nineteenth century, when the Polish state did not exist, the modern Polish nation took shape on the basis of ethnic and religious bonds and in opposition to neighboring countries to which the Polish dream of independence was indifferent or hostile. Anti-Semitism, just as in all of the countries of the region where Jews lived, was an ideological binding agent for a broad political camp called National Democracy. That anti-Semitic sentiment was fueled by the Russian authorities following the principle of *divide et impera*. Already in the interwar period, anti-Semitism was a permanent and natural component of the radical ideology of the nationalist Right. Strong anti-Semitic sentiments could also be found in the rhetoric of the dignitaries of the Catholic Church. Poland, tucked between Nazi Germany and Stalinist Russia, could not establish regular relations with its ethnic minorities, including the Jewish community. In comparison with her totalitarian neighbors, Poland remained, relatively speaking, a haven for Jews. Nevertheless, in the 1930s, Jews felt and indeed were discriminated against more and more by the anti-Semitic hit squads, by persecution of Jewish students, that is, the so-called bench ghetto at universities, and in an atmosphere in which there were calls for pogroms.

However, in the years of the Nazi occupation, the Polish nationalist and anti-Semitic Right, unlike its counterparts in the majority of other European countries, did not choose the path of collaboration with the Nazis but actively participated in the anti-Nazi underground. Polish anti-Semites fought Hitler, and some helped rescue Jews, although to do so was punishable by death. Here we have a specifically Polish paradox—in occupied Poland, one could be at the same time an anti-Semite, a hero of the anti-Nazi resistance, and a participant in the rescue of Jews.

A few years ago, Jan Błoński, one of the most eminent Polish intellectuals, published an essay on this very paradox in the *Tygodnik Powszechny*. He recalled a well-known appeal made by the Front for the "Revival of Poland," published in August 1942. The appeal's author was the famous Catholic writer Zofia Kossak-Szczucka. The appeal reads as follows:

> In the Warsaw Ghetto, behind a wall, isolated from the world, a few hundred thousand condemned await their death. There is no hope of rescue for them, and no help comes from anywhere.
>
> The total number of Jews killed has reached over a million now and it grows every day. All die: the rich and the poor, the old, women, men, youngsters, babies, Catholics perishing with the names of Jesus and Mary on their lips, and those of the Jewish faith. All of them are guilty simply because they were born into the Jewish nation sentenced by Hitler to extinction.
>
> The world has been watching this crime, the most horrifying in all human history—and the world remains silent. The slaughter of millions of defenseless people is happening in universal, sinister silence. The executioners keep silent; they do not boast of what they are doing. Neither England nor America raises any objection, and even influential international Jewry remains silent, though it was formerly so sensitive to every harm done to its own. Poles too remain silent. The Polish political friends of Jews limit themselves to protest notes, while the Polish opponents of Jews are indifferent to a matter alien to them. The Jews as they perish are surrounded only by Pilates, washing their hands.
>
> This silence can no longer be tolerated. Whatever the reasons for it, it is evil. Whoever keeps silent in the face of murder becomes an accomplice in the murder. He who does not condemn consents.
>
> Therefore, we Polish Catholics hereby take a stand. Our feelings toward Jews have not changed. We have not stopped considering them the political, economic, and ideological enemies of Poland. Moreover, we realize that they hate us even more than they do the Germans, and consider us responsible for their misfortune. Why and on what basis? That remains a mystery of the Jewish soul, but it is a fact repeatedly confirmed. However,

our awareness of those feelings does not excuse us from the duty to condemn those crimes.

We do not want to be Pilates. We have no means of actively preventing the German murders; there is nothing we can do to save anyone; but we protest from the bottom of our hearts, gripped by compassion, indignation, and horror. Our God, the God who does not permit killing, demands that protest of us.

We also protest as Poles. We do not believe that Poland can profit in any way from German atrocities. To the contrary. In the stubborn silence of international Jewry, and in the German propaganda that is already trying to blame the slaughter of the Jews on Lithuanians and...Poles, we sense plans for hostile action against us. We also realize how poisonous the seed of murder can be. The forced participation of the Polish nation in the bloody spectacle happening on Polish soil may easily produce indifference to harm and sadism, but above all, it may breed the dangerous conviction that one's neighbors may be murdered with impunity.[1]

This extraordinary appeal, full of nobility and courage, and clearly tainted with anti-Semitic stereotyping, illustrates well the paradox of the Polish attitude toward the dying Jews. In keeping with anti-Semitic tradition, it insists on perceiving Jews as the enemy; but, in keeping with the tradition of Polish heroism, it calls on people to help the Jews in their plight.

After the war, the very same Kossak-Szczucka described this paradox in a letter to a friend:

One day back then, on the Kierbedź Bridge, a German noticed a Pole giving alms to a hungry Jewish boy. He rushed at them and ordered the Pole to throw the child into the water or else he would shoot both the Jewish boy and the inopportune alms giver. "You can't help him," the German jeered. "I will kill the boy one way or the other. He doesn't have a right to be here. If you drown him, you can walk away; otherwise, I will kill you. I'm counting to three. Now, one...two..." The Pole gave in, broke down, and threw the boy over the railing to the river. The German patted him on the back.

---

1. Zofia Kossak-Szczucka, "Protest," *Wikipedia*.

Braver Kerl. They went their separate ways. Two days later, the Pole hanged himself.

The later life of Poles whose consciousness bore the scars of being helpless witnesses of a crime must have been accompanied by a special trauma that was revived in every debate on anti-Semitism, Polish–Jewish relations, and the Holocaust. After all, deep in their subconscious, people in Poland remember that they moved into the apartments left behind by the Jews who were herded into the ghettoes and later murdered by Germans.

Polish public opinion is diverse, but nearly every Pole reacts sharply to the occasional Jewish accusation that Poles "suckle anti-Semitism with their mother's milk," and particularly to accusations of Polish participation in the Holocaust. For anti-Semites, of whom there are not few on the margins of Polish political life, these attacks are powerful proof that there exists an international Jewish conspiracy against Poland. Ordinary people who came of age during a time when either the truth about the Holocaust was falsified or silence was kept perceive such accusations as a grave injustice. It is for the latter that the book *Neighbors,* by Jan Tomasz Gross, came as such a shock. It revealed the truth about the murder of sixteen hundred Jews in Jedwabne, committed by Polish hands.

It is very difficult to describe how great a shock *Neighbors* was. The heated reaction to Gross's book can be compared to Jewish reactions to the publication of Hannah Arendt's *Eichmann in Jerusalem.* Arendt described how some Jewish groups collaborated with the Nazis:

> The Jewish Councils of Elders were informed by Eichmann or his men of how many Jews were needed to fill each train, and they made out the list of deportees. The Jews registered, filled out innumerable forms, answered pages and pages of questionnaires regarding their property so that it could be seized all the more easily; they then assembled at the collection points and boarded the trains. The few who tried to hide or to escape were rounded up by a special Jewish police force.
> We know how the Jewish officials felt when they became instruments of murder—like captains "whose ships were about to sink and who succeeded

in bringing them safe to port by casting overboard a great part of their precious cargo," or like the saviors who "for the price of a hundred victims saved one thousand people, and for the price of a thousand, ten thousand."[2]

Jewish critics promptly asserted that, according to Hannah Arendt, the Jews themselves implemented the Shoah.

Some of the Polish reactions to Gross's book were equally emotional. The average Polish reader was unable to believe that anything like Jedwabne could have happened. I must admit that I could not believe it myself: I thought my friend Jan Tomasz Gross had become the victim of a hoax. Still, the murders in Jedwabne, preceded by a brutal pogrom, did happen, and that must burden the collective conscience of Poles just as it does my individual conscience. The Polish debate on Jedwabne has been going on now for a few months. It has been serious, thorough, sad, and also full of horror, as if the whole society had suddenly been asked to take up the burden of that horrific crime of sixty years ago. As if all Poles were being asked to admit their guilt and to beg collectively for forgiveness.

I do not believe in collective guilt or in collective responsibility, apart from moral responsibility. So I often reflect on what my individual responsibility is, and my own guilt. Certainly I cannot be held responsible for that mob of murderers who set fire to the barn in Jedwabne. Likewise, the residents of Jedwabne today cannot be blamed for those murders. When I hear calls to admit my own Polish guilt, I feel as wounded as the current residents of Jedwabne do when they are interrogated by journalists from around the world. But when I hear that Gross's book, which reveals the truth about the crime, is a lie concocted by the international Jewish conspiracy against Poland, then the feeling of guilt grows within me, for these untruthful contemporary excuses are, in reality, a rationalization of that crime.

I write this chapter cautiously, and, weighing my words carefully, I repeat Montesquieu's statement: "I am a man by nature; I am a Frenchman

2. Hannah Arendt, *Eichmann in Jerusalem* (New York: Viking Press, 1963), pp. 115–16.

by chance." It is also by chance that I am a Pole with Jewish roots. Nearly all of my family was devoured by the Holocaust, and my close relatives could have perished in Jedwabne. Some of them were Communists or relatives of Communists; some were craftsmen, merchants, or perhaps rabbis. But all of them were Jews, according to the Nuremburg Laws of the Third Reich. They all might have been herded into that barn set on fire by the hand of a Polish murderer. I do not feel guilt toward the murdered ones, but I do feel a sense of responsibility. Not for the fact that they were murdered—I could not have prevented it. But I do feel responsible for the fact that after their deaths they were murdered again—they did not get a decent burial, they were not mourned, and the truth of that atrocious crime was not revealed; instead, a lie was repeated for decades. Now, here I am clearly culpable. Out of lack of imagination or lack of time, out of opportunism and spiritual laziness, I never posed certain questions and never looked for their answers. Why was that? After all, I was among those active in revealing the truth about the Katyń massacre, and I demanded that the truth be revealed about the Stalinist trials and the victims of the Communist apparatus of repression. Why did I not search for the truth about the murdered Jews of Jedwabne? Perhaps, subconsciously, I feared the cruel truth about the Jewish fate during that time.

But the crazed mob of Jedwabne was not unique at the time. In all of the countries conquered by the Soviet Union after 1939, the summer and fall of 1941 marked horrific crimes against the Jews. Jews died at the hands of their Lithuanian, Latvian, Estonian, Ukrainian, Russian, and Belorussian neighbors. I think it is high time that the whole truth about those dreadful events be revealed. I will do my best to contribute to that work. As I write these words, I feel like a perfect schizophrenic: I am Polish, and my shame over the murder in Jedwabne is a Polish shame; but I also know that had I happened to be there at the time I would have been murdered as a Jew.

Who am I, then, writing these words? Well, by nature I am a man, and I am responsible to other people for what I have and have not done.

By choice, I am a Pole, and I am responsible to the world for the evil my compatriots have wrought. I do feel that way without any external compulsion; it is my choice, my will, and the deep urging of my own conscience. But as I write these words, I am also a Jew, who feels a deep sense of kinship with those who were murdered as Jews. From the latter perspective, I must state that anyone who tries to abstract the crime of Jedwabne from the context of the era, and who tries on the basis of that crime to make generalizations, to claim that only Poles (and all Poles) behaved that way, is guilty of a lie as abominable as the lie told for so many years about the crime in Jedwabne.

Clearly, it might have happened that a Polish neighbor snatched one of my relatives from the hands of the executioners who were shoving him into the barn. There were many Polish neighbors like that, and thick is the forest of Polish trees growing along the Avenue of the Righteous among the Nations of the World at Yad Vashem in Jerusalem. I also feel responsible to those people who gave their lives to save Jews, and I feel guilty toward them—for in both the Polish and the foreign papers I read so much about the murderers who killed Jews, and I register the deep silence about those who rescued them. Do murderers really deserve more notice than the Righteous? The primate of Poland, the Polish president, the Polish prime minister, and the rabbi of Warsaw have spoken almost with one voice to say that the homage paid to the victims of crime in Jedwabne should serve Polish–Jewish reconciliation in truth. There is nothing I want more. Should it happen otherwise, that will also be my fault. I will be responsible for it.

GLOSSARY

GUIDE TO EVENTS AND PEOPLE

ANDERS, GENERAL WŁADYSŁAW (1892–1970) Commanding officer of the army formed in Russia by Polish prisoners released as a result of the Soviet–Polish pact of 1941; after the war, commander of the Polish armed forces in exile.

BEREZA Concentration camp for political prisoners, set up by the Polish government in 1934.

BRZEŚĆ In September 1938, on Józef Piłsudski's orders, several leaders of the Center-Left Coalition were detained in a military prison in the Brześć fortress.

BUJAK, ZBIGNIEW (B. 1954) Solidarity leader from the Warsaw region.

CIMOSZEWICZ, WŁODZIMIERZ (B. 1950) Polish left-wing politician; prime minister from 1996 to 1997.

DECEMBER 13 On December 13, 1981, martial law was imposed by the government of General Wojciech Jaruzelski.

DMOWSKI, ROMAN (1864–1939) Founder and ideologue of the National Democratic Party (Endecja), the main current of the Polish Right.

GEREMEK, BRONISŁAW (1932–2008) Historian of medieval France and politician; a protagonist of the Round Table negotiations; later, minister of foreign affairs and delegate to the European parliament.

GIEDROYĆ, JERZY (1906–2000) Founder, publisher, and editor in chief of *Kultura*, the foremost political periodical of the émigré community in the post–World War II era.

GIEREK, EDWARD (1913–2001) First secretary of the Polish Communist Party, 1970–1980.

GOMUŁKA, WŁADYSŁAW (1905–1982) First secretary of the Polish Communist Party, 1943–1948 and 1956–1970.

GRUNWALD PATRIOTIC ASSOCIATION An "independent" group created in the 1960s and affiliated with the nationalistic and anti-Semitic wing of the Communist Party.

HERBERT, ZBIGNIEW (1924–1998) Eminent Polish poet and essayist.

HOME ARMY (AK, OR ARMIA KRAJOWA) Underground Polish military forces during World War II.

JASIENICA, PAWEŁ (1909–1970) Writer, author of popular books on early Polish history; hounded to death by the party establishment.

JEDWABNE Site of the mass murder, on July 10, 1941, of the Jewish population by a portion of the Polish inhabitants of the town.

KATYŃ Name of a forest in which much of the systematic killing by the Soviets of more than 20,000 Polish officers, prisoners of war; took place in 1940.

KISIELIEWSKI, STEFAN (1911–1991) Essayist, novelist, and composer; published in *Tygodnik Powszechny* and *Kultura*.

KISZCZAK, CZESŁAW (B. 1925) Minister of police during the period 1981–1990, architect of the martial law regime, and then a protagonist of the Round Table negotiations.

KOŁAKOWSKI, LESZEK (1927–2009) Philosopher, historian, and writer, the most influential teacher of his generation; in exile since 1968 in Great Britain and the United States; author of, among other works, *Main Currents of Marxism.*

KUROŃ, JACEK (1934–2004) Dissident and politician who spent nine years in Communist prisons; author (with Karol Modzelewski) of the "Open Letter to the Workers' Party"; founder of the Workers' Defense Committee (KOR); later, minister of labor in the first two post-Communist governments.

LIPSKI, JAN JÓZEF (1926–1991) Essayist, historian of Polish literature, and political activist; member of the Workers' Defense Committee (KOR).

MAZOWIECKI, TADEUSZ (B. 1927) Catholic writer and politician, founder of the Catholic periodical *Więź*, adviser to Solidarity, and, later, prime minister of the first post-Communist government.

MIEROSZEWSKI, JULIUSZ (1906–1976) Political writer, émigré; published mostly in *Kultura,* advocating acceptance of the postwar status quo and reconciliation among the formerly warring parties.

MIKOŁAJCZYK, STANISŁAW (1901–1966) Politician, prime minister of the Polish government in exile during World War II; later, deputy prime minister in postwar Poland before going back into exile.

MILLER, LESZEK (B. 1946) Left-wing politician; prime minister during the period 2001–2004.

MIŁOSZ, CZESŁAW (1911–2004) Poet, essayist, novelist, and translator; from 1951, in exile from Poland; from 1961, professor of Slavic languages and literature at UC Berkeley; Nobel Prize for Literature, 1980.

MYCIELSKI, ZYGMUNT (1907–1987) Composer and music critic; author of *Diaries*; published in *Tygodnik Powszechny*.

NARUTOWICZ, GABRIEL (1856–1922) Professor of hydraulic engineering at the Technical University of Zurich, he directed the construction of many dams in Western Europe. First president of the newly liberated Poland, he was assassinated in 1922.

NORWID, CYPRIAN (1821–1883) Poet, painter, and sculptor; he died in obscurity in exile in France.

PIŁSUDSKI, JÓZEF (1867–1935) Polish revolutionary and statesman, field marshal, and first head of state and dictator of the Second Polish Republic, as well as head of its armed forces.

RASZEWSKI, ZBIGNIEW (1925–1992) Theater historian, writer, and diarist.

ROUND TABLE AGREEMENTS The 1989 negotiations between representatives of the opposition and of the authorities, which led to the gradual transfer of state power from the Communist Party to Solidarity.

RYWIN, LEW (B. 1945) The principal figure in the corruption scandal of 2002, when Leszek Miller was the prime minister of Poland. Rywin, a Polish film producer, proposed to *Gazeta Wyborcza* that, in exchange for $17.5 million, he would help legislate an amendment to the media law favorable to the plans of Agora, the publisher of *Gazeta Wyborcza*.

SECOND REPUBLIC Poland between the two world wars.

SŁONIMSKI, ANTONI (1895–1976) Poet and essayist, renowned for his cutting wit; Michnik was his secretary in the early 1970s.

SŁOWACKI, JULIUSZ (1809–1849) Romantic poet; died in exile in France.

SOLIDARITY Independent labor movement created in August 1980 in Gdańsk, and abolished by the Jaruzelski government through the imposition of martial law in December of 1981.

TISCHNER, REVEREND JÓZEF (1931–2000) Philosopher, essayist, published in *Tygodnik Powszechny*.

TUROWICZ, JERZY (1912–1999) Leading Polish Catholic journalist; founder and editor in chief of *Tygodnik Powszechny*.

TYGODNIK POWSZECHNY [UNIVERSAL WEEKLY] Newspaper edited by members of the open, ecumenical Catholic intelligentsia; Pope John Paul II was one of its early authors.

WAŁĘSA, LECH (B. 1943) Legendary leader of the Solidarity movement; later, president of the Polish Republic.

WOJTYŁA, KAROL (1920–2005) Cardinal of the Polish Church; later, Pope John Paul II.

WORKERS' DEFENSE COMMITTEE (KOR) Opposition group founded in 1976; the first independent institution of East European dissidents, its members represented many political persuasions; KOR dissolved itself during the Solidarity period (1981).

WYSZYŃSKI, CARDINAL STEFAN (1901–1981) From 1948 until his death, primate of Poland; staunch defender of the Catholic Church against Communism; under house arrest from 1953 to 1956.

ŻEROMSKI, STEFAN (1864–1925) Eminent writer, called "the conscience of Polish literature"; author of novels that promoted social responsibility and patriotic values.

INDEX

Text:	10.75/15 Janson MT Pro
Display:	Janson MT Pro
Compositor:	Westchester Book Group
Printer and binder:	Maple-Vail Book Manufacturing Group